of General
the Trans

more knowledge but not
more understanding.

He Will Save You from the Deadly Pestilence

He Will Save You from the Deadly Pestilence

The Many Lives of Psalm 91

PHILIP JENKINS

OXFORD
UNIVERSITY PRESS

OXFORD
UNIVERSITY PRESS

Oxford University Press is a department of the University of Oxford. It furthers the University's objective of excellence in research, scholarship, and education by publishing worldwide. Oxford is a registered trade mark of Oxford University Press in the UK and certain other countries.

Published in the United States of America by Oxford University Press
198 Madison Avenue, New York, NY 10016, United States of America.

Library of Congress Cataloging-in-Publication Data
Names: Jenkins, Philip, 1952- author.
Title: He will save you from the deadly pestilence : the many lives of Psalm 91 / Philip Jenkins.
Description: New York, NY, United States of America : Oxford University Press, 2023. |
Includes bibliographical references and index.
Identifiers: LCCN 2022029903 (print) | LCCN 2022029904 (ebook) |
ISBN 9780197605646 (hardback) | ISBN 9780197605660 (epub)
Subjects: LCSH: Bible. Psalms, XCI—Criticism, interpretation, etc.
Classification: LCC BS1450 91st .J46 2022 (print) | LCC BS1450 91st (ebook) |
DDC 223/.206—dc23/eng/20220808
LC record available at https://lccn.loc.gov/2022029903
LC ebook record available at https://lccn.loc.gov/2022029904

DOI: 10.1093/oso/9780197605646.001.0001

1 3 5 7 9 8 6 4 2

Printed by Sheridan Books, Inc., United States of America

Contents

Acknowledgments

I am blessed to work in the Institute for Studies of Religion (ISR) at Baylor University, where my talented colleagues include David Jeffrey, Byron Johnson, Tommy Kidd, and Gordon Melton. Special thanks go to Jeff Levin, who is extremely knowledgeable about the Talmud and Jewish tradition, and so generous in sharing that knowledge. Thanks also to other Baylor colleagues, including Beth Allison Barr, Alan Jacobs, and Ralph Wood. I greatly appreciate the advice and comments of Kathryn Hume, Jason McCloskey, and Peter J. Thuesen.

Heidi Olson Campbell provided excellent research assistance.

Deepest thanks to my long-standing editor at Oxford University Press, Cynthia Read. Sadly, her retirement now means that this is the last book that we will work on together.

As always, special thanks to my wife, Liz Jenkins.

Note on Usage

The psalm that forms the subject of this book has been known under various names. Traditionally, Catholic and Orthodox Christians have called it Psalm 90, while the Protestant and Jewish usage refers to 91. As I will explain, that numbering has also shifted over time, which potentially can cause even greater confusion. Throughout the present book, for reasons of consistency, I will use the "Psalm 91" label, except where 90 appears in direct quotations. St. Augustine, Thomas More, and Thomas Merton all spoke lovingly of what they called Psalm 90, but in reporting their remarks here, I will write as if they were commenting on 91.

1

Under the Shadow of the Almighty

Discovering Psalm 91

> And [the Devil] brought him to Jerusalem, and set him on a pinnacle
> of the Temple, and said unto him, If thou be the Son of God, cast thy-
> self down from hence: For it is written, *He shall give his angels charge*
> *over thee, to keep thee: And in their hands they shall bear thee up, lest*
> *at any time thou dash thy foot against a stone.* And Jesus answering
> said unto him, It is said, Thou shalt not tempt the Lord thy God.
> —Luke 4:9–12, King James Version, c. 95 CE

Although the story of Christ's temptation in the wilderness is one of the most famous in the New Testament, few modern readers will grasp its multiple ironies. The Devil is quoting Psalm 91, vv. 11–12, which he properly cites as scripture with the appropriate phrase "it is written," *gegraptai*. He is thus following the form of scriptural discourse approved among the most respected rabbis. In Jesus's time, this psalm was one of the most powerful weapons in the arsenal of Jewish exorcists, because its words were so effective in driving away demons, yet on this occasion, Satan himself utters them. In modern terms, it is as if a cinematic vampire were brandishing a crucifix. For neither the first nor the last time in its history, that psalm was appearing in a surprising and even shocking context, on the porous frontiers between the holy and the demonic.[1]

Even people with good knowledge of the Bible and of Jewish or Christian history might be amazed to find how phenomenally popular and ubiquitous a scripture 91 has been, and still remains. It is in fact one of the most commonly cited writings from the Hebrew Bible, one of the most actively used and most widely beloved. Its words and images are reflected in liturgy, devotional writings, and (extensively) the visual arts. It still occupies a prominent place in popular culture both within North America and globally. The fact

He Will Save You from the Deadly Pestilence. Philip Jenkins, Oxford University Press. © Oxford University Press 2023.
DOI: 10.1093/oso/9780197605646.003.0001

that the psalm appears in adapted or mildly disguised versions can cause us to ignore or underestimate its presence: the cherished contemporary hymn "On Eagle's Wings" is a freely adapted version.[2]

For over two millennia, 91 has played a pivotal role in both Christian and Jewish discussions of theology and politics, of medicine and mysticism. Through that history, the evolving uses of 91 allow us to map developing ideas about religion and the supernatural. Depending on the context of the reader in any given era, Psalm 91 is prophylactic; it is triumphalist; it is messianic; it is millenarian and apocalyptic; it is therapeutic. In different ages, it has borne many different names: the Song of Evil Spirits, the Soldier's Psalm, the Trench Psalm, and, most concisely, the Protection Psalm. As the Song of Plagues, it has gained a whole new relevance in an age of global pandemic.

Frequently, as in that tale of Jesus and Satan, 91 has both reflected and shaped changing concepts of evil and the demonic. It can be read as a lesson in exalted monotheistic theology, but it was and is used for purposes that are overtly magical and troublingly superstitious. Even citing its title or opening words can constitute a powerful form of spiritual protection, a statement that can be made of very few other biblical texts. As perils and threats have changed and evolved in various societies, so interpretations of Psalm 91 have developed to accommodate each new reality. The psalm's language about demons and evil forces has repeatedly come into play when Christianity encounters other religious traditions. When European empires spanned the globe in the sixteenth and seventeenth centuries, Catholic priests and missionaries relied on 91 to defeat the hostile local deities and spiritual forces they discovered in Mexico or Paraguay.[3]

At every stage, interpretations of 91 have to be understood in the larger context of social, spiritual, and practical concerns. A biography of Psalm 91 is also a history of critical themes in Western religion.[4]

Discovering Psalm 91

Given the very long shadow that 91 has cast, it is almost shocking to realize how short it is, 112 words in the original Hebrew, or some 300 words in a standard English translation. I will quote the full English text here, using the familiar King James version. As I will explain, not just are translations abundant, but they vary substantially in words and themes, going far beyond mere nuances of meaning. But for present purposes of general introduction, the King James is quite adequate:

Psalm 91 (King James Version)

1 He that dwelleth in the secret place of the Most High shall abide under the shadow of the Almighty.

2 I will say of the LORD, He is my refuge and my fortress: my God; in him will I trust.

3 Surely he shall deliver thee from the snare of the fowler, and from the noisome pestilence.

4 He shall cover thee with his feathers, and under his wings shalt thou trust: his truth shall be thy shield and buckler.

5 Thou shalt not be afraid for the terror by night; nor for the arrow that flieth by day;

6 Nor for the pestilence that walketh in darkness; nor for the destruction that wasteth at noonday.

7 A thousand shall fall at thy side, and ten thousand at thy right hand; but it shall not come nigh thee.

8 Only with thine eyes shalt thou behold and see the reward of the wicked.

9 Because thou hast made the LORD, which is my refuge, even the most High, thy habitation;

10 There shall no evil befall thee, neither shall any plague come nigh thy dwelling.

11 For he shall give his angels charge over thee, to keep thee in all thy ways.

12 They shall bear thee up in their hands, lest thou dash thy foot against a stone.

13 Thou shalt tread upon the lion and adder: the young lion and the dragon shalt thou trample under feet.

14 Because he hath set his love upon me, therefore will I deliver him: I will set him on high, because he hath known my name.

15 He shall call upon me, and I will answer him: I will be with him in trouble; I will deliver him, and honour him.

16 With long life will I satisfy him, and shew him my salvation.[5]

I should stress that the division of verses is a relatively modern practice, dating only from the sixteenth century in the Christian tradition.

The psalm imagines the believer surrounded by dire threats, but passing through unscathed. Thus girded, the faithful would encounter enemies both material and spiritual, yet remain secure. 91 is strikingly comprehensive in enumerating the threats and dangers that an individual might face in a pre-modern society, or indeed in any place or time. Diseases and plagues of various kinds are mentioned, as are perils that might come from regular human enemies, or from enchanters. The reference to "a thousand falling at your side" need not refer to warfare, although it can easily be applied in that way. It can equally well apply to a plague or pestilence. As was common knowledge through much of human history, war was inevitably accompanied by plagues and famines, and all those evils were commonly attributed to supernatural causes, including God's punishment for a people's sins.

In the face of these multiple evils, the psalm is lavish in offering images of protection, including (depending on the translation) fortress, refuge, rampart, shield, sheltering wings, and shadow. The psalm promises personal supernatural and angelic protection. All those blessings are promised to the believer, and in terms that are both absolute and unequivocal: these are the benefits that *will* come to the person who places full trust in God. That believer is not requesting protection, but asserting that it already exists. The final section assures the believer of uplifting or elevation, which might be material or spiritual. The psalm easily lends itself to mystical interpretations.[6]

Readers and Believers

Psalm 91 has supplied both Jews and Christians with a refuge in time of trouble of all kinds, including supernatural assault, deadly plague, and worldly violence. Just how attractive its words have been is demonstrated by the strikingly diverse range of prestigious commentators and authors who have used or expounded it through the millennia, often in lofty terms.

Just to take one of the most influential commentators, when Augustine of Hippo wrote his commentary on the psalm around 400 CE, his text (in English translation) ran to almost 6,700 words: that is, over twenty words of his own thoughts for each one contained in the psalm itself. That compared to just 450 words in which he discussed what today is the far more highly regarded 23rd Psalm, or 1,500 words for the scarcely less popular Psalm 1. Even the richly messianic Psalm 8 only merited 4,400 words. Martin Luther was scarcely less enthusiastic, and he often quoted the psalm in contexts where to modern readers, at first sight, it seems irrelevant. Luther lived and breathed 91, and in this he was far from unique in that early modern era. So frequently was the psalm cited and commented upon that we could in theory write a book-length study on the history and reception of each of three or four of the most beloved verses. Several books actually do offer a history of the noonday demon, a menacing figure found in Latin translations of our psalm's v. 6. Another weighty example is v. 13, about treading on and trampling dangerous creatures, words that we will encounter very frequently in this study.[7]

No less surprising than the passion inspired by 91 in earlier eras is the relative lack of interest in other biblical texts that today are seen as so inspiring. In modern times, the beloved 23rd Psalm has become the common refuge in time of mortal threat (the valley of the shadow of death), and we readily assume that this has always been the case. Throughout the Middle Ages and the early modern era, however, that psalm was far less appreciated than 91, which remained the principal deathbed prayer until well into the nineteenth century. Nor did the 23rd offer anything like the same incentive to create visual representations.[8]

The Demonic Realm

In part, 91 attracted such deep and enduring interest because of what it could teach about the nature of supernatural evil. For much of the premodern history of Jews and Christians alike, we are dealing with a world that drew little distinction between supernatural possession and illness in body and mind, or between healing and exorcism. Otherworldly causes were also assumed for other misfortunes and disasters, which were all too rarely seen as simple happenstance. That was certainly true of the biblical world out of which 91 emerged. That view accepted the existence of ubiquitous and powerful evil spirits, which were confronted by angelic forces of good. Both demons and angels found explicit warrant in 91, which is in fact one of a tiny number of biblical texts to describe guardian angels on anything like the model that we know so well from medieval and later depictions. The move away from those assumptions about suffering and misfortune was slow, gradual, partial, and strikingly late, and can be traced through successive comments on, and practical applications of, our psalm.[9]

Scholars commonly describe charms and amulets deployed to resist evil as *apotropaic*, from the Greek words meaning "to turn away," and 91 has never lost those apotropaic functions. The psalm has an age-long history as a material symbol, from the amulets and talismans that were so common in the ancient Mediterranean world to the camouflage bandanas that are now popular in the U.S. military; it appears on masks to defend against the coronavirus. Surveying the sheer abundance of early and medieval Christian material objects that use the psalm in some way, scholar Thomas J. Kraus has described 91 as "the most widely attested text of the Bible." In this sense, it is actually better attested than the Lord's Prayer.[10]

If post-Enlightenment thought has consigned ideas of exorcism and demon-fighting to the despised realm of superstition, that was certainly not the case for most of Christian (or Jewish) history. In the early years of the Common Era, educated believers and religious institutions thoroughly accepted that demonic framework. Many Talmudic references show erudite rabbis not only believing absolutely in demons, but seeking defense against them through the use of prayers and protective objects. For Jews and Christians, Psalm 91 was everywhere. It was a mainstay of the earliest concepts of Christology, the triumphant vision that is often called the Christus Victor theory of atonement. When the evangelists report how Satan quoted the psalm in the wilderness, we have to read that episode in a larger framework intended to teach profound lessons about the meaning of Jesus Christ, of his crucifixion and resurrection, and his triumphant victory over dark forces. Tracing the psalm's subsequent history among Jews and Christians shows how very gradual was the separation between the faiths in their basic assumptions, and how thoroughly each accepted very similar ideas of those evil forces. The two faiths found common ground in 91.

Through the Borderlands

Across all human societies, some moments and events are believed to be especially dangerous or troubling. When understood in a supernatural context, these are the times when demons or dark forces will take advantage of weakness and instability. People thus exposed need protection. In Western religion, Psalm 91 has commonly served as an ideal defense for these times of transition.

This text is to be used by those crossing perilous frontiers, and seeking protection on the way. Historically, those liminal experiences have included marriage and childbirth, as well as embarking on travel in times when that was far more perilous than it is today. As Jesus himself discovered, you were likely to hear the words of 91 while traveling in a wilderness, whether literal or figurative. Many stories attest to the use of 91 by or for those on the border-land of life and death, seeking safe and easy passage from this life. On a daily basis, people face literal darkness during the transition to sleep and night. In every one of these instances, we repeatedly find 91 invoked, whether through prayers, spells, or amulets. People use it to face the darkness, however they conceive it.

I have mentioned the psalm's obvious relevance to warfare, and many features of 91 make it appropriate for use in times of combat. For this reason, the psalm has often had a strong and unusual gender appeal. Particularly in the modern world, women have customarily played the leading role in shaping popular devotion. The appeal of 91, however, has usually been masculine-oriented. Its subject matter lends itself to traditionally manly concerns of combat and competition, with a heavy emphasis on individu-alism, even a strikingly modern and radical form of individualism. The psalm after all imagines "you" (singular) taking refuge in God, and receiving all those blessings and immunities. It is ideal for the embattled, a hymn for the stubborn. Its appeal to the combative (and thorny) Martin Luther needs little explanation. This statement about gender appeal must be qualified, as 91 has a whole history of its own in Marian devotion, in the cult of a dis-tinctly martial Virgin Mary. But the masculine quality has become steadily more prevalent in modern times, when 91 could be said to represent a mas-culine bridgehead in popular understandings of scripture.[11]

SUP ASP: The Power to Trample

Beyond offering protection, the psalm is fundamentally concerned with the assertion of power, which has both spiritual and political dimensions. In both cases, 91 assumes a vision of combat and violent struggle against forces of evil or darkness. One verse above all is central to that narrative: v. 13, which promised the power to tread on or trample various beasts. The Vulgate Latin promised that *super aspidem et basiliscum ambulabis, et conculcabis leonem et draconem*: "you will walk upon the serpent and basilisk, you will trample the lion and the dragon."[12] (The creatures specified varied greatly between translations, and visual representations often reduced the number from four to two, the lion and the serpent.) In the spiritual realm, such an act of subjugation and suppression was the proper function of holy beings, whether that meant Christ, the Virgin Mary, or saints, who conquered Satan, demons, or the forces of death. In modern times, evangelicals and charismatics find here a foundation for theories of what has become known as spiritual warfare.

The motif has been extremely common in Christian art through the centuries, in sculpture and architecture as well as painting and manuscripts, amulets and inscriptions. In various media, it occurs often in Europe's medieval cathedrals and parish churches. In the ninth century, a royal Frankish workshop produced the so-called Douce Ivory, a sumptuous carved figure of Christ in triumph, who bears a book with the letters IHS XPS SUP ASP. These are abbreviations for two phrases that were so common in medieval church art as almost to constitute clichés, and thus did not need to be spelled out in full. Modern readers with any knowledge of the Christian heritage would likely recognize IHS XPS for "Jesus Christ," but the other acronym would be more challenging. In fact, the terse SUP ASP stands for "super aspidem," and the image duly shows Christ trampling the four creatures.[13]

That thirteenth verse became a standard vehicle for Christian discussions of political power, authority, and domination, and how those concepts were represented in visual form. Following the creation of Christian states from the fourth century onward, successive writers on 91 presented those lethal beasts in different ways, as representing rival kings, or heretical movements, or pagan peoples resisting conversion. One of the greatest representations of the theme dates from the sixth century, in a Ravenna mosaic that was directed against Arian heretics. Another dazzling work, a Baroque sculpture from Munich in the 1630s, showed the Virgin Mary suppressing Protestants and Jews. In any case, the act of trampling belonged to the true Christian ruler, so that v. 13 became a centerpiece of political ideology and iconography from late antiquity into the age of absolutism and beyond. These were, after all, societies that acknowledged no serious division between the political and the religious. For over a thousand years, that verse shaped the self-image of kings and emperors, and how they defined their worldly role.

The right to be portrayed as trampler was fiercely contested, as rival political forces sought to appropriate that image, and the legitimacy and power that went with it. Originally the privilege was intimately associated with the imperial office, before it was borrowed by secular kings or pretenders. In the high Middle Ages, popes enjoyed great success in establishing their own dominant status. Some of these psalm-derived images could be fiercely controversial. One late medieval myth told how a twelfth-century pope had subjugated a German emperor, placing his feet on the royal neck and reciting the *super aspidem*. Although the story was false, it offered a perfect epitome of what critics of the papacy wanted to believe about that office and its arrogant overreach. As such, the legend became one of the most quoted and illustrated themes in Protestant polemic from the sixteenth century until the late nineteenth. When in turn both royal and papal regimes stumbled during the revolutionary years of the nineteenth century, the radical successor states and movements appropriated the trampling imagery for their own purposes.

The Monks' Charter

Just how influential these themes were is difficult to appreciate unless we understand the way that so many communities and individuals encountered the psalm, and so thoroughly internalized it. Of course, individuals read the text or heard it read, perhaps in a liturgical context. But the psalm held a special role for the Christian monastics who were for so long the preservers of literacy, and the source of so much of what is recorded from earlier eras.[14]

From earliest times, the monastic movement stressed the role of spiritual combat, and monks and hermits used 91 so frequently that the psalm became a charter document of the whole enterprise. For over a thousand years after the fall of the Roman Empire in the West, monks and religious of various kinds undertook much of the official and ecclesiastical work demanding literacy. They supplied most of the historians, chroniclers, and commentators, and a large share of the administrators and bureaucrats of Christian states. They also commissioned much of the cultural product of the age, in music as well as the visual arts. In the West, virtually all those monastics ended every single day of their clerical lives with the service of compline, in which 91 was a fixture, precisely because it fortified Christians against the hazards of darkness and the night. How could those frequent reciters and listeners help carrying its words into those other contexts? How could they not think of asps and lions?

Such monastic discourses produced some surprising by-products. Throughout late antiquity and the Middle Ages, readings of 91 served as vehicles for quite sophisticated explorations of psychology and psychological states, including anxiety and depression. The key text involved the "noonday demon," which featured in some alternative translations in v. 6 in place of the "destruction that wasteth" in the King James Version. As monastic writers examined their own conditions and those they saw around them, they often returned to that demon, and in trying to comprehend him, they analyzed themselves. Just as alchemy represents the prehistory of later chemistry, so these demonic speculations supplied a foundation for later psychology.[15]

The Psalm's Dilemma

Beyond inspiring faith and confidence, 91 raised some of the key theological questions that have so often arisen in the Judeo-Christian tradition, but which were here encountered in acute and memorable form. People place their total trust in God, they pray and lead holy and generous lives, and according to the explicit words of 91, they are immune from demonic assault and misfortune. The psalm's warranty is clearly stated: if you take refuge in the Most High, then there shall no evil befall thee. So firm and explicit is this affirmation that in modern times, 91 offers a vital justification for the influential global movement known as the Prosperity Gospel, which promises faithful believers wealth, health, and blessings in the present life. They need only name and claim the blessings they have been promised, to speak the Word of Faith.[16]

Observed experience shows that such assertions are false, or extraordinarily naive. While it is pleasing to be assured that the faithful person will alone survive a cataclysm that kills thousands all around them, such a statement simply clashes with reality. Disasters sometimes do indeed afflict good and faithful people but leave the deeply ungodly quite unscathed. And if the psalm's final verse promises long life, we can point to many great and holy people who died at tragically early ages, even by the standards of premodern societies. Jesus himself probably died in his early thirties. For many modern readers, the psalm's confidence is more of an obstacle than an attraction. It sounds like the Psalm of Pollyanna.

Nor is such an observation confined to cynical modern times. As we will see, the biblical Book of Job sought to understand why God permits bad things to happen to good or even saintly people. As Job struggles to understand the calamities he has experienced, he is confronted by the ultra-pious and superficial Eliphaz the Tamanite, who argues that if Job is suffering, it must be because of something he has done to anger God, some secret sin. If Job denies having sinned, he is deceiving himself and others. Already in this ancient setting, Eliphaz supports that argument by offering a close paraphrase of Psalm 91, which may have been composed not too long before:

> Thou shalt be hid from the scourge of the tongue: neither shalt thou be afraid of destruction when it cometh. At destruction and famine thou shalt laugh: neither shalt thou be afraid of the beasts of the earth.[17]

As Job says, he dearly wishes that he could find some such sin that might have provoked divine wrath, but he has tried, and found nothing. So why must he suffer? How can he avoid the conclusion that in his case at least, God has been arbitrary and even unjust? The reader is obviously meant to sympathize with Job, and to condemn the crude spiritual outlook of Eliphaz and, by extension, of 91. If not rejecting the psalm itself, then the author of Job is challenging popular misconstructions of it. If this is not the only instance where one biblical book specifically targets a passage in another, such intrascriptural sniping is not common. Even when the text first comes into historical view, the psalm was provoking skeptical resistance, and the theological issues that it raised were already troubling its readers.

Christians faced the same dilemmas. In 397 CE, the Church Father Jerome addressed a pious Christian correspondent who was blind. As Jerome noted, many holy people were sick or troubled, while it was all too evident that many pagans, Jews, and heretics were flourishing indecently well. That contrast seemed to make nonsense of the psalm's promise that evil or plague would not come near the true believer. Why did God not show an explicit preference for his faithful people in their everyday lives? What, indeed, was the point of prayer, at least as it might affect conditions in this present worldly reality? Jerome has to explain why God allows the righteous to suffer, and inevitably returns to the classic statement of this seeming paradox in the Book of Job itself—a work that we might call the anti–Psalm 91.[18]

Plague and Disease

Jerome's homily gets to a perennial issue at the core of Western religion: namely, the need to explain the existence of evil in a world ruled by a God who is both all-powerful and all-just. This is the project of theodicy, which has inspired so many learned tracts. That issue was all the more crucial, and wrenching, in a world that attributed natural calamities such as epidemics to the divine will and divine judgment, not understanding the forces actually at work. The precise and literal words of 91 brought the question into stark relief, most glaringly in the context of plague and pestilence. It was at such times that faithful believers turned most enthusiastically to 91: for protection and guidance, but also in the hope of understanding the theological implications of the crisis.

I will argue that the psalm originated as a response to an assault of epidemic disease in ancient Israel. Depending on the translation, we can read as many as five or six words or phrases directly relevant to disease (although, as we will see, some other versions considerably underplayed that element). So if a faithful person prayed 91 with all confidence and humility, then surely they would be immune from infection? But as experience showed, that was not the case. During outbreaks of disease, a great many people died in appalling circumstances, and many of the sufferers were to all appearances devout or even saintly Christian believers, the very people who should have been sheltered under the divine wings. Why did that happen?

We properly recall the Black Death of the fourteenth century as a signal catastrophe, but plagues and pandemics continued to rage in Europe long afterward, and were very destructive on many occasions between the sixteenth and nineteenth centuries. It is scarcely possible to understand the history of Western responses to plague and disease in those times without following the sermons, tracts, and commentaries directly inspired by 91. Some preachers and authors did indeed assert that believers could survive solely by invoking the psalm. Until surprisingly modern times in the West, medical writers commonly cited the psalm as an invaluable supplement to worldly cures. Other thinkers wondered how those who devoutly appealed to 91 could still perish.

Over time, we see the emergence of new opinions, which sought one of two solutions to the psalm's dilemma. Either they read the ills and plagues of 91 as metaphors or interior realities rather than literal pestilence and war, or else they held that the promises of protection and safety applied only in the heavenly realm. A faithful person could indeed die from plague or war, but would be granted salvation, and in that sense only evil would not befall him. The evils referred to in the biblical text were thus spiritualized, and so were the blessings promised to defend against them. These interpretations avoided the crude materialism advocated by an Eliphaz, but they did open commentators to the charge of invalidating quite explicit promises of worldly benefit. A skeptic might object that they were removing the divine assurances from any prospect of empirical testing or disproof.

Although these controversies arose directly from confrontation with disease, they had much wider application, and indeed marked a fundamental shift in Western thought. Debates arising from 91 had a powerful impact in concepts of divine intervention in human affairs, and of providential action as such. Today, at least in the West, most educated Christians or Jews would find a resort to 91 or other spiritual weapons questionable in times of disease or pandemic, at least unless accompanied by strictly secular means of securing health and protection. Historically, that change represents a revolutionary transformation in approaches to prayer and the perceived scope of divine intervention in everyday life. But as we will see, that more skeptical approach did not win over all audiences, and strongly materialistic readings of 91 remain very much alive today.

High and Low

A biography of 91 tracks other crucial shifts in concepts of religion, and indeed, it maps the evolving frontiers of religion as such as well as the vocabulary we use to describe it. In every time and place, people do many things that are oriented to supernatural realms. Some of those actions are conventionally described as religious, while others fall into the less desirable and often stigmatized categories of magic or superstition. I have characterized different concepts of religion as high or low, respectively. In the modern West, "high" religion implies solid, informed faith, based on the institution and its approved practice and scriptures, and grounded in serious theology. The "low," in contrast, involves vernacular practices, mere folk religion, which are not grounded in serious or educated thought. Praying to a deity is religion. Seeking to command a deity or spirit by means of ritual words or behavior is magic.

As we explore the realities of lived religion, those lines become much fainter. The legendary Duke Ellington famously observed that all music is in fact folk music, as he had never heard any music made by horses. By the same token, we might challenge the reality of "folk religion," as it all falls on the larger spectrum of lived human religion, of what folk do. The high/low distinction becomes thoroughly suspect when traced through history. In earlier eras, religious institutions themselves practiced and thoroughly approved of many things that to a modern eye look distinctly magical and superstitious; over time, those institutions increasingly moved toward defining such practices as worthy of condemnation.[19]

As we trace the history of Psalm 91, we see repeated debates over the proper role of actions designed to persuade or influence the supernatural world. Throughout its history, and even today, the psalm's advocates proclaim its wonderful powers: often, the words must be spoken in particular ways, or repeated a certain number of times—perhaps forty, to recall Jesus's time in the wilderness. Even today, praying 91 for ninety-one straight days is a common devotion. Commentators learned and simple alike have found deep significance in the psalm's very number, and noted that a given person lived for ninety-one years, or that a military unit bore that number. When COVID-19 struck, the psalm's enthusiasts delightedly noted the blessed symmetry that offered 91 as a sovereign antidote to 19. Claims and legends about the psalm's powers are expressed through elaborate storytelling, a process that in different societies is undertaken through folktales and sermons, printed pamphlets and books, and, spectacularly in the modern world, through online resources. Together, these materials constitute a substantial body of vernacular tradition or mythology, which both creates and sustains faith in 91.[20]

The idea that spiritual power rests in precise words, formulae, or numbers seems like the essence of superstition, although it is not difficult to find esteemed monks or rabbis who followed such practices in bygone days. According to some interpreters, the story of Christ's encounter in the wilderness was intended to warn against just such magical uses of scripture: if Satan himself could use the potent exorcistic quote, then obviously words alone were not going to protect the believer. As the story is reported in the gospels, Jesus followed many other distinguished rabbis in urging piety and obedience to God's commandments, rather than the ritualistic use of the text alone. By the seventeenth and eighteenth centuries, we can speak of something like our modern distinction between religion and superstition. But the distinction between the two approaches, between high and low, is a question of time and place, rather than any essential quality.

The Psalm as Scripture

Psalm 91 offers multiple obstacles for anyone believing in the plain and obvious truth of sacred scripture, simple and unadorned. Of course, interpretations of 91 have varied enormously over time, to accommodate the changing
needs and circumstances of its readers. Societies made the translations they
needed. But such pressures have reshaped the psalm itself, as successive
translations have produced divergent and even irreconcilable meanings. This
is not the only scriptural text of which that can be said, but 91 does pose such
problems in abundance.

Those shifting interpretations raise the question about determining
what is authentic or real scripture. The Septuagint translation turned the
"destruction that wasteth" in v. 6 into a "noonday demon," and that concept survived in Catholic and Orthodox Bibles into the last century. In
Christian history, that was the meaning a majority of believers found in the
psalm, and many preachers and commentators expounded it. They treated
it faithfully as revealed scripture. We can agree wholeheartedly that the
noonday demon did not represent the original intent of the psalm's original
composers, but does that mean that the figure can simply be dismissed as
a linguistic blunder? Surely when something is so very widely venerated as
scripture, then that fact in itself entitles the text to be treated as part of the
biblical tradition.

Nor are matters wholly self-evident even when we agree what the original
text actually says. Although the Hebrew text of Psalm 91 is reasonably clear,
subsequent generations have differed enormously on the exact meaning of
particular words and phrases, and about the tone or emphasis of the whole
work. Already in the third and second centuries BCE, the Septuagint Greek
translation made the work much more overtly and systematically anti-
demonic, and that approach was carried over into the Vulgate Latin translation undertaken by Jerome in the fourth century CE. That move into Greek
also affected the numbering. The Hebrew tradition calls this 91, and that is
the practice of later Protestants. Roman Catholics and Orthodox followed
the Septuagint in knowing it as Psalm 90. And as I have suggested, 90 and 91
differed not just in their numbers but in their implications and, accordingly,
in the iconography and musical treatments that each inspired. During the
early modern period, when Protestants and Catholics glared at each other
across Europe's confessional frontiers, it is scarcely too much to say that each
side read and esteemed quite different psalms.

One specific example shows how interpretations of the psalm have evolved over time. One of its most famous phrases concerns "the terror by night," a phrase that has been a gift to modern-day writers of sensational fiction and film. But what does it mean? The Hebrew seems straightforward enough: *miPachad lay'lah*, in which *pachad* means "dread," "fear," or "terror." The Septuagint Greek reads that faithfully as *phobou nukterinou*, which in Latin becomes *timore nocturno*. But "nightly fear" can be interpreted in various ways, and "terror by night" is not the only option. Other English translations are subtly but significantly different, including "the terror of the night" (Douai-Reims) or "the terror of night" (New International Version, NIV).[21]

Just on the basis of the translations, are we speaking of a special kind of terrifying evil most often found in the night? Or of the night itself? Nor is it obvious whether we are speaking of a terror of one specific thing, or of a more generalized menace. Some commentators have read *pachad* as the personal name of an individual demon, Pachad. Others see it as a metaphor for some pressing danger, such as heresy or (for Martin Luther) Judaism. Or it might be a psychological phenomenon. In explicating the verse, Thomas More noted that a man who gave way to trivial imaginary fears made himself vulnerable to being overcome by an enemy. The psalm's phrase might refer to a well-grounded fear of literal nighttime dangers such as surprise military attack or robbery. Around 1700, the English Puritan Bible commentator Matthew Henry was comprehensive:

> When we are retired into our chambers, our beds, and have made all as safe as we can about us, yet there is *terror by night*, from thieves and robbers, winds and storms, besides those things that are the creatures of fancy and imagination, which are often most frightful of all.[22]

Those are possible and very diverse readings of one short phrase, but similar things can be said about almost every word of this dense text. As each generation read the psalm according to its own needs and fears, so those successive readings make 91 a diagnostic tool for approaching the larger religious history.

A Life

I have spoken of the present book as a biography of the psalm, and that metaphor applies very well to a literary work that has evolved so much during the course of its existence, one that has assumed so many guises in different eras and settings. Already in its earliest years, it enjoyed a precocious and controversial significance: witness its use in the Book of Job. Over time, it has grown, evolved, matured, and mutated. Like the human subject of a major biography, the psalm has had a significant impact upon the individuals and societies with which it has come into contact. The psalm has mingled with celebrities (and not just the Devil), and shaped great events and movements. On occasion, it has fallen into really bad company. Its life story illuminates many of those wider worlds.[23]

That life continues today. So much of the mythology once associated with 91 is extinct, at least for educated people in the West, who have no time for explanations based on the demonic. Yet the psalm itself remains vigorously alive as a device for spiritual protection, even in the most advanced societies. Never absent from the landscape of popular culture and faith, the psalm returned vigorously to view during the pandemic that began in 2020. On a larger canvas, 91 is currently enjoying a spectacular vogue in the Global South, where it is beloved among casualties of globalization and mass urbanization, among border crossers and refugees, not to mention among gangsters and convicts. As a (still) valuable tool against demons, it has gained a whole new lease on life for use in struggles against witchcraft.

But throughout the world, a great many Jews and Christians find enormous spiritual wealth in the psalm without any belief in its protective powers, which they would reject as superstitious. Their readings point to the text's real spiritual treasures as an affirmation of trust in divine love and justice, transcending death. That is evidently true of the many millions who devoutly sing the hymn "On Eagle's Wings," and they are profoundly moved by the experience.

If this is indeed a biography, then it lacks one of the critical features of such a work—namely, a time of decline and death. Such an eclipse, if it ever does occur, is still far off. We seek in vain for an obituary.

2

A Thousand Shall Fall at Thy Side

How a Plague Prayer Became a Song Against Evil Spirits

> As Moses was going up to heaven, he recited the psalm against evil
> spirits which begins with *He that dwells in the secret place of the Most
> High, will abide in the shadow of the Almighty.*[1]
> —Midrash Tehillim, date uncertain

About 500 CE, Jewish scholars in Babylonia, ancient Iraq, compiled a collection of legal and ritual decisions that were collectively known as "instruction," or Talmud. Despite their relatively late date, these texts included much authentic material dating back to the time before the destruction of the Second Temple four centuries before, traced through a series of authorities. One of these tractates, known as Shevuot or "Oaths," hauntingly recalls the consecration of an addition to the old Temple's courtyard, and the music that accompanied it, with harps, lyres, and cymbals. After the psalms of thanksgiving and celebration, the clerical choirs sang Psalm 91, remembered as "the Song of Evil Spirits, which begins: 'He that dwells in the secret place of the Most High.' And some say that this psalm is called the Song of Plagues." "The Song of Evil Spirits" is *shir shel pega'im,* and changing one letter makes it "the Song of Plagues," *nega'im,* suggesting the dual purposes for which it was employed. That special association with the Temple helps account for the psalm's role in the story of Jesus's temptations.[2]

That is excellent evidence for how 91 was regarded in this era, but many questions remain about its beginnings and early history. Just how old was the psalm at that point? What was its original context or purpose? Did it always have those demonic associations?

I will argue that 91 appeared in the fifth or the fourth century BCE, and that it was first directed against plagues before becoming more comprehensively "demonized." But the degree of uncertainty is considerable, and two

He Will Save You from the Deadly Pestilence. Philip Jenkins, Oxford University Press. © Oxford University Press 2023.
DOI: 10.1093/oso/9780197605646.003.0002

hundred years of detailed scholarly analysis have left plenty of room for debate. Virtually nothing we can say about that early history will not find a counterargument from some accredited expert. Was 91 even intended to be a freestanding text, or was it to be read as part of a larger work? What we can say confidently is that this element of controversy and contestation dates to very early times, and even then, translators and commentators differed widely with respect to its meaning and interpretation.[3]

Psalms

Today, 91 is one item in the biblical Book of Psalms, one of a familiar collection of 150 pieces. The psalms were originally designed as worship music within the ancient Temple, both the First Temple, which stood from the mid-tenth century BCE through 587/586 BCE, and the Second, which was restored in the fifth century BCE. The word "psalm" comes from a Greek term referring to stringed instruments; the Hebrew term for the biblical book is *Tehillim*, or Praises. Our 91 shares many features with the genres and poetic devices of the psalms as a category, especially in its use of parallelism, or reiterating and reinforcing an original idea: "He will cover you with his feathers, and under his wings you will find refuge."[4]

But in many ways, 91 fits poorly with the larger collection. If we list the most common categories into which psalms are divided, then 91 stands out by its stubborn refusal to fit into any of the available slots. Many psalms are obviously intended for liturgical use in the Temple. Some are designed for use in a royal context, celebrating great events such as a coronation or marriage. There are songs of personal piety, of thanksgiving, of repentance and penitence. There are didactic psalms that teach about the Law, or divine wisdom. But as Robert Alter remarks of 91, it "does not belong to any obvious cultic genre of psalms." To quote another scholar, "It is not a hymn, a lament, or even a prayer of trust." We categorize it by what it is not. If the psalm is not exactly an outlaw, it is an outlier.[5]

One unusual feature of our psalm is deciding who exactly is speaking, and to whom, as the text shifts between the first, second, and third persons, in a way that has been described as "bewildering." A modern English translation like the NIV supplies obvious and helpful divisions, marked by line breaks, and some passages are designated as quotations. None of those indications feature in the original, and neither, of course, are the verses themselves identified or numbered as separate units. In our present v. 2, we are introduced to a human "I," and then vv. 3–13 are directed to "thou," who is also human. This uses a second person singular, but it is not clear whether it might be applied in some collective sense. These verses all promise things that "he" (unquestionably in this case meaning God) will perform—how *he* will save or deliver *you*. Presumably, these promises are asserted by the "I" of v. 2. In the closing, vv. 14–16, God himself speaks in the first person. The shifting use of second and third persons suggests that it was performed or chanted antiphonally. That might imply a liturgical Temple setting, although, as we will see, other settings can be imagined.[6]

One line in the psalm may support this Temple setting. In v. 4, the "thou" is told that he will take refuge under the wings (Heb: *kanaph*) of God, being covered by his pinions. This is a familiar metaphor for divine protection, but the word *kanaph* occurs quite frequently in the context of the Temple, with respect to the winged cherub figures that guarded the Ark of the Covenant. Those wings are referred to repeatedly in the phantasmagoric vision of Ezekiel, around 600 BCE. The protection being promised would thus be especially associated with the Temple structure itself. In some scholarly reconstructions, the psalm was to be recited by pilgrims arriving at the gate or portal of the Temple, as part of a hypothetical "liturgy of the Temple gate."[7]

One rival suggestion should be considered. As a text collected as a psalm, 91 would have been used in the Temple, and likely over a period of centuries, but just possibly it had a prehistory before that point. It might have originated as a kind of exorcism or healing ritual used in a private setting in the household religion of ancient Israel, a tradition that often emerges in the archaeological record, but far less commonly in written sources. That would explain the psalm's antiphonal and performative quality. But wherever and whenever it began, it was incorporated into the formal religious cult, and was interpreted accordingly.[8]

Through the centuries, there have been many opinions about the identity of the speaker or speakers, and even more about their intended audience. A strong early tradition attributed most or all of the psalms to King David, who ruled around 1000 BCE, although 91 is unusual in its alleged connection to Moses (we will return to that question). Jesus himself clearly accepted the idea of Davidic authorship of the psalms in general. In the case of 91, many interpreters (both Jewish and Christian) imagine David speaking in the opening lines, and then making a promise specifically to his son, Solomon.

This was a standard Talmudic assumption, although some authorities thought the different blessings might come from different sources. Perhaps David offered the first half, and Solomon's mother, Bathsheba, the second. However fringe that last suggestion might have been, it demands attention as a rare proposal for finding a female voice in the biblical text. As to the psalm's destined audience, the promises might be more generally applied than to one named individual, perhaps even to David's people as a whole.[9]

If we move away from the hypothesis of celebrity authorship and under-play the "I," then the individual receiving blessings and protections might be the king who ruled at the time of composition. In that case, 91 might fit with other royal psalms, but as I will suggest, that is probably not correct, and a strong case can be made for its origins in a kingless age. Later generations exercised much ingenuity in identifying that singular "thou" of the promises, whether it was the individual believer or else (a common theme) some especially blessed individual, such as the messiah.[10]

Plague

Taken in isolation, it is not obvious when or why a given psalm was written. Davidic theories would place 91 around the start of the first millennium BCE, but modern critical scholarship is skeptical about any such linkage, and psalms are variously dated anywhere from the tenth century through the fourth, or indeed later. Virtually no psalm offers any kind of internal evidence that allows for more precise dating. Several psalms (such as 45 and 72) assume the existence of a king, but of itself that fact is scarcely helpful in determining exact dating. Israel had kings in the several centuries before the Babylonian Exile and captivity of the sixth century BCE, but these royal-oriented pieces might also refer to much later monarchs, even as late as the second century BCE. Psalm 137 is rare in offering any more exact suggestion of chronology, in that case a reference to the Exile. In that case at least, we can say that the psalm had nothing to do with King David.

But 91 does offer some important indicators of its original context. The thrust of the psalm is that the believer who relies on God will be delivered not just from generic evils and threats, but from pestilence or plague. This indicates that it was intended not for any regular or recurring holiday or pilgrimage, but for a specific and isolated disaster. It reads like a liturgy inspired by a severe biological onslaught.[11]

The Hebrew text of the psalm includes several words that explicitly refer to plague or disease, such as *deber* (which occurs twice). *Deber* appears fifty times in the Hebrew Bible, and on every occasion it refers to some variant of "pestilence." Other words in 91 are more ambiguous, such as *qeteb yashud*, "the destruction that wasteth" (v. 6), or the *nega* of v. 10. This latter term can mean a mark or scourge, but more commonly refers to an infection or disease that leaves marks, such as leprosy, and the KJV does indeed translate it as a plague. The disease interpretation is all but certain. More tenuously, in v. 12, the line about "dashing your foot against a stone" uses a word for "dash" or "smite" that is commonly used as a metaphor for plague. The accumulation of disease-related words in such a short text is remarkable. And the image of thousands falling dead around the speaker (v. 7) suggests a time of signal catastrophe, such as a plague.[12]

That plague theme is more unusual than might at first appear in a biblical setting. Plague is a very familiar Old Testament concept, especially in the context of the Exodus from Egypt, but neither the specific word *deber* nor related words such as those for "pestilence" and "disease" are common in the Book of Psalms. Even when they do occur, these references are generally either metaphorical or historical. Besides the two occurrences in 91, *deber* only appears in one other psalm, in a list of the evils that God sent against Pharaoh's Egypt in the time of Moses. In all the 150 individual texts, plague-related words appear in at most eight psalms and even there, they are not central to the main argument or discussion. Such diseases appear variously as symbols of divine wrath, as generic evils from which God will deliver, or else as references to the Plagues of Egypt. None of these texts necessarily suggest any contemporary outbreak or pressing danger.[13]

Psalm 91 is unique in implying the clear and present danger of an actual contemporary pestilence. Conceivably, it reads so unusually because it represents the sole survivor of a specialized literary category that would once have existed in greater abundance.

Which Plague?

If we accept the plague reading, then two historical moments have appealed to generations of commentators as possible contexts for 91. Ancient Israel, like other Middle Eastern societies, viewed pestilence as a divine visitation, and commonly interpreted occurrences as the work of supernatural beings.

In one story in the book of 2 Samuel, God's anger against King David was expressed by a destructive plague (*deber*), implemented by an "angel," and it is only stopped when God commands the angel to stay his hand. That is the only recorded story that would fit with the psalm's attribution to David, and as such, it remained popular with many Jewish and Christian commentators in the Reformation era and beyond.[14]

But unmooring the psalm from David leaves plenty of other alternatives to choose from, as probably no century in Israelite history lacked epidemic outbreaks of some sort. One popular choice for biblical commentators on 91 was an event from 701 BCE, in the time of King Hezekiah. When the fearsome Assyrian king Sennacherib attacked Jerusalem, he was forced to withdraw after being assailed by a plague. As the Bible reports, "That night, the angel of the LORD went out and put to death a hundred and eighty-five thousand in the Assyrian camp." Yet the Israelites themselves suffered no harm, exactly fitting the psalm's promise of standing safe while thousands fell around them. So attractive was this story as the origin of 91 that it caused some agony for scholars who desperately wanted to believe it but who were reluctant to abandon the Davidic connection. In the fifth century CE, the Christian scholar Theodoret of Cyrus referred repeatedly to Hezekiah in his popular commentary on 91, but was forced to revert to approved orthodoxy in concluding:

> Blessed David, in fact, perceived with spiritual eyes from a distance the situation of blessed Hezekiah, and seeing how with hope in God he overthrew the army of the Assyrians, he uttered this psalm to teach all people how great an abundance of goods trusting in God yields.

We can see what Theodoret wanted to say, had he dared.[15]

A Book Within a Book

Unlike Theodoret, we are not bound to link 91 to any particular scriptural episode or individual, allowing us to range widely in our search for possible plague-related contexts, and we can seek out other writings to which it bears some resemblance. To begin with, we need to know something about how we got our Book of Psalms—the Psalter—as we know it in our Bibles. Those who are not Bible scholars might be surprised to learn that 91 exists not only within that venerated collection, but also within an identifiable book-within-a-book.[16]

The location of a given psalm within the collection tells something about the context in which it was understood. Although today the canonical number of psalms is 150, there are references to, or reminiscences of, many others. One text found at Qumran claims that David composed 3,600 psalms. Various now-orphan texts were once regarded as psalms in various times and places, and some of those pieces survived into later Christian churches. That points to the issue of editorship, and why given psalms show up as they do and in the canonical context that we know today. Why did some community find that arrangement or selection valuable? If this does not give us an exact date of origin for a given text, it does show how it was read at a very early date.[17]

At some point, a group or individual made the decision to limit the category of psalms to what we know today. When they did that, they also brought those individual psalms together into a unified book, with the sequence that we have known over the last two millennia. Crucially, they divided the collection into five units or "books," the final psalm in each being concluded with a special praise to God, a doxology. The five books can be divided as follows:

Book 1 (1–41)
Book 2 (42–72)
Book 3 (73–89)
Book 4 (90–106)
Book 5 (107–150)

That structure has been widely accepted, and it is consecrated in the popular modern English-language Bible translation, the NIV. It is not hard to deduce that those five books are intended to echo the five books of the Torah. Medieval rabbis extolled the Psalms as a second Pentateuch and their supposed author, David, as a second Moses. We have to read Psalm 91 in the context of that Fourth Book.[18]

The Psalter, with its fivefold division, reached its final form at some point after the early fourth century, and it must have been in place by the time of the Bible's translation into Greek, the Septuagint, which was undertaken between 270 and 120 BCE. As we know from many other sources, the third century was a time of intense literary and spiritual creativity in Israel, marked by a fascination with eschatology—the end times—and with messianic ideas. That background helps us understand that final organization of the Book of Psalms as it then emerged. Whatever the editorial goal, the compilers sorted the psalms in an order that seemed appropriate to them, even if the guiding principle is not obvious to modern readers. A general consensus holds that the first three books are earlier than the last two, but the gap in time may not be large.[19]

Three in One, One in Three?

According to this five-book reconstruction, special weight attaches to the psalms of transition, which represent introductions or conclusions to the "volume" in question, and which declare or restate key themes. These are sometimes compared to hinges, or seams. The Third Book ends with Psalm 89, which praises David, but then goes on to lament how the misdeeds of David's descendants have led to crisis and disaster for the nation. The obvious context for that condemnation would be the fall of Jerusalem and the Babylonian Exile. We would naturally expect the opening psalm of the Fourth Book to announce its agenda, but here we run into a problem. Depending on how we read it, that strategic "hinge" constitutes either Psalm 90 alone or some combination of 90 through 92. So was 91 originally freestanding, or has it been detached from a larger unit?[20]

Those three psalms have many features in common. Almost certainly, we are meant to read them together as a sequence, and modern scholars often analyze them in this way, as a triptych. Psalms 90 and 91 are close in theme and vocabulary, and some Hebrew manuscripts present them as a unity. If not a triptych, we are at least dealing with a diptych.[21]

The three psalms can be summarized:

90: Attributed to Moses, this psalm stresses the weakness and frailty of the human in the face of the divine. It proclaims God's absolute sovereignty and eternity, compared to which human realities are as nothing: human lives are utterly transient, and leave no trace. Humans should learn their total dependence on God and live accordingly.

91: Anyone who places such absolute trust in God will be immune to multiple dangers and snares. Because the believer gives that trust, God will deliver and exalt him.

92: The wise believer who places complete trust in God will see how evildoers perish. Those who follow God will succeed and flourish; those who oppose him will be destroyed.

The three together represent a call to return to absolute trust in God. In the context of the five-book structure, they suggest a thorough reconstruction or reimagining of Israel after the collapse depicted in 89. We might speak of reformation or rededication.[22]

Those three, 90–92, seek a basis for authority quite distinct from their predecessors, lacking as they do any obvious references to kings, or to the royal covenant that was such a theme of the previous book. Also, they ground themselves on Moses rather than David. Moses is explicitly cited as the author of 90, which by this reading must predate David by at least two centuries. God, we are to remember, had his purposes for Israel long before David's time, and those continue to work themselves out. The text of 91 as we have it offers no attribution of authorship, just possibly because it was seen as a continuation of the explicitly Mosaic 90. Over the next two millennia, at least some thinkers, Jewish and Christian alike, claimed 91 as Mosaic. That attribution was increasingly confined to a stubborn minority, however, as so many commentaries and translations credited it to David, but the Mosaic idea never entirely died.[23]

This reconstruction still does not give us a date for 91, which might well have originated independently before being repurposed as part of that triptych. That indeed would be my argument, given 91's strong plague associations, which are scarcely relevant to the psalm's present location. Perhaps 90 and 91 really were composed together, and later separated; or else the two originated separately before being combined and harmonized as we have them now. Was 90 even composed as a kind of prequel to 91? Whatever we conclude, this framing offers important lessons for how the compilers of the Psalter wanted 91 to be read, and that interpretive strategy helps us resolve some of the thorny theological points that have troubled many generations of readers. If 91 in itself does not answer our questions, we might need to look more closely at those two neighboring contributions. Psalm 90 pleads with God for certain assurance of aid, and 91 offers that assurance in stark terms. It is so certain and unequivocal, even disturbingly so—does it really imply that *no* evil would befall the godly believer, none whatever? Such statements become more comprehensible when placed alongside their neighbors.[24]

It should also be said that if the compilers of the Fourth Book wanted its readers to use 91 in that context, they enjoyed only limited success. Over the following centuries, when 91 enjoyed so much popularity for spiritual protection in everyday use, only rarely was it deployed together with either of its neighbors, at least in their full-text versions. (Jewish versions often expanded 91 by borrowing a verse of 90 or 92, but never more than that.) If the Fourth Book was intended to contextualize or even tame 91, the effort scarcely succeeded.

Job and the Writings

With whatever caveats, we can say that 91's position in the Fourth Book points to a date after the Exile. Supporting that date are its close connections with other biblical writings of that era. Drawing those parallels helps us understand how the psalm was originally read.

In the Hebrew tradition, the Book of Psalms is listed among the Writings, the Ketuvim, which together with the Torah and Prophets (Navi'im) constitute the Bible. What Christians call the Old Testament, Jews call the Tanakh, an acronym for Torah, Nav'im, and Ketuvim. The collection of biblical Writings conventionally places Psalms alongside the Books of Proverbs and Job, although the exact sequence differed somewhat in ancient times. The Fourth Book of the Psalter finds a great many echoes in those two other biblical books, which may help us date its psalms, including our 91. Job and Proverbs are generally dated in the post-Exilic or Persian period of Israel's history, stretching from the fifth century through the third century BCE, and a time without kings.[25]

Like Job and Proverbs, the Fourth Book presents a sublime monotheism that is almost beyond human comprehension, and the Book is fascinated by the idea of the Wisdom through which God created all things. The Wisdom theme was a powerful component of Jewish thought in the Second Temple era, and it found early expression in Proverbs. Psalm 91 in particular finds thematic parallels in both Job and Proverbs, and really nowhere else in the Hebrew Bible. One powerful resemblance is to a passage in Proverbs (3:21–26), which declares the blessings and protection that will attend the righteous person who follows wisdom and understanding, and which has echoes of 91. Scholars differ (of course) over the exact direction of influence, which text influenced which, but the two works clearly inhabit the same intellectual world.[26]

The parallels to Job are even closer, and quite a few words and usages appear in Job and Psalms but infrequently in the rest of the Hebrew Bible. Just to take one example of many, when Psalm 91 speaks of "the terror by night," the Hebrew word is *pachad*, which features forty-nine times in the Hebrew Bible. Nine of those uses occur in Psalms, ten in Job, and four in Proverbs. I am not claiming any precise scientific analysis here, but the Job parallels are frequent. The other place we find verbal echoes of 91 is in Jeremiah, but this is a very large book, in fact the longest in the Hebrew Bible, with an appropriately extensive vocabulary.[27]

As I have noted, Job even includes a prickly conversation with Psalm 91 itself. After Job has suffered his various calamities, he receives a visit from a series of figures who collectively have been known as "Job's Comforters," although "comfort" is scarcely what they are offering, as their lessons and lectures are dark indeed. One, Eliphaz the Tamanite, asserts that God will not punish a truly righteous person, so if Job is indeed suffering, it must be because of some dreadful act he has committed. He uses what is surely a summary of 91 to preach that the one who accepts God's correction will escape the evils of plague, war, famine, destruction, and wild animals.[28]

The Age of Angels

Since discussions of biblical texts often range across lengthy historical periods, it might be useful to recapitulate here what I have argued about Psalm 91 and what we can say with any degree of confidence. I have suggested that 91 was composed in response to a plague outbreak. As to a date, it probably originated in the fifth or fourth century, when it was known and used by the author of Job. In the fourth century (perhaps) 91 was integrated into the fivefold structure of the emerging Book of Psalms. That general chronology finds other support when we look at the larger worldview of Israel in those post-Exilic times, which suggests that we should date 91 later rather than earlier in the story. If 91 is unusual in its concentration on plague, it is also distinctive because of how it treats angels, which became vastly more important in Hebrew religion during these later centuries. That new spiritual environment also explains how that plague psalm was transmuted into a song against evil spirits.

During the Second Temple era, most aspects of Israelite society's world-view were transformed, rapidly and thoroughly, and not just because of the political crisis associated with the Babylonian Exile. In spiritual terms, the sixth century BCE was a revolutionary period during which strict mono-theism became established as unquestioned orthodoxy in Israel. That in turn forced pious believers to rethink many aspects of the supernatural. As God became exalted as an absolute and transcendent being, it became ever more difficult to imagine such a deity interacting easily or personally with his human subjects, or intervening so readily in their affairs. That demanded a new emphasis on God's messengers, the angels, and older scriptures were ed-ited to show that it was these figures who had conversed with human beings, rather than God personally. The Septuagint translation of the Bible system-atically reduces any sense of direct divine interactions with human beings.[29]

Angels helped to resolve newly pressing difficulties in understanding the existence of evil. In earlier times, evils could easily be blamed on the malev-olence of a multitude of rival deities, but the new monotheism demanded other explanations for the everyday ills that afflicted humanity. From about 300 BCE onward, Hebrew society developed a strong belief in angels as messengers implementing God's commands, but also in demonic forces as the sources of evil. Seeking to preserve the belief in God's absolute su-premacy, thinkers developed stories claiming that even those demonic forces themselves originated as angels who had fallen into rebellion. As a general rule, the more clearly a text speaks of angels and demons, the later it is likely to be.[30]

Angels and demons became the source of much speculation in this era, with the now-lost Book of Noah (mid-third century BCE) as a pioneering text. Over the following two centuries, those same ideas resurfaced in mul-tiple once-popular scriptures and writings, such as 1 Enoch, which describes noble archangels and rebellious evil angels of the kind that would so domi-nate Christian thought through the time of John Milton and beyond. A whole literature concerned the angels and demons associated with individuals, as either guardian figures or tempters. In the Book of Tobit, from around 200 BCE, the archangel Raphael disguises himself to guard the faithful Tobias as he goes forth to confront the monstrous demon Asmodeus. People were very concerned about demonic threats, as manifested in sickness, misfortune, or outright assault.[31]

Against that background, we look again at the words of 91, and specifically the promise in v. 11 that "he shall give his angels charge over thee, to keep thee in all thy ways." Such a promise of a (literal) guardian angel or angels sounds commonplace enough in the Judeo-Christian inheritance, but in the context of Psalms, it is anything but that. Of the 150 psalms, unambiguous references to angels, *malak*, feature in just seven, and most depict angels generically, whether serving God or else striking and punishing his enemies. In only two psalms, 34 and 91, is there any sense of individual protection, of a guardian angel. The distinctive usage in 91 would be singularly appropriate if in fact the text was intended for protection in time of plague, and therefore against the harmful workings of ill-intentioned spirits or angels. Our psalm promises that the angels would be benevolent, and would work for the protection of the believer. That angelic v. 11 might even have inspired the Book of Tobit, the plot of which tells precisely how an angel takes charge of a human and guards him.[32]

Whatever its origin, this theme of the protective angel contributed to 91's popularity in the spiritual world of the Second Temple era.

The Psalm as Weapon

As people became ever more disturbingly aware of the threatening spiritual universe around them, they ransacked the scriptures for texts that could be deployed for protection. Over and above those protecting angels, other words in 91 appealed to the spiritually fearful and besieged. It is not difficult to take the psalm's catalog of threats and hazards—such as *qeteb*, "destruction," and *deber*, "plague"—and to personalize them as actual demons to be named and subjugated. Many scholars have drawn parallels between such key words in our psalm and the names of demons or spirits in the societies surrounding the Israelites, such as the Canaanites and Phoenicians. Also, the format of 91 resembles protective spells and incantations that are recorded in those neighboring societies, including charms to be used against snakes and against nocturnal terrors. The psalm fits almost too well into the cultural environment of the ancient Near East.[33]

Whether or not the psalm's composer intended to create a magical text, the resulting work readily lent itself to such purposes. Psalm 91 proved ideal for warfare against demons or evil forces. Just how perfect it was is apparent if we compare it with other possible rivals, which at first sight were not uncommon. The very next psalm, 92, imagines the destruction and scattering of enemies, evildoers, and "workers of iniquity," Other psalms pray for deliverance from enemies, who might be construed as spiritual or demonic. But 91 offers a comprehensive range of such invocations, presented in the form of direct unconditional assertions of actual deliverance rather than just the believer's hopeful prayer.[34]

So ideal was 91 in these contexts that it almost reads as if it were directly intended to serve such purposes of "turning away"—of what we have encountered as apotropaic functions. If Psalm 91 was not a direct product of this emerging age of angels, it was from the third century BCE that it came into its own, and in the process it underwent some remarkable transformations.[35]

Demons and Dragons

Themes of spiritual combat came to the fore when the psalm was translated into the Greek of the Septuagint, in the third or second century BCE. That Septuagint translation tells us a great deal about understandings of the psalm in the new environment, and in Jewish diaspora communities.

At first sight, it might seem curious to pay so much attention to a translation as opposed to the original text, as we naturally assume that the Hebrew is more authentic and archaic than the Greek. But the Septuagint undoubtedly preserved many early readings and understandings. Just to take a minor example, I have already mentioned the question of numbering the psalms. The Hebrew Masoretic text reads Psalms 9 and 10 as discrete texts, while the Greek Septuagint correctly understands them as one unified work, which it calls Psalm 9. Whatever the merits of the decision, it affected the numbering of the following hundred or so psalms. What the Hebrew text calls Psalms 11–113, the Greek calls 10–112, and Hebrew 91 refers to Greek 90. The Protestant translators of the Reformation era decided to follow Hebrew usage.[36]

The Septuagint version of 91 has several distinctive features, including an attribution to David, but it is in its "spiritual" aspects that it most surprises. Of course, the angels are present in the translation, but so, unexpectedly, are demons and even dragons. Exactly how those sinister creatures emerged requires some explanation. If we found just one instance, we might attribute it to a translator's bias or even error due to carelessness or ignorance. But so frequent are the examples, with all tending in similar directions, that we must see them as examples of a systematic tendency toward monstrous and otherworldly interpretations.[37]

I have stressed the several clear disease references in the Hebrew text, all of which are subverted or minimized in the Greek. In v. 6, for instance, "the destruction that wastes at noonday" is neither personalized nor necessarily supernatural. It almost certainly refers to disease, and parallels the previous phrase about the pestilence that walks in darkness. The Hebrew combines *qeteb*, "destruction," with *yashud* or *yšwd*, a word that implies "despoiling" or "destroying." But a very similar root to *yšwd* gives the word *shed*, which appears in another psalm as a devil or demon who receives human sacrifices. The Greek translators decided that the "destruction that wasteth" was in fact such a demon, who operated at midday and who therefore became the midday demon, *daimonion*. That Greek word, *daimonion*, did not originally have the grim implications of our "demon," but it increasingly did in the Second Temple world, and very much so in the age of the New Testament. We recall that the translation of the Septuagint stood very close in time to the outpouring of the angels-and-demons literature that I have already described, in works like the Book of Noah or Tobit, or the earliest sections of 1 Enoch.[38]

That "demonic" change was part of a larger transformation of the psalm's meaning, away from its explicit connection to plague and pestilence. In a standard modern English translation, we have a deadly pestilence (v. 3) as well as a pestilence and a plague (v. 6), and these verses provide a context into which other menaces (arrows and terrors) can easily be fitted as metaphors. The Septuagint consistently undermines that element. In v. 3, the "noisome pestilence" (KJV) becomes a harmful or troublesome "word," *logos*, giving rise to centuries of commentary about the devastating effects of ill-considered speech or slander. If it was indeed an error, it was easy enough, a confusion of the Hebrew word *deber*, "pestilence," with *dabar*, "word." It should be said, however, that some scholars think that the "word" reading represented the psalm's original intent, possibly in the sense of the "word" of a magic spell.[39]

Whatever the exact process here, "plague" is also displaced at v. 6, where *deber* becomes a generic "thing." "The pestilence that walketh in darkness" now becomes "a deed [or, rather, thing, *pragmatos*] that travels in darkness." The word *pragmatos* is almost comically nonspecific, and we might be tempted to translate it as "thingamajig." As we have seen, in v. 10, the Hebrew *nega* can mean a "marking" disease, and probably does here, but the Septuagint prefers the looser metaphor of "scourge."[40]

As read in the Greek, and presumably as understood by the third- or second-century Jews who made the translation, the psalm is much less about the threat of disease than that of spiritual or demonic enemies. Just why the translators thus de-plagued the text is mysterious. At the time of translation, plagues of various kinds continued to be a very familiar part of life in the Middle East and in the Hellenistic empires, and we might think that a scripture designed to combat such menaces would be both useful and popular. But demons, broadly defined, must have been seen as a more immediate and palpable threat.[41]

That would explain some other surprising readings in the Greek text. One of the psalm's most oft-quoted lines (v. 13) promises domination over ferocious and venomous animals, which was a greatly valued power in a Mediterranean world beset by dangerous creatures. Just which animals the psalmist intended has been subject to much debate, and the list as we normally have it contains some oddities. The word that we usually translate as "serpent" or "dragon" is notoriously flexible. The Hebrew word *tan*, "jackal," shares a root with *tannin*, which usually means a regular snake or serpent, but can also signify a monster or sea serpent. At several points in the Hebrew Bible, the two meanings (snake and jackal) are confused, so passages that were originally intended to refer to desert-dwelling jackals have been twisted to apply to serpents. Conceivably, 91 too originally paired the lion and the jackal, which would make more sense than the serpent or dragon that we have presently. Nor do we know if the psalm always intended victory over literal rather than symbolic animals. Even at the earliest stage, it might have implied trampling metaphorical enemies, such as rival kings or chieftains. By the third century BCE, however, the animals mentioned were acquiring supernatural and demonic dimensions.[42]

In a dependable English translation, the Hebrew text promises victory over "the lion and the cobra . . . the great lion and the serpent" (NIV). For reasons that are not obvious, the Septuagint Greek changes the order in which the creatures appear, listing "*aspida kai basiliskon . . . leonta kai drakonta.*" Probably this was done to create a euphonious and balanced effect in the Greek, rather than to suggest a different hierarchy of menace. But that Greek catalog of creatures is also more zoologically imaginative. Both the basilisk and the dragon can refer to actual reptiles, but each is credited with special powers in Hellenistic lore. A basilisk, literally a "little king," is a snake that can kill with a look. The Hebrew word *tannin*—which now became the

Greek *drakon*—is complicated. It can mean an ordinary snake, but later it developed into something more mysterious and threatening, such as a sea serpent. Whatever the original intent, *tannin* now morphed into a dragon. This latter word in turn comes from a root meaning "to see," indicating the creature's incredible powers of vision used to detect prey. We are not far from the Satanic dragon of the New Testament (see Chapter 4).[43]

Into a Wider World

The Septuagint popularized many words that have subsequently supplied much of the West's vocabulary in spiritual matters, not least the words "angel" and "demon" themselves. But beyond those terms, the translation's shift of interpretation cast a very long shadow. The Septuagint was the version of the Bible used by early Christians, and by Greek-speaking churches up to the present day. Those Christian readers thus inherited the "spiritual warfare" and demonized reading of the psalm, rather than its more primitive emphasis on plague.

So also did Latin readers of the Vulgate of St. Jerome, who in the fourth century CE faithfully reproduced the image of the "noonday demon." Meanwhile, the *pragmatos* that wandered in darkness became for Latin readers a *negotium*, an equally ill-defined business or matter, as in our "negotiate." At v. 10, the Vulgate followed the Septuagint in turning a "mark" (or marking disease) into a scourge, *flagellum*, as in the word "flagellation." In consequence, the explicitly plague-oriented readings of the psalm were unknown to the vast majority of Christians until the Reformation and the sixteenth century. Demons, in contrast, were freely available. The Latin also followed the Greek in the order in which the creatures were listed in v. 13, beginning not with lion and cobra, but with *aspidem et basiliscum*.[44]

That Latin story is more complicated than it might appear. Jerome was a superb scholar with excellent Hebrew, and he well understood the problems of the Septuagint version. Accordingly, he produced two separate and quite different Latin translations of the Psalter, one closely dependent on the Hebrew, the other, the *Versio Gallicana*, following the Septuagint. That "Hebrew Psalter," *versio juxta Hebraeos*, was quite faithful to the original. Verse 6, for instance, retains the reference to plague, *peste*, and at 10, the "mark" is a *lepra*, suggesting leprosy, rather than a scourge. Nor is there a noonday demon. Although this more accurate rendering survived in some limited areas of

emerging Christendom, it largely faded from general use by the ninth century CE. Crucially for later Christian history, it was the Septuagint-derived
Vulgate that was adopted enthusiastically by the Western church, and it dominated psalm interpretation until the Reformation. Henceforth, I will refer
to that Greek-derived "Gallican" version simply as the Vulgate translation,
which remained the standard Psalter of the Roman Catholic church until the
twentieth century.[45]

Although we naturally think of the medieval church mainly in its Western
and Latin dimensions, in early times the Eastern and Syriac-speaking
Christian communities were enormously significant, and widespread ge-
ographically. The version of 91 that they knew leaned heavily toward the
Septuagint readings. The Syriac did keep the plague at v. 10, but not in either
v. 3 or v. 6. Likewise recalling the Septuagint's use of the "harmful word," v. 3
promises deliverance not from the pestilence, but from "talking of vanity,"
and in v. 6, the reference to plague has been replaced by a sinister "word."
The noonday demon here becomes a "wind that bloweth in the noonday."
This may refer to the fearsome *simoom,* the "poison wind" that is such a dangerous feature of Middle Eastern climates, but again, it cannot naturally be
interpreted as a plague or disease.[46]

The other key translation of this and other psalms appeared in the Targum.
As the Hebrew language fell out of use among Jewish people, it was widely
replaced by the Aramaic that was the usual vernacular for Jesus and his first
followers. Probably by the first century CE, translators would render biblical
texts into Aramaic versions or interpretations (in Aramaic, *targum*), at first
in oral form. Those translators usually added some extra commentary as they
went, so their presentations constituted a kind of homily. During the early
centuries of the Common Era, those presentations gradually began to be
written down; they survive to illustrate the popular understanding of texts
in this period. In the case of Psalm 91, the interpreter has turned the text
into a dialogue between David and his son, Solomon. It is thus Solomon who
will be released from the snare. For our purposes, the new "vernacular" version looks strikingly like the Septuagint in underplaying plague and instead
stressing demons to an almost obsessive degree. In v. 3, the noisome pestilence has become "death and tumult." And vv. 5 and 6 now read:

> You will not be afraid of the terror of *the demons that go about in* the night,
> nor of the arrow *of the angel of death that he shoots* in the daytime, nor of
> the *death* that goes about in the darkness nor of *the company of demons*

that destroy at noon. [Words in italics represent the Targum's changes, interpolations, or additions.]

The word "plague" does survive in v. 10, but it is qualified as "no plague *or demon.*"[47]

Normal Demons

The Septuagint approach to 91 was no quirk of an individual translator, but genuinely reflected an early and enduring Jewish interpretation. Moreover, that view was in no sense confined to "sectarian" Jewish groups, a term that historians detest because it suggests that any one form of Second Temple Judaism could be described as mainstream or small-*o* orthodox. Usually, the hypothetical "mainstream" Judaism is identified with the ancestors of what became the rabbinic or Talmudic tradition, which is duly retrojected into the earlier era. In fact, the demonic interpretation appealed across partisan or sectarian boundaries and was as mainstream and generic as could be. That approach is powerfully apparent in the (quite extensive) records we have of the Jewish world around the turn of the Common Era. The conspicuous exception was the elite party of the Sadducees, who stubbornly denied any belief in angels or spirits.

I have already quoted the Talmudic text known as Shavuot, but other tractates likewise place the psalm's "demonic" interpretation in the context of the Jerusalem Temple, and of its "mainstream" priests and Levites. In a discussion on amulets and using scripture as a means of healing, the fourth-century CE Rabbi Yudan recalls that "they would recite the Psalm of the Afflicted in Jerusalem," presumably before the fall of the Second Temple in 70 (the title can also be translated as "Song of the Possessed"). The tract quotes the opening of Psalm 3 and then includes only the first nine verses of 91, a limitation mentioned elsewhere. Such references confirm that the Shavuot passage is accurately reflecting how 91 was used in that earlier period.[48]

Abundant evidence of the psalm's usage can also be found in the Dead Sea Scrolls. In the mid-second century BCE, a dispute over the succession to the Jewish high priesthood led to the defection of a breakaway group or faction, who created a thriving settlement at Qumran, near the shore of the Dead Sea. Over the next two centuries, this group, which had a close relationship to the historical Essenes, collected and developed a sizable body of literature, much of which concerned themes of spiritual warfare, of the conflict between Light and Darkness, and (of course) of angels and demons. Naturally, they treasured such works as Tobit and 1 Enoch, and the substantial Enochic literature has a close relationship to that Essene world. But they also saw those broad themes well represented in the canonical Book of Psalms, which was by far the biblical book most frequently represented in the surviving Scrolls. They found the Psalter rich in texts foreshadowing the messiah and the messianic age, which would succeed the present polluted world.[49]

The Qumran believers valued Psalm 91 as a practical weapon in their ongoing spiritual struggles. About 60 CE, a scribe at Qumran compiled a series of four songs intended to exorcise demons and to heal the stricken (the text is known as 11Q11, or alternatively, 11QApocrPs). All four were attributed to David. Three of the texts are not known elsewhere, but the fourth is basically the Psalm 91 we know, with a few additions. It includes a different conclusion, ending "and they answered amen, amen." This shows that the "song" was intended for communal or liturgical use and, in the context, as part of a defensive ritual against evil forces.[50]

The other three songs are only partially preserved, but they indicate exactly the themes and ideas that we have already observed in the context of 91. Song 1 is centrally concerned with exorcism, it speaks of a dragon, and it uses the number seventy, which often appears in connection with demons. Song 2 recalls the magical powers of Solomon, it imagines combat against the demon Abaddon, and it invokes the healing archangel Raphael, whom we already know from the Book of Tobit. Song 3 is intended to defend against demonic attackers in the night, who are imagined with horns, and it also invokes angels. Although its canonical status was unchallenged, Psalm 91 was already found in marginal and even disreputable company, in a world of exorcists and demon-fighters.[51]

Through the centuries, many scholars have speculated about possible connections between the world of Jesus and his earliest followers and the traditions of the Essenes and of Qumran. Whatever those connections might have been, there is no doubt the earliest Jesus movement was in its first few decades a Jewish sect and, further, that it was absolutely rooted in ideas of healing and exorcism. Psalm 91 was very much part of that movement and its belief system. Just how significant the psalm was emerges from the famous scene of Christ's temptation in the wilderness, and the other Gospel passages that build upon that episode.

3

Lest You Dash Your Foot Against a Stone

Finding Christ in the Psalm

Under the figure of scorpions and serpents are portended evil spirits, whose very prince is described by the name of serpent, dragon, and every other most conspicuous beast in the power of the Creator. This power the Creator conferred first of all upon His Christ, even as the ninetieth Psalm [i.e., 91st] says to Him: *Upon the asp and the basilisk shall Thou tread; the lion and the dragon shall Thou trample under foot.*[1]

—Tertullian, c. 210 CE

Through the centuries, many artists have depicted the harrowing episode of Christ's temptations in the wilderness. Some depict Jesus in dialogue with the tempting Devil himself, while others focus on a solitary Jesus, who presumably is battling these temptations as inner impulses and psychological conflicts. Hearing these seductive calls to action, Jesus must decide whether to reveal his supernatural status by some flamboyant miracle, by casting himself off the Temple. At that point, he hears the assurance of Psalm 91 that the angels will bear him up. But he resists, faithful to God.

Two of the four gospels recall the strange scene in which the Devil himself quotes the exorcist's psalm. Viewed by itself, it might seem like an isolated or even quirky reference. We easily miss the sequel that occurs later in the New Testament itself, most explicitly in Luke, and which completes the wilderness story. When we place the temptation scene in its larger context within the New Testament, both the episode and the psalm become central to the early Christian narrative. In Luke's gospel, indeed, Psalm 91 becomes the charter of the Jesus movement and of the church. As an indispensable mainstay of early Christian belief, the psalm shaped both the writing of the gospels and their later interpretation.[2]

He Will Save You from the Deadly Pestilence. Philip Jenkins, Oxford University Press. © Oxford University Press 2023.
DOI: 10.1093/oso/9780197605646.003.0003

Temptations

The authors of the four gospels presented their story in the context of the Bible as they knew it, and they often contextualized actions or events by quoting scriptural texts, to show how Jesus was fulfilling prophecies. The Book of Psalms is the source most commonly used this way in the New Testament: when the dying Jesus uttered the words "My God, My God, why hast thou forsaken me?," he was quoting the opening of Psalm 22. Like the Qumran community before them, the earliest Christian writers thought in psalms, and searched them for words and images that could be understood as messianic. As the early churches sought to comprehend Jesus's relationship with God the Father, they drew on a select group of psalms to create their Christologies. Such texts as Psalms 2 and 110 were the means by which Jesus's followers made their case, and they provided the scriptural foundation for early polemics between Jews and Christians. We need not be surprised, then, to find 91 playing a major role in a gospel story, or being used to construct a theological system.[3]

Even so, the use of 91 is distinctive. It differs in several ways from those other psalm-derived proof texts, not least in being quoted by the Devil personally. Whereas other psalms were used to illustrate or explain specific moments in Jesus's career, the gospels use 91 to construct a whole narrative arc. That begins with the wilderness encounter, which carries such special weight in Jesus's career. The three synoptic gospels—Mark, Matthew, and Luke—all place that scene in a prominent position in their narrative, following Jesus's baptism by John the Baptist. In each case, the temptation leads directly to the beginning of Jesus's mission, and the calling of his disciples.

Each synoptic gospel frames the wilderness episode in terms of Psalm 91. Mark offers the shortest account, stating only that Jesus was "tested by Satan, and he was with the wild beasts, and the angels were ministering to him." Even if we had that account alone, without the other gospels, the juxtaposition of wild beasts and angelic protection would suggest 91. Both Matthew and Luke knew Mark's gospel, and as each of them developed it the references to 91 became quite explicit. The fact that Matthew and Luke offer broadly similar accounts that do not derive from Mark means that they are drawing on a now-lost proto-gospel called Q, although they use that material in different ways.[4]

Three Rejections

Matthew and Luke differ both in detail and in their general concept. In Matthew, the psalm is used in the second of three temptations, and his Devil offers a slightly compressed version of 91. In Luke, 91 is the basis for the third and culminating temptation, and that reflects its critical position in his narrative. Luke integrates the Psalm 91 material into a complex sequence although the denouement does not follow on immediately. In musical terms, it is as if a leitmotif is here introduced, and listeners have to await its reappearance. To understand this, we need to analyze Luke's account of the wilderness encounter in some detail.

The Devil tempts Jesus three times. So you are hungry? he asks. Then turn these stones to bread.

He takes Jesus to a high mountain. Look at all the world's kingdoms, he says. Just worship me, and I will give you all of them.

Then the Devil takes Jesus to a high point on the great Temple itself and urges him to throw himself off. Does not Psalm 91 say that angels will protect him, so that he will not so much as dash his foot? What better way for a messiah, a Christ, to prove his status to the world, and to show that he is guarded by angels?

Luke and Matthew agree that on each occasion Jesus refuses the temptation, and three times he quotes a verse from Deuteronomy. More specifically, he draws on a section of that book that in modern Bibles appears as chapters 6–8, immediately following the giving of the Ten Commandments. To the first suggestion (in Luke's sequence), he responds that man shall not live by bread alone. Nor will he worship Satan, responding, "Thou shalt worship the Lord thy God, and him only shalt thou serve." To the suggestion about throwing himself off the Temple, he replies, "Do not put the Lord your God to the test."[5]

Jesus grounds himself absolutely in the Torah. In this era, Deuteronomy (literally, the "Second Law") often served as the epitome of the whole Law, but it had a special relevance to this episode because it was so powerfully associated with Israel's wandering the wilderness in ancient times. In Hebrew, Deuteronomy is known as Devarim, "Words"—the words of Moses that he delivered in this barren setting. It is ideal in foreshadowing the wilderness of Jesus's own time. When Jesus quotes words that are attributed to Moses, he presents himself as a new version of that holy figure. In some accounts of 91, as we have seen, the psalm was attributed to Mosaic authorship, and we may well be meant to recall that here.[6]

Three Triumphs

From early times, commentators expressed puzzlement that the citation of 91 in the wilderness scene was oddly incomplete. As reported, the Devil quoted what we would call the psalm's vv. 11–12, but he did not proceed to v. 13, in which the fall of evil forces is signaled, and which, moreover, contained those evocative messianic references to trampling and serpents. Naturally, thought some, the Devil would not want to undermine his argument by citing such an embarrassing line. Origen noted this failure to follow through. In fact, however, if we read Luke's gospel as a whole, that very v. 13 shortly reappears, centrally and memorably, as Jesus openly proclaimed his messianic mission. Jesus caps Satan's quotation.[7]

In two chapters, 9 and 10, Luke presents a series of critical episodes that upend and reverse the Devil's challenges in the wilderness, and Psalm 91 is pivotal to this story, specifically the allegedly missing v. 13. Among the four gospels, this story appears in fully developed form only in Luke. This may mean that he constructed those connections himself or, more likely, that he alone preserved an ancient narrative of the movement's beginnings.[8]

Luke's wilderness account features three temptations, which we might summarize as the miraculous feeding; the ascent and the call to worship; and the invocation of Psalm 91. These three reappear, in that very same sequence, in Luke's later two chapters. We first encounter the famous scene in which Jesus miraculously feeds the five thousand. When invited by the Devil to turn stones into bread, he had quoted the Deuteronomy passage concerning manna, the miraculous bread from heaven, and had refused to be provoked into performing a miracle. Yet in Luke 9, he performs exactly such an act, in a way that is meant to evoke the giving of manna. Jesus responds to the Devil's challenge, but entirely in his own way, and in his own time.

After that miraculous feeding, Peter acknowledges Jesus as the messiah. There then follows another reversal of the wilderness episode. The Devil had "led him up to a high place" to tempt him with worldly power. In Luke 9, it is Jesus who takes the initiative in "leading people up" when he takes his apostles "up to a mountain." There he is transfigured in divine glory, and appears with Moses and Elijah, as God proclaims his Sonship. Again, this scene reverses the earlier one. Jesus will indeed go up to a high place where he will receive immeasurable power, far beyond mere kingly rule, and he will achieve it through his obedience to God, not Satan.[9]

We then move directly on to Jesus's sending out the disciples, in what is effectively the foundation of the church. Here again, the story overturns an earlier temptation, specifically the Devil's use of Psalm 91. Jesus sends out his seventy-two disciples (or seventy; manuscripts differ), with healing as a core part of their mission. In each village, they should "heal [*therapeute*] the sick who are there." At the time, the boundaries between healing and exorcism were slim to nonexistent, as was the distinction between the sick and the possessed. Jesus is dispatching exorcists, not paramedics. On their return, the disciples joyfully report their triumphs, but they do not mention healing or "therapy" in any sense that we might recognize. Instead, they recount overcoming devils, *daimonia*:

> And the seventy returned again with joy, saying, Lord, even the devils are subject unto us through thy name. And he said unto them, I beheld Satan as lightning fall from heaven. Behold, I give unto you power to tread on serpents and scorpions, and over all the power of the enemy: and nothing shall by any means hurt you.[10]

In this last verse, 10:19, Jesus is remembering and paraphrasing our psalm's v. 13. Reinforcing the identification is the assurance that nothing will hurt the believer, which recalls 91's "no evil shall befall thee."

The Great Reversal

As we have seen, Jewish interpretations of v. 13 over the previous two centuries had transformed the psalm's animals into threatening spiritual beings, and that exactly fits the context here. One phrase here can be interpreted in various ways. The Greek text of Luke 10:19 promises triumph over "the power of the enemy," *ten dynamin tou echthrou*. But what does that last word, *echthros*, mean here? Literally it means an enemy, a hostile force or person, and that is how it is rendered in most English translations. It is the word used when Jesus tells his followers to love their *enemies*. But it can also mean The Enemy, in the sense of the Devil. (The Greek text gives no clue about issues of capitalization or punctuation.) As this text was interpreted in later centuries, that "enemy" became ever more explicitly Satanic.[11]

We are not told the means by which the disciples undertook their healing of body and soul, still less the exact words they used, but in the context of the passage, it would make excellent sense if they were deploying 91, perhaps as part of a package of other songs and formulae. We have already seen how the Qumran community recorded such songs within a generation of the events described here. If in fact Jesus's followers had undertaken their mission by deploying 91, it would be wholly appropriate for Jesus to reassert that text in praising and reaffirming their victories. For Luke, Jesus is accepting the Devil's original challenge and overcoming it. Satan had invited Jesus to plummet from a pinnacle of the Temple; instead, he himself has fallen from Heaven. Point by point, the wilderness story has come full circle.

We note that the creatures to be trodden here include "snakes and scorpions," although the latter does not appear in our psalm. But this does recall a verse in Deuteronomy that stands adjacent to the others cited earlier and which refers to "snakes and scorpions" in the context of the *eremos*, wilderness. This leaves little doubt that the later passage harks back to the temptation dialogue, and that the two scenes are united by Psalm 91.[12]

Matthew's Trappers

Although all three synoptic gospels use 91 to frame the temptations scene, only Luke makes it such a core part of his gospel. But Matthew too returns to the psalm in a later episode. All the synoptic gospels tell the story of Jesus's opponents trying to trap him on the issue of paying tax to Roman authorities, which Jesus resolves with his famous words about rendering to Caesar the things that are Caesar's, and to God the things that are God's. But in Matthew's gospel the exact language used to describe the attempted trapping is distinctive. In Matthew's chapter 22, Jesus's Pharisaic opponents plan to "trap him in his words," which leads to the famous dialogue about taxation. This phrase is a reference to the psalm's v. 3.[13]

In modern English translations, no such verbal linkage is obvious, but in the Septuagint that Matthew and his readers were using, the fowler's snare or trap (*pagidos*) in 91 was followed immediately by the harmful *logos* or word. In Matthew 22, the Greek text about "trapping in words" reads *pagideusosin en logo*. In the psalm, the hearer will be delivered *ek **pagidos*** *thereuton kai apo **logou** tarachodous*: from the hunter's snare and from the dreadful word. As in Matthew's gospel, and in no other obvious contemporary examples, trapping is linked to words. Once that allusion registered, a contemporary hearer would see the Pharisees as the would-be hunters laying their snares, yet failing, because God would deliver the faithful. As the psalm was read at the time, this would also frame the Pharisees in demonic mode.[14]

This passage in Matthew 22 has a clear verbal echo earlier in that same gospel, when the Pharisees similarly plot together against Jesus, in this case to destroy him rather than to trap him. The relevant line, in chapter 12, comes immediately before a heated row with the Pharisees about casting out demons, *daimonia*, invoking Beelzebub, and other appropriately diabolical themes. That exchange leads into a passage about good and bad words, by which one may be condemned or acquitted. Jesus's remarks here read like a homily on the psalm's verse about "bitter words." The whole passage offers a neat parallel to and prefiguring of the chapter 22 episode; at every point, Psalm 91 lies in the background.[15]

Just as the temptations mark the beginning of Jesus's career, so the lengthy dialogues in Matthew's chapters 22–25 foreshadow its end. The use of the psalm in these exchanges tells the reader how to understand Jesus's opponents, the Pharisees and teachers of the Law, and also prefigures their defeat. They are serpents, a generation of vipers, and any attentive reader of 91 knows that such sinister beings will be duly trodden down. In their combination of serpents, demons, traps, and bitter words, Matthew's dialogues leave little doubt about their scriptural source.[16]

More allusively, Mark's gospel suggests 91 in its vision of subjugating the forces of evil and chaos. Throughout the gospels, the fact that Jesus is "Son of God" is an explosive secret, to be revealed only very gradually to humans, although the Devil uses the title in the wilderness accounts of Matthew and Luke. In Mark, Jesus encounters a demon-possessed man, and the demon offers a startling and explicit recognition of his true identity, calling him "Jesus, Son of the Most High God." Jesus exorcises the man, driving the evil spirits into the bodies of the famous Gadarene swine. That "Most High" title, *hypsistos*, is not commonly used in the New Testament, but it recalls the term applied to God in the opening verse of 91. Just like Satan in the Wilderness, Mark's demon is acknowledging Jesus's status and placing it in the context of the psalm that is destined to subjugate himself and his sinister kind. Evil forces are good at quoting 91.[17]

Christ the Conqueror

Even as it was compiling the writings that became the New Testament, the church was giving a central place to 91 as a means of comprehending and explaining Jesus's life and death. In their writings, Luke, Matthew, and other believers were contributing to that theological work. Whether or not 91 had messianic connotations during Jesus's lifetime, it rapidly acquired them after his death. The psalm supplied the lens through which the stories about him were viewed retroactively, and the framework for later reporting.

Psalm 91 proved so suitable for this Christological work because of its vision of evil forces being defeated and overthrown—in the psalm's language, trampled and trodden down. From earliest times, Jesus's followers believed that he had been crucified and then resurrected from the dead, but the exact meaning or purpose of those events had to be determined. Early theories of atonement suggested that Christ's death was paid as a kind of ransom to Satan to redeem the souls of humanity, who otherwise would have been eternally lost by reason of original sin. Medieval and later theologians modified this theology in various ways, adding the idea that in his death, Christ made a kind of legal satisfaction for the insult to God's honor. Christ stood in for human beings through a "substitutionary" atonement.

But in the church's earliest days, theologians paid at least as much attention to the resurrection as the crucifixion, to the act of victory as much as that of ransom or substitution. They emphasized the liberating effects of Jesus's death and resurrection, as Christ's act of triumph freed human beings from the powers of sin and death, which hitherto had held humanity in bondage. The New Testament letter to the Ephesians declares that as Christ ascended he became like a victorious warlord: "he took many captives and gave gifts to his people." (This is another example of using a psalm as a messianic proof text, in this instance 68.) For centuries, this Christus Victor idea was reflected in literature and art by images of Christ triumphing over those defeated and humbled spiritual foes.[18]

The gospel writers were intimately familiar with this theme of the risen Christ meeting and defeating the Devil and his servants, and they projected it back into their accounts of what Jesus said and did during his earthly life. Knowing as they did that Jesus of Nazareth was Christus Victor, how could that fact not dominate their accounts, framed so naturally in the familiar ideas of Psalm 91? Naturally, then, that theme of Christ's triumph is critical to passages like the temptations in the wilderness.

The Messiah's Psalm?

In the Christian tradition, Psalm 91 became closely attached to the messianic idea. It is not entirely clear how that connection arose. Why does the Devil (as we are told) draw on that particular psalm, following directly after the suggestion "If you are the Son of God . . ."? That framing would be exquisitely appropriate if 91 already had well-known messianic implications, so that when Jesus was facing a very specific test of his role, the "you" who would not dash his foot against a stone was not just any random believer, but the messiah. Would early readers have recognized the psalm in that context? Was there a preexisting messianic interpretation of 91 in Jewish thought, perhaps among the Essenes?[19]

No text in the Qumran collection or elsewhere proves such a linkage. But in the context of contemporary messianic expectations and the scriptures commonly used to support them, the psalm fits extremely well. The messiah envisioned at Qumran, for example, would certainly trample down evil forces and subjugate dangerous creatures. He would also be attended and guarded by angels. The gospel writers are well aware of those associations, and later passages suggest that Jesus could theoretically call on legions of angels to fight on his behalf. In the third century CE, the Church Father Origen scorned the idea that the Christ imagined in his time would need that angelic aid or protection, as he was quite capable of performing any wondrous deeds entirely on his own account. In this sense, the Devil was committing an exegetical blunder. But that is anachronistic, and a messianic Jesus thus assisted and accompanied made wonderful sense in the Jewish context of the first century CE. As we have seen, 91 was unusual among psalms in its inclusion of attendant angels.[20]

Of the several key texts in which Jews of this time found potent messianic significance, two in particular had close parallels to 91, notably in the theme of subjugating or controlling dangerous forces. One evocative passage in the Book of Isaiah speaks of "a rod out of the stem of Jesse." That Rod or Branch would institute a glorious new age in which the behavior of dangerous animals would be transformed and tamed. Those animals include the serpent and lion, and the Septuagint uses the same terms that we find in our psalm's v. 13: the snake is an *aspidon*. According to readings of Isaiah in the Second Temple era, the messiah is the one who will transform the natural order in such a revolutionary way.[21]

Even clearer is the analogy with the Book of Malachi, a short and cryptic work that raises a great many questions about origin and authorship. That book's concise chapter 4 is packed with phrases and ideas that were read as messianic, and they were popular at Qumran. The chapter prophesies the return of the prophet Elijah before the end times, and references to that figure abound in the New Testament (as in Luke's transfiguration story). One verse in Malachi promises that "you" will trample the wicked or lawless, an action that was commonly taken to apply to the forthcoming messiah. In the Septuagint, the verb used for that trampling is *katapateo*, which also features in v. 13 of our psalm. Another passage in Malachi suggests that the final crisis will arrive when God sends his messenger (in the Septuagint Greek, his *angelos*) not just to earth, but specifically to the Temple. Satan, as we know, invites Jesus to hurl himself from that same building. Early Christians would find it difficult to read 91 without thinking of those passages from Malachi, which were such standard components of the messianic dream.[22]

Of Dragons and Serpents

Whether or not the messianic reading of 91 was an early Christian innovation, the idea quickly gained strength and merged with other themes in the emerging theological system. Not only did the psalm imagine the defeat of evil forces, but it spoke of the dragon or serpent that now stood as the most potent symbol of Christ's cosmic foes.

The psalm's v. 13 offered believers a promise of victory over evil, of trampling the lion and the dragon, *leonta kai drakonta*. The identity of that dragon was made quite clear by the Book of Revelation, which contains all thirteen uses of the word "dragon" in the whole New Testament. Eleven of these occur in one sustained narrative in chapters 12 and 13, where the Dragon (usually capitalized in modern usage) makes an unsuccessful attempt to destroy a holy woman and her child. Later Christians naturally enough identified the pair with the Virgin Mary and Jesus. This Dragon is a symbol of ultimate evil, who is identified with the Roman Empire. But if in fact the Dragon was literally Satan or the Devil, the whole of 91:13 reads as a triumph over evil forces to be trampled or trodden down. As Satanic evil became strongly identified with reptilian or "draconian" imagery, 91 came into its own, gaining a theological importance it has never lost.[23]

The Greek vocabulary of that v. 13 demands attention. The first verb used here is quite mild, something like "walking over," but the second, which in English becomes "trample," is violently forceful. The original Hebrew *ramas* has that connotation, as does the Septuagint Greek verb *katapateo*. Applied to a living creature, such treatment, such "stamping" or "stomping," is certainly pictured as lethal. In the adaptation in Luke 10:19, the word for "tread" comes from the Greek *pateo*, which suggests an arrogant triumph. The theme of treading or trampling was reinforced by other serpent- and dragon-related texts that are intimately related to that Psalm 91 verse, and these usually traveled together. In early and medieval Christian writings, Psalm 91 was seldom found alone and unaccompanied. Apart from 91 itself, these related passages were:

> Genesis 3:14–15: God pronounces curses on the serpent who has tempted Eve. God tells the serpent, "I will put enmity between you and the woman, and between your offspring and hers; he will crush your head, and you will strike his heel."
> Luke 10:19: Jesus promises his disciples the power "to tread on serpents and scorpions."
> Romans 16:20: St. Paul prophesies that "the God of peace will soon crush Satan under your feet."
> Revelation 12:1–9: The Dragon attacks the woman clothed with the Sun, but is defeated and cast from Heaven.

Together with 91, this sequence of texts laid a foundation for core themes in nascent Christian theology.[24]

In the Genesis account of Adam and Eve, God prophesies eternal enmity between the serpent and the human race. When that text was originally written, it made no reference to Satan or the Devil, but over time that identification became self-evident. As early Christians contemplated the meaning of Christ's death, they thought back to the original Fall, which he was now reversing. The brief Genesis passage inspired so much pious speculation in later Christian writing that it is sometimes called the Protoevangelium, the First Gospel. Almost certainly, Luke was recalling this verse when quoting Jesus's promise in his 10:19, and juxtaposing it with 91. In addition to the image of crushing, the word used for enmity in the Septuagint version of Genesis, *echthran*, has the same root as the Enemy identified in Luke. (As we will see in Chapter 6, the fact that the Latin Vulgate gave the crushing role to "she," *ipsa*, provided a scriptural foundation to later devotion to the Virgin Mary. Marian theologies also found support in the Revelation story of the woman and the dragon.)[25]

Such texts made it natural to apply that "crushing" idea to Christ himself, or his saintly representatives, and this remained a standard Patristic and medieval biblical interpretation for over a millennium. To take one example of many, around 710 England's Venerable Bede composed a long-popular exposition of Revelation. Discussing the dragon hurled to the earth in Revelation 12, Bede turned both to Genesis and 91: "For to [Satan] it is said, 'Earth shalt thou eat all the days' [Genesis 3:14]; and in this earth he is bruised by the feet of the saints, as it is written, 'Thou shalt tread upon the asp and the basilisk.'"[26]

The other verse in this group comes at the end of Paul's Letter to the Romans. After offering a list of greetings and acknowledgments, Paul condemns troublemakers who spread dissent, and then foretells the future crushing of Satan. The phrasing is curious. The verb Paul uses for "crush," *suntribo*, can be translated as "break" or "smash," and it usually stands by itself as a powerful expression of aggressive action. It might indicate a blow from a fist or a weapon. It just does not need the extra words "under your feet," which have presumably been added to conform with the trampling or treading that we find in Genesis, as well as in our psalm. The phrasing sounds closer to the Luke verse than to Genesis, and thus refers back to 91.[27]

As I have noted, 91 was by no means the only psalm used to frame the emerging understandings of Christ. Another popular reference was Psalm 8, which was also read as a vision of Christ ruling over all things, which were put "under his feet," and Paul alludes to this in 1 Corinthians. However, it is easy enough to tell which of the two psalms, 8 or 91, is being recalled at any given time, as allusions to 91 always use a violent vocabulary of trampling, treading, or smashing.[28]

Irenaeus

That intertwined group of verses suggests how very early the psalm-derived trampling or crushing tradition stands in the Jesus movement. Paul wrote Romans around 60 CE, before the temptation accounts in Mark (c. 75) or in Matthew and Luke (90s CE). The lost gospel we know as Q might date to the 50s or 60s. The "trampling" idea thus precedes the writing of any of our gospels in the form in which we know them. The confrontation with the dragon in Revelation is somewhat later, likely from the last decade of the first century.

Explicit references to 91 appear in the earliest attempts at systematic Christologies. A classic statement of the Christus Victor idea occurs in the work of Bishop Irenaeus, writing far from Palestine in the distant western land of Gaul. In his comprehensive denunciation of heresies and alternative forms of belief, around 180 CE, he combined Luke's reminiscence of 91 with the Ephesians passage I quoted earlier, about the triumphant Christ taking many captives:

> For the Lord, through means of suffering, *ascending into the lofty place, led captivity captive, gave gifts to men,* and conferred on those that believe in Him the power *to tread upon serpents and scorpions, and on all the power of the enemy,* that is, of the leader of apostasy. Our Lord also by His passion destroyed death, and dispersed error, and put an end to corruption, and destroyed ignorance, while He manifested life and revealed truth, and bestowed the gift of incorruption.[29]

Irenaeus then integrated the actual words of 91 into his larger discussion of Eden, the Fall, and Christ's redemption of humanity, juxtaposing the Genesis verse about Eve and the serpent. That serpent brought about the fall of Adam, the first man, which would be reversed and nullified by Christ, the second man, who would in turn trample serpents and other dangerous beasts. The incorporation of the various core texts I have mentioned is thorough and intricate:

> For this end did He put enmity between the serpent and the woman and her seed, they keeping it up mutually: He, the sole of whose foot should be bitten, having power also to tread upon the enemy's head; but the other biting, killing, and impeding the steps of man, until the seed did come appointed to tread down his head, [Genesis 3:15]—which was born of Mary, of whom the prophet speaks: *Thou shalt tread upon the asp and the basilisk; thou shalt trample down the lion and the dragon*—indicating that sin, which was set up and spread out against man, and which rendered him subject to death, should be deprived of its power, along with death, which rules [over men]; and that the lion, that is, Antichrist, rampant against mankind in the latter days, should be trampled down by Him; and that He should bind *the*

dragon, that old serpent [Revelation 12:9 and 20:2] and subject him to the power of man, who had been conquered so that all his might should be trodden down.[30]

Already for Irenaeus, Psalm 91 was a key messianic prophecy, a type or foreshadowing of Christ.

Moving Westward

In the earliest Christian centuries, Greek was the commonest language of Christian thought and debate. Over time, however, Latin grew in importance, and from the end of the first millennium the Western church and its Latin Vulgate Bible played an ever more central role within Christendom. No less than Greek Christians, Latin-speakers readily appreciated the connections and cross references between these various texts.

When the New Testament was translated into Latin from the second century, the word for trampling became *calcare*, which is related to "heel," *calcaneum*. To use a related modern word, to be "recalcitrant" is to kick out with the heel. In Luke 10:19, Jesus is promising that his followers will literally "heel down" the evil beasts and the powers of the Enemy. Jerome's fourth-century Vulgate reads: *Ecce dedi vobis potestatem* **calcandi** *supra serpentes, et scorpiones, et super omnem virtutem inimici.*[31]

As they read the Genesis verse in Jerome's Vulgate, Catholic Christians found another reference to "enmity," *inimicitias*, and the "heel" offered an immediate link to *calcare*, "treading": *Inimicitias ponam inter te et mulierem . . . ipsa conteret caput tuum, et tu insidiaberis* **calcaneo** *ejus.* In Genesis, the serpent receives the right to strike at human heels; in Luke, the faithful believer could "heel down" those same snakes and serpents. In the parallel verse in Psalm 91, the Vulgate promised: *Super aspidem et basiliscum ambulabis, et conculcabis leonem et draconem.* The verb *ambulare* suggests a gentler kind of walking or "ambling," in contrast to the more aggressive "treading down," which is referred to with *conculcabis*.

That v. 13 text, the "*super aspidem*," would have a vital and enduring history within Western Christendom. A key founder of the Latin Christian intellectual tradition was Tertullian, who wrote in North Africa in the generation after Irenaeus. He was thoroughly acquainted with the idea of the triumphant Christ and with Psalm 91. He remarks that Satan was himself "the old serpent" who tempted Christ in the wilderness, so it was very fitting that Christ should trample him. In his invocation of that verse, as in the example I quoted at the beginning of this chapter, Tertullian would have many successors in the Latin West. Both lions and serpents featured frequently in early Christian literature and art, together with other beasts both real and imaginary. In themselves, they need not recall Psalm 91. But when they are combined, as in "the lion and the serpent," then the psalm is undoubtedly being recalled, and such instances are easy to find.[32]

I have mentioned the familiar modern distinction between high and low approaches to religion, and the impossibility of applying that dichotomy to premodern times. Believers in these centuries saw nothing incongruous about mingling seemingly very different kinds of divine triumph, of the resurrection as a cosmic phenomenon, and of spiritual warfare in everyday life. A text like 91 at once provided spiritual and practical resources for exorcists and for humbler spiritual practitioners as well as esteemed thinkers., It is all but impossible to draw any demarcations between those two worlds. In village streets and in the schools of cathedrals and monasteries, the same verses of promise and protection could be read with equal enthusiasm.

4

The Terror by Night

A World Full of Demons and Enchanters

> What is meant by the words *A thousand may fall at thy side*? The Holy
> One, blessed be He, gives to each Israelite ten thousand angels who
> guard him and help him on the way. One precedes him, exclaiming:
> Pay homage to the likeness of the Holy One, blessed be He. He does
> this because the entire world is filled with spirits and demons.[1]
>
> —Rabbi Yehoshua ben Levi, c. 240 CE

In the sixth century CE, near Luxor in Egypt, a monastic scribe composed a
substantial volume intended for strictly practical use by Christian believers.
He compiled key texts that were to be copied onto smaller objects, either
pieces of parchment or else utilitarian objects, to offer protection from evils
of all kinds. Commonly, these texts use the opening words of a key work, the
incipit, rather than a whole text, although they might be even more random
in their selection. Among the writings chosen for this purpose are the Lord's
Prayer and the canonical gospels, and it is in this noble company that we find
Psalm 91, one of the texts most frequently encountered in this settings. If it
was not the only Old Testament text deployed in this way, it was by far the
most common. Beyond amulets, the psalm features often on bowls, rings,
and armbands; some inscribed it on door lintels, on church walls, and on
tombs. In a world constantly assailed by demons and enchanters, Psalm 91
was everywhere.[2]

If medieval Christians and Jews were bitterly at odds over virtually every
issue of theology and scriptural interpretation, at least they could agree on
the value and purposes of this one psalm, as a weapon for everyday self-
defense. In the twelfth century, Christian scholars in France compiled what
would for centuries be the standard collection of biblical commentaries, the
Glossa Ordinaria, which was the source for countless tens of thousands of

He Will Save You from the Deadly Pestilence. Philip Jenkins, Oxford University Press. © Oxford University Press 2023.
DOI: 10.1093/oso/9780197605646.003.0004

sermons. Echoing the familiar Jewish label, Christians too knew 91 as "the hymn against demons."[3]

Assuming the reality of demonic and angelic realms, the psalm profoundly shaped discussions about those other worlds, spawning a whole clerical study of demonology. It also sparked debate about the proper limits of using scripture against evil forces. The psalm gave rise to acute questions about defining the appropriate limits of religious practice.

Words of Power

In the Jewish worldview, demons were inconceivably abundant. One rabbi of the third century CE opined, "There is not a piece of ground which supports one *roba* of seed, in any part of the world, that does not contain nine hundred *kabs* of demons." We do not have to translate the quantities too exactly to grasp the point that demons were ubiquitous and threatening. That quote comes from a typical Talmudic dialogue on 91, a text that shaped Jewish thinking on demons and the best way to counter them.[4]

Across the spectrum of Jewish sects and schools, 91 was esteemed as a bulwark against demonic powers, as well as against material manifestations of disease or plague. This was much evidenced in amulets and protective objects. In any society where literacy rates were low, and where the ability to write conveyed rank and prestige, the particular words and letters of a text carried special force. In one Jewish amulet designed to protect women in childbirth, we find what at first appears to be a meaningless jumble of letters, but which in fact represents the first letters of each word in the psalm's first nine verses. This practice of using first letters bears the name *notarikon*, literally "shorthand," and it was very widespread. At first sight just as nonsensical were the amulets that took 91 and the great proclamation of the Shema (Deuteronomy 6:4)--so fundamental to Jewish life and practice—and presented the words of the two texts alternating with each other.[5]

Wherever Jewish societies used scriptural texts for protection, 91 featured prominently. Between the fifth and the eighth centuries, Jews in what we would now call Iraq and Iran inscribed the psalm on incantation bowls intended to protect a home. These were placed at the threshold, or in corners. These objects are all the more interesting when we recall that they were created in roughly the same times and places as the Babylonian Talmud was being compiled: these were the exact sort of material items that were exercising the minds of the sages of the day. We might ask how many of those rabbis and their scribes were working in houses defended by such bowls, or some similar manifestation of 91.[6]

Such practices continued for centuries. In eleventh-century France, the venerated commentator Rashi cites two specific verses that were popular for amulets in his time. One, from Exodus, referred to the Israelites escaping the plagues visited on the Egyptians, and the other was 91's reference to the terror by night and the arrow by day. People wore amulets containing such texts and placed them on their animals. Reciting scriptural texts also protected against demons, and you might choose the Shema, or 91.[7]

Adding significantly to the psalm's status and popularity is the fact that it opens with several of the holy names and titles of God, an awe-inspiring barrage of spiritual power. In English translation, the opening verses read as follows, with transliterated Hebrew originals in brackets:

> He that dwelleth in the secret place of the Most High [*Elyon*] shall abide under the shadow of the Almighty [*Shaddai*]. I will say of the LORD [*YHWH*], He is my refuge [*machseh*] and my fortress [*matswd*]: my God [*Elohim*]; in him will I trust.

In a very short space, we read not just the sacred YHWH, the unsayable four-letter Name or Tetragrammaton, but also the divine titles Elyon, Shaddai, and Elohim and the descriptors "my Refuge" and "my Fortress." Such names acquired immense magical force in later centuries, and also served to inspire mystical contemplation. In the Middle Ages, a typical incantation to command demons and spirits involved a recitation of "the Most Holy and glorious Names," which would include among others Shaddai, Elohim, Elyon, Adonai, and the Tetragrammaton. Citing just the opening two verses of 91 was in itself a mighty assertion of power. Some practitioners used the method of *notarikon*, using the initial letters of its words to create a magical word of power.[8]

Adepts could increase the already impressive list of divine names by prefixing the beginning of 91 with the last verse of Psalm 90. Depending on the transliteration, that began *Vayehi No'am* or *Vihi Noam* ("Let the beauty of the Lord"), a phrase that gradually became a standard name by which Jews referred to this expanded version of 91. Another method of augmenting the psalm's potency was by repeating its final verse, doubling its last letters to produce yet another divine name. The psalm became firmly established in works of ritual magic as well as exorcism, and appears prominently in the sixteenth-century manual *Shoshan Yesod ha-'Olam* (*Lily, Foundation of the World*), which was intended for practical occult use. As we will see in Chapter 8, that tradition would cross over into the European and Christian esoteric world.[9]

The psalm appealed to those inclined to seek mystical and esoteric dimensions in scripture. One great source for such material is the lengthy discourse in the Midrash Tehillim, the Midrash on Psalms, which belongs to what in Christian Europe would be known as the Early Middle Ages. After debating claims for authorship by David and Solomon, the Midrash Tehillim definitively attributes 91 to Moses, and placed its composition at a critical moment in the formation of the Jewish people—namely, the divine encounter at Sinai. In this view, "the secret place of the Most High" meant nothing less than the divine presence itself. Reputedly, Moses used the psalm while entering the cloud above Mount Sinai. It would be hard to imagine a more prestigious origin story—although it does not specifically state that Moses composed the psalm on this occasion, rather than using an already existing text.[10]

That Mosaic link became even more significant with the emergence of Qabala as a well-defined school of mystical teaching. The core idea of Qabala assumes a direct secret transmission of knowledge from Moses, and Qabalists delved enthusiastically into the "Mosaic" psalms 90 and 91. The connection to Moses's ascent features in the thirteenth-century Zohar, one of the most important works of Qabala.[11]

The Psalm and the Demons

An extensive demonology can be reconstructed from rabbinic exchanges over 91. In reading the psalm, the sages regularly gave personal identity to the terms and concepts listed there, and then let their imaginations run free in describing what these monstrous creatures might actually look like and how they would behave.

One popular use of personification was *qeteb* (*ketev*), Destruction, as in the destruction that wastes at noonday. As we have seen, the Septuagint had already presented that figure as a literal "demon," and later Jewish thinkers elaborated that thought. Around 500 CE, one tractate in the Babylonian Talmud, Pesachim, notes:

There are two types of *ketev* demons, one that comes before noon in the morning and the other one comes in the afternoon. . . . The *ketev* in the afternoon is called *ketev yashud tzaharayim* [the destruction that wastes at noonday] . . . , and it appears inside the horn of a goat and revolves around inside it like a sifter.[12]

A midrash on the Book of Lamentations harks back to 91 when it describes this *qeteb* as "full of eyes, scales, and hair . . . whoever looks at it falls down dead." Very likely, that language was inspired by the mythical basilisk, which featured in the psalm's Greek translations.[13]

The Midrash Tehillim expounds at length the various demons believed to be mentioned in 91. On the destruction that wastes at noonday, Rabbi Judah noted only that this was a demon active at that time of day. Rabbi Khunna was more creative in describing the demon Bitter Destruction as

covered with scale upon scale and with shaggy hair and he glares with his one eye and that eye is in the middle of his heart. . . . He rolls like a ball and from the seventeenth day in Tammuz to the ninth day in Av he has power after the fourth hour in the day and up to the ninth hour. And every man who sees him falls upon his face.

Commentators debated what kind of evils the psalm was enumerating, and whether they involved literal demons or more metaphorical evils and sins. Over time, the demonic interpretations triumphed and became commonplace. Rashi explained that in the psalm's text, "Pestilence, etc., Destruction: These are names of demons: one destroys at night, and one destroys at noon."[14]

While expatiating on demonic forces, some rabbis also offered far more mundane interpretations of the threats and even annoyances against which the psalm was efficacious, challenges that fell considerably short of plague or demonic assault. Reading the psalm's promise that "No evil shall befall you" in the mid-third century CE, Rabbi Yirmeya (Jeremiah) viewed this in a limited and domestic way:

This means that you will be frightened neither by bad dreams nor by evil thoughts. "Neither shall any plague come near your tent," means that you will never find your wife with the uncertain status of a menstruating woman when you return from a journey.[15]

Listing the evils that could befall the pious, and against which the psalm could offer protection, also offered the opportunity for some religious polemic. In the tractate Sanhedrin, in the Babylonian Talmud, after the reference to bad dreams, the author proceeds with his own interpretation:

> "Nor shall any plague come near your tent" means that you will not have a child or student who overcooks his food in public, i.e., sins in public and causes others to sin, such as in the well-known case of Jesus the Nazarene.

Plagues and curses could take many forms, one of which was the spawning of the Christian religion.[16]

Inevitably, 91 inspired discussion of angels and their roles, and especially the appealing promise of a protective angel. The Midrash Tanchuma (seventh century CE?) explained the psalm's v. 11 thus:

> When a man performs one precept, one angel is assigned to guard him; when he performs two precepts, two angels are given to him; when he performs all the precepts, many angels are assigned to him, as it is said: *For He will give His angels charge over thee.* Who are these angels? They are the beings who will protect him from demons, as it is said: *A thousand may fall at thy side, and ten thousand at thy right hand. . . .* What is meant by *may fall*? It means that they force [their opponents] to surrender to him.

But those protective angels wielded a two-edged spiritual sword, threatening the ordinary believer who fell into sin. If one who sinned in secret hoped to escape the day of judgment, he would be disappointed. "The two ministering angels who accompany a person will testify against him, as it is stated: 'For He will give His angels charge over you, to keep you in all your ways.'"[17]

Against the Darkness

Most readers may have cherished the psalm's protective qualities, but thoughtful commentators were troubled by the use of scripture as a form of magic or incantation. Talmudic sages respected the psalm's power and used it freely themselves for protective purposes, especially for night prayer. Most agreed that it should be prayed on a daily basis. Even so, they warned that while apotropaic uses were acceptable, there were strict limits. To pray for healing and protection was highly desirable. It was a very different matter to assert that repeating the words or letters of a particular text would somehow compel God or his angels to supply such protection.[18]

Rabbi Yehoshua ben Levi, whom we have already encountered, indicates the fine line to be walked in such practices. He declared that "one is prohibited from healing himself with words of Torah," which seems explicit enough, yet at the same time, we know that he used protective verses from Psalms 3 and 91: "[He] would recite these verses to protect him from evil spirits during the night and fall asleep while saying them." When challenged to explain the apparent discrepancy, he replied that "to protect oneself is different, as he recited these verses only to protect himself from evil spirits, and not to heal himself." Apotropaic uses were acceptable, but curative ones were not. Other rabbis were not as forgiving, and forbade any use of scripture either in healing or for protection.[19]

But such qualms did not prevent the psalm from retaining a pivotal place in Jewish approaches to darkness and night, both literal and figurative. Indeed, modern Jewish practices and liturgical custom often echo those Talmudic discussions and commands. Psalm 91 remains fundamental to rituals surrounding death and dying. The psalm is said seven times during the funeral service, as the pallbearers stop on several occasions to repeat its words. When the casket is lowered into the grave, the rabbi repeats 91 together with the prayer for repose, El Maleh Rachamim. The psalm also features prominently in regular Jewish liturgy, which in so many ways builds upon the precedent of the ancient Temple. Psalm 91 forms part of the Pesukei d'Zimra, the "verses of singing" that feature in daily morning services, and which are duly expanded for Sabbath worship. The psalm is still thought highly appropriate for evening and nighttime use, and is naturally included in the bedtime prayers that accompany the Shema. In this usage, the psalm's last verse is said twice, probably to produce another divine name.[20]

A Theology of Trampling

In their reading of 91, Christians shared the same Second Temple inheritance as Jews, and looked to the same traditions of spiritual warfare. Jews and Christians lived in a common greater Mediterranean world, in which the use of amulets and apotropaic devices was all but universal. So, of course, were fears of darkness and night. Christians, like Jews, incorporated 91 into their liturgies. But the Christian experience had certain key differences from that of Jews. For one thing, Jewish readings and uses drew on various parts of the psalm, while Christians overwhelmingly focused on one key portion, v. 13. Whether quoted directly from the psalm or else through the adaptation in Luke, this verse was so commonly cited in early and Patristic Christian writings that it became something like a slogan of the faith, an epitome of what the faith offered, and a boast of its power.[21]

Christians and Jews also differed in their approach to permissible religious symbolism. Jews mainly confined themselves to texts and words, although incantation bowls did offer crude visual sketches of the demons who were to be bound and disabled. Such artifacts would never depict Moses or a biblical figure in the act of combatting evil entities. Christians, in contrast, felt free to depict human and animal forms, including sacred figures of Christ or the saints. That predilection added immensely to the appeal of v. 13: it was not difficult to construct an image of a human trampling or dominating animals, which even in its roughest form would announce the scriptural connection.[22]

That theme of domination over animals was reflected in the very common depictions of saints, which appeared in icons and pilgrimage souvenirs such as flasks for holy water or oil. In Egypt, the power of the saints was demonstrated by their power over the tamed and submissive animals that flanked them. That might include the canonical four beasts named in the psalm, but it also extended to antelopes or crocodiles, the latter serving well as "dragons." Such stories of domination commonly feature in the lives of Coptic saints and holy men. Apa (Father) Timothy ruled a herd of desert antelope; Apa Poemen subjugated reptilian demons. The best-known such saint was Menas, whose shrine was a renowned center for healing and pilgrimage, where visitors could obtain a wide range of memorabilia. Menas is commonly shown flanked by camels, but crocodiles also appear: demons took many forms. This theme had a special resonance in Egypt and other lands where pagan deities had so often been represented in animal form. Egyptian gods had regularly been depicted dominating dangerous beasts by standing on them or holding them in their hands; the transition to Christian iconography was easy. The scorpion reference in Luke had a strong resonance to the mythology of Isis and Horus.[23]

The Christian assertion of resurrection constituted another sharp difference with rabbinic Judaism. Christ himself increasingly occupied the place of honor as the victor over evil forces, and over the forces of death itself. That ultimate victory invited visual portrayal in funerary memorials, which became popular after the empire's conversion, when Christian symbols could be displayed publicly. One early example comes from Gerona in Spain, where in the mid-fourth century a sarcophagus depicted Christ standing on a lion and a snake. Another example just as clearly derived from 91 comes from fifth-century Ravenna, and the type then becomes quite common in tomb monuments.[24]

Christ's central role is apparent from images on one very common domestic object, a small earthenware lamp mass-manufactured using a double mold. A surviving example shows a standing Christ, identified by the cross he carries, treading underfoot a lion, dragon, asp, and basilisk. In the fifth or sixth century CE, such objects might have illuminated thousands of homes in Christian North Africa. We can debate just what were the intentions of those who purchased such lamps for use in their homes. For many, surely, using such a lamp supplied spiritual protection, when the owner lit the light to confront the growing darkness, and the intimidating forces that would be at their most dangerous during the nighttime. Literally, the psalm lit up Christian homes.[25]

Holy Words

Christians also used texts for spiritual protection. We see this in one Egyptian amulet that has been painstakingly reassembled from papyrus fragments, and which dates from the early Christian centuries. Typical of so many such objects, it included on the front the text of Psalm 91, and on the back the Lord's Prayer, from Matthew's gospel (both of course in Greek). The psalm thus occupied pride of place even above the gospel text. The document was then folded five times, to allow it to be carried or positioned effectively.[26]

Egypt has left many examples of amulets that use those texts, often in abbreviated form. A typical example might just include the psalm's opening words, "The one who dwells in the shelter of the Most High," with the remaining promises and blessings simply assumed. But the fact that Egypt has been so prolific in preserving such relics does not mean that they were uniquely common here; rather, they happened to survive in this notably dry climate. Residents of Italy or Gaul were scarcely less likely to defend themselves by such means, which commonly meant using the words of 91.[27]

Optimistically, from the perspective of high religion, we might suggest that a believer kept such a written item as a means of recalling the inspirational words of scripture and the prayer appropriate to times of peril. In reality, the fact of wearing such an amulet says nothing whatever about the religious faith or identity of the wearer, or whether she or he could actually read the protective words. If we assume that the wearer was in any sense a Christian, the amulet held virtue and power because it contained words of special power, whether or not they were to be read with any understanding. Usually, such amulets had also been blessed in some way, commonly by approved clergy or monks, or else by ritual specialists. That added to the special power of such items, which was evidently magical in nature. That was clearly true when the words of 91—usually v. 13—were tied to domestic animals, to protect them from harm.[28]

While they recognized the strength of popular faith, clerical elites were disturbed to see Christian clergy assuming the role of magicians or enchanters, especially if they were selling such items for gain. Reciting Psalm 91 was a laudable form of prayer, but writing its opening verse on a scrap of cloth intended for retail was a shady form of spiritual exploitation. In the 360s, the church council held at Laodicea condemned clergy who made amulets, "which are chains for their own souls. And those who wear such, we command to be cast out of the Church." Such statements can readily be found recurring over the following centuries, suggesting the very limited effectiveness of such attempts at prohibition.[29]

Monsters

Also recalling their rabbinic counterparts, Christians exercised much ingenuity in determining exactly what forms of menace were enumerated in 91. Although it never achieved anything like the central role of the dragon or serpent, the basilisk likewise acquired diabolical connotations. The basilisk has a lengthy history in Roman and Hellenistic science, but the vast majority of its appearances in Christian lore and art can be traced back to this single potent verse in Psalm 91. For Origen, Satan was "the basilisk and the petty ruler of all serpents. Your poisons are more harmful than those of other snakes, for as soon as you see someone, you kill him." In the fifth century, Augustine believed similarly that "the basilisk is the king of serpents, as the devil is the king of wicked spirits." Theodoret of Cyrus said that in mentioning the asp and basilisk the psalmist "hinted at the extremity of evil, the former injecting deadly poison, the latter causing death on sight."[30]

As Eastern Christian scholars approached the relevant scriptures, they had the inestimable advantage of firsthand acquaintance with the Greek of the Septuagint. In the eleventh century CE, the Byzantine scholar Euthymios Zigabenos properly located the origin of the word "dragon" in a root suggesting vision, and used v. 13 as the basis for a whole literature based on the dangers of the evil eye. As Euthymios noted, "The basilisk is the *baskania* [evil eye], for just as he has destruction in his eyes, so *baskania* causes destruction through the eyes." Psalm 91 was the prized resource against such a threat, and its words commonly appeared on amulets intended to ward off assaults by the evil eye.[31]

Of Monks and Demons

The greatest single difference between Jewish and Christian uses of 91 is that in the Christian context, the psalm found a welcoming home in a large and enduring institution—namely, that of monasticism. From early Christian times, the psalm has an exceedingly rich monastic history, which was critical given the key role of monks and nuns in writing and editing texts throughout the Middle Ages and beyond, and creating visual art and music. As they read it, Psalm 91 enumerated both the dangers of their profession and the means of overcoming them.

Christian monasticism originated in the third century CE, most famously in Egypt, but with important manifestations in Syria. Through the centuries monastics would acquire many functions, but in the earliest times they were above all spiritual warriors, who confronted and defeated the forces of evil. Monks and hermits wrestled with temptations and demonic assaults, commonly in waste places, in literal or figurative deserts. They resorted to such places not just to escape the world, but to seek out and destroy the evil forces that dwelt there. In such front-line settings, 91 was of paramount value. The explicit quotation from the psalm found in the gospels is set in the wilderness or desert, *eremos*, the root of the word for "hermit."[32]

One pioneering settler of the *eremos* was the Egyptian monastic founder St. Antony (c. 250–356), whose biography, by the great patriarch Athanasius, exercised a vast influence on later church practice. Athanasius quotes one sermon that Antony delivered (in Coptic) to his fellow monks, which made the fight against demonic forces central to their task. The monks should not fear the demons, who would be defeated by their holy practices and who had a healthy fear of what true Christian believers might inflict on them:

> Wherefore they do all things that they may not have any that trample on them, knowing the grace given to the faithful against them by the Savior, when He says, *Behold I have given to you power to tread upon serpents and scorpions, and upon all the power of the enemy.*

Such texts shape much of Antony's discourse about defeating and expelling demons, which is best achieved by singing psalms. Together with Satan, says Antony, "are placed the demons his fellows, like serpents and scorpions to be trodden underfoot by us Christians."[33]

In his conclusion to the lengthy work, Athanasius warns pagans "that the demons, whom the Greeks themselves think to be gods, are no gods, but [Christians] also tread them under foot and put them to flight." That "trampling" acquired an all too material form following the Roman Empire's conversion to Christianity in the fourth century CE. Inspired by such pious examples as Antony, the monks took the lead in destroying the temples of the pagan gods, which were represented in animal form, invoking 91 in justification. For centuries afterward, monks and hermits continued to attract legends of their prowess in fighting literal demonic forces. The ninth century Byzantine saint and wonder-worker Ioannikios used the psalm to slay a mighty dragon that was troubling a country region.[34]

By the late fourth century, monasticism had become a standard feature of the Eastern churches, where it was shaped by venerated Fathers like Basil the Great (330–379). That tradition was then imported into Latin Western Europe, where it flourished mightily. One key figure in that transmission was John Cassian, who about 415 set up a pioneering monastery modeled on Eastern lines, near Marseille. A voluminous writer, John offered detailed instruction for the monastic life, and for spiritual practice more generally. All these pioneers lauded 91 as a weapon against evil forces.[35]

In 384, St. Jerome wrote to the noblewoman Eustochium Julia, who had taken vows of perpetual virginity and was about to embark on a life comparable to the most severe regimes followed by Antony's followers. The resulting letter became a famous manifesto of stringent asceticism, together with a bitter condemnation of contemporary corruption and worldly decadence. But as Jerome warned, "We are hemmed in by hosts of foes, our enemies are upon every side." The prospective Desert Mother would need the strongest resources of prayer and scripture, and he quoted Psalm 91's vv. 5–7. In the spiritual struggles, it was safe to assume that thousands would fall from the ascetic path, but she, ideally, would stand faithful.[36]

John Cassian cited the psalm to show that particular demons operated at specific times of day, notably noonday, but he often returned to the "treading" motif. One of his more surprising uses of the psalm came when he attacked a critic for engaging in selective quotation, a kind of literary debate in which we would not expect a demonic allusion. But as John says, the critic is acting just like Satan himself during the temptation of Christ, when he quoted vv. 11–12 but failed to make the obvious transition to v. 13, which would have identified him as a demonic serpent: "So then you also bring forward a part and omit a part; and quote the one to deceive; and omit the other for fear lest if you were to quote the whole, you might condemn your own deception." Their total immersion in the psalm allowed its monastic devotees to escalate personal feuds to the Satanic dimension with scant delay.[37]

As the Shadows Gather

In the sixth century, those Eastern examples profoundly influenced such major figures of the Latin church as Benedict of Nursia, the founder of Benedictine monasticism, and Pope Gregory the Great. Monasteries and convents spread to all parts of the Christian world, and their very diverse functions and activities made them central to economic activity as well as to cultural and spiritual life. However much they differed in their origins and traditions, what all such houses had in common was the position of the psalms as the centerpiece of prayer and worship. Monks and nuns recited the whole Psalter frequently, and must have come to know the texts intimately. The Psalter became the indispensable foundation of European Christian faith.[38]

Throughout these centuries, writers explored 91 for the practical guidance it offered monks, hermits, and ascetics about the hazards they faced. In Ireland, where monasticism early gained a strong foothold, monks incorporated the psalm into the lengthy prayers they developed as a kind of spiritual armor against a list of evils. Such prayers bore the name of a breastplate, *lorica*, and a typical example prays for delivery from all evils, from poisons (or: magic potions), from envies and from evil eyes, ears (?), and from the dangers of the pit and of darkness, from the demon, and from the arrow that flies by day, from the trouble (or: pestilence) that walks through the darkness.[39]

One distinguished pioneer of Western monasticism was Cassiodorus, a leading figure in the violent politics of sixth-century Italy, who reputedly lived from 487 to 585. In the 540s, he retired to a monastery that he founded at Vivarium in Calabria, where he undertook the heroic task of rescuing the vanishing works of antiquity. Among his many writings, he produced his *Exposition of the Psalms*, which is lavish in its praise of 91:

> This psalm has marvelous power, and routs impure spirits. The Devil retires vanquished from us through the very means by which he sought to tempt us, for that wicked spirit is mindful of his own presumption and of God's victory. Christ by His own power overcame the Devil in His own regard, and likewise conquers him in ours. So this psalm should be recited by us when night sets in after all the actions of the day; the Devil must realize that we belong to Him to whom he remembers that he himself yielded.[40]

Like the Jews of that time, Christians agreed that 91 should be sung or chanted on a daily basis, which placed the psalm in a very privileged category. Christians in this era advocated using any and all psalms in prayer, and some offered suitable rotations to work through the full Psalter over a short period, but 91 was rare in being deployed each and every day. Its blessings were indisputable. As Theodoret declared, "Everyone who is guided by this song is made secure in his life, and with his trust in the Savior makes a prayer."[41]

That regular usage contributed to creating the evening prayer service of Compline, in which generations of monks and religious would encounter 91 on a daily basis, over and above special days of feast or fast. The Christian Compline tradition was probably begun by Basil the Great, but Benedict introduced it to the West, giving it its later Latin name, *completorium*, marking the completion or end of the day. The Western Compline used 91 alongside two other psalms, 4 and 134, and that general structure persists today in Catholic and Anglican services. Today, the service may provide a psychological blessing, a shedding of daily cares before moving to a new stage of relaxation, but in its origins it was intended to fortify the believer against the perils of the darkness and sleep.[42]

It is hard to overstate just how pervasive that liturgical usage was. One famous monk of a later generation warned of the dangers that could arise during contemplation, when so many devils "stand to profit if they can destroy and exhaust us with false lights and raptures of their own devising." But believers could stand secure. He quotes the psalm that is

> chanted every night in the monastic Complin[e] when the shadows fall upon the cloister and the monks are ending their day of prayer. "I will be with him in trouble. I will rescue him and honor him." The angels are at our side, holding us up lest we should dash our foot against a stone. We could not travel through the forest that the spiritual life has now become unless His power carried us onward, where we tread upon the asp and the basilisk and never feel their sting, and never suffer harm! *Altissimum posuisti refugium tuum*. We have made the Most High God our refuge. The scourge will never touch us.

The monk was Thomas Merton, writing in 1953, when Dwight Eisenhower was president of the United States, and when IBM was marketing the first mass-produced computer.[43]

Merton's words remind us that the psalm asserted the power of angels as much as demons, and monastics heard those teachings just as frequently. As the rabbis fully realized in these same centuries, angels and demons alike are necessary protagonists in the vision of spiritual warfare. Angelology, as much as demonology, drew reliably on 91. The great Christian theologian Thomas Aquinas, in the thirteenth century, used our psalm repeatedly in his discussion of the actions and behavior of angels. At first sight, angels did not and could not know specific "singulars," nor could they guard individuals. But the psalm's verses clearly asserted the contrary. Yes indeed, angels knew and guarded individual men and women.[44]

The Noonday Demon

Some ages were less florid than others in the menagerie of demons that monks imagined arrayed against them, but one figure was of enormous and enduring concern even to thinkers whom we might not view as obsessed with spiritual combat. This foe was the psalm's noonday demon, who was understood as the special enemy of the individual monk's well-being and stability.

The demon took two forms, one celebrated, the other less so. The more famous manifestation was *acedia*, the distraction or depression to which even
the holiest ascetics could fall prey. But the cunning demon could also strike
through temptations to claim excessive holiness, which could delude a pious
monk into spiritual arrogance, self-deception, and ultimate ruin.

From earliest times, monastic writers warned of *acedia*, which might
even make ascetics dream of returning to the secular world. John Cassian
remarked that "this is akin to dejection, and is especially trying to solitaries,
and a dangerous and frequent foe to dwellers in the desert; and especially
disturbing to a monk about the sixth hour." Modern observers might use
the language of anomie or apathy, combined with a nonspecific anxiety. But
in understanding acedia, Western monks turned to the noonday demon,
daemonium meridianum.[45]

At the end of the fourth century, the Egyptian-based Desert Father
Evagrius described acedia as

> the most oppressive of all the demons. He attacks the monk about the
> fourth hour and besieges his soul until the eighth hour. First of all, he makes
> it appear that the sun moves slowly or not at all. . . . Then he compels the
> monk to look constantly towards the windows, to jump out of the cell. . . .
> And further, he instils in him a dislike for the place and for his state of life
> itself, for manual labor and also the idea that love has disappeared from
> among the brothers and there is no one to console him.[46]

As he instructed monks how to organize their daily lives, St. Basil specifically commanded that 91 be incorporated into the noonday prayers, "to en-
sure deliverance from the demon of noon-day." John Cassian likewise made
that connection, relying on the opinion of many Eastern elders. Theodoret
suggested his own reason for how such a demon might be able to take advantage of human weakness at that vulnerable point in the day: "It is not
unlikely that those schemers against humankind after a heavy meal launch
an assault as though to a prey prepared for them, and easily enslave those
deprived of care from on high." Had they been able to exchange ideas on
amiable terms, monks and rabbis would have found substantial areas of
agreement in their diagnoses of supernatural evil, and of demons' daily
schedules.[47]

Concern about the noontide devil resurfaced with each new revival of monastic zeal and organization. In the twelfth century, Western monasticism

enjoyed a vast resurgence, led by the saint of the Cistercian order, Bernard of Clairvaux, who became one of the most influential figures in Latin Christendom. His writings were still cherished in monastic communities four centuries later. Bernard's sermons focused on the practical needs and dangers facing his fellow monks, and like his predecessors, he found much wisdom in 91. In modern terms, his concerns are at once pastoral and psychological. He quoted vv. 4–6 as a perfect summary of the temptations those monks would face in their daily round, in each case equating one of the fearful threats to a specific challenge. "The terror of the night," for instance, meant the inability to concentrate on the eternal blessings that made daily sufferings bearable. The arrow that flies by day is vainglory; the pestilence that stalks the darkness is hypocrisy.[48]

The False Light of Noonday

But the greatest danger was the noonday demon, here viewed not as depression or *acedia*, but as the temptation to pursue unrealistic and excessive holiness. However devout they might seek to be, monks faced constant threats of evil spirits who lay in ambush, preparing their arrows. Rather than just striking at noonday, this was a dark demon who assumed the bright light of noon in order better to deceive. As Bernard wrote of this monster:

> He will tempt and overthrow his victim by suggesting what appears to be good, by persuading him, unsuspecting and unprepared as he is, to commit evil under the guise of good, unless the Sun from heaven shines into his heart with noontide brightness. The tempter really appears like noon, clothed in a certain splendor, when he comes with the suggestion of an apparently greater good. . . . The task of the noontide devil is to lay ambushes for the perfect, those persons of tried virtue who have survived all other temptations: pleasures, applause, honors.

Put in secular terms, we often make our worst and most destructive decisions when we think we are doing things that are self-evidently helpful and positive. Biographical accounts of Cistercian monks and nuns report how aspirations to lead hyper-pious lives often led to disaster, as these would-be saints fell prey to the noonday demon. Some suffered despair, even to the point of attempting suicide.[49]

As we will see in Chapter 5, in the fourth century St. Jerome had interpreted the noonday demon in the context of the deceptive false light offered by heretics. That understanding strongly influenced later medieval writers. Around 1390, the cleric Walter Hilton wrote the earliest known mystical treatise in English, *The Scale of Perfection*, which was widely read and copied. Hilton warned his readers "of the Midday Fiend that feigneth light as if it came out of Jerusalem, and is not so":

> Light of knowledge, that is feigned by the fiend to a dark soul, is showed betwixt two black rainy clouds. Whereof the upper cloud is presumption and exalting of himself, and the lower cloud is the down-putting and disdaining of his neighbor.[50]

Hilton was almost certainly the author of a substantial commentary on our psalm, which built on Bernard's interpretation, but with a strictly contemporary twist. As would-be contemplatives sought to achieve the divine vision, they needed to be constantly aware of the risk of falling into the deadly error of believing themselves to be divine. In the context of the time, Hilton was warning against the alarming heresy of the Free Spirit, a radically antinomian view in which deceived believers came to see themselves as literally divine and above sin, the error of "autotheism." Across fourteenth-century Europe, that Free Spirit movement gave abundant employment to inquisitors and executioners, and Hilton was anxious to prevent would-be mystics from falling into the same lethal snare:

> This is the last temptation . . . subtly assailing high souls in kind that come as it were to the state of perfection. And it is called the Midday Fiend, forasmuch as the spirit of *thesternesse* [darkness] comes shining like to an angel of light . . . shewing to a soul the height of itself and of his state of living with a blind pride, and bringeth into the soul wonderful knowing and singular conceits that seem full true. And makes a soul believe that he is himself in the height of contemplation and in the perfection of love high above all the common life of other good men. And that he may therefore live just as he pleases, for he is made so free and so high in grace, and so burning in love, that he shall not sin, and that he may not sin . . . That every deed that another man might do as sin, in him it is virtue and well done, and that he may lawfully do it if he pleases.[51]

The figure of the noonday demon long persisted in later vernacular translations, and entered popular parlance. Over time, it was the discussions of *acedia* that were best remembered, while (perhaps regrettably) the analyses of spiritual arrogance and overreach—of those "ambushes for the perfect"— were consigned to academic histories of spirituality and heresy. Explorations of *acedia* came to constitute a sizable genre, and they were often very percep- tive psychologically, not least in suggesting ways in which besieged monks might resist the threats to their everyday functioning. Even today, popular writers and self-help texts invoke "demonic" language metaphorically in ac- counts of depression and ennui. The fundamental vocabulary was a legacy of Psalm 91, and it assumed constant demonic assault, to a degree that we might miss if we only know the standard English translations.[52]

The Devil as Hunter

One core theme in the spiritual warfare literature derived directly and ex- plicitly from the psalm: namely, the vision of the Devil as hunter, with in- dividual humans as his prey. This grew out of one of the several verses that contained minor mistranslations. The Hebrew original of v. 3 refers to the snare of the trapper, almost certainly of birds, and that is reflected in modern English translations. As we have seen, the Greek Septuagint used a word that more commonly signifies the hunter who deployed his traps, likely against other animals besides birds. In Western and Latin Christianity, that hunter imagery was consecrated by Jerome's Vulgate, which again referred to the hunter, *venantium*, rather than the fowler. That gave rise to a whole litera- ture about the Devil as hunter, deploying the familiar vocabulary of hunting, trapping, and ensnaring.[53]

Jerome followed the Septuagint in linking the trap to evil words, rather than the correct "pestilence," and that error left a long shadow on scholarly commentaries. As writers struggled to make sense of this, many suggested that bad or improper words could lead people astray, and thus into the hands of that diabolical hunter. In his commentary on 91, St. Augustine noted that "many have fallen into the hunter's net through a harsh word. . . . The Devil and his angels spread their snares, as hunters do: and those who walk in Christ tread afar from those snares." The lesson was that even seemingly minor words or temptations could be deadly snares that would draw believers into the way of destruction. So saturated were monastics in the psalm that they drew from it multiple lessons about their life and conduct. Over the next millennium, monks and ascetics were constantly reminded that they were potentially prey to subtle and often concealed Satanic hunters, who set traps wherever they could. Such a steady drumbeat of warnings inevitably created a deep suspicion of worldly things and their temptations.[54]

In the process, the whole concept of hunting was tarnished and given a disreputable cast. Jerome himself remarked that in the whole of scripture, "never do we find a hunter that is a faithful servant; we do find faithful fishermen." Ordinary believers heard the same messages, and very frequently. In the late fourteenth century, Geoffrey Chaucer included in his *Canterbury Tales* a near-sermon of the sort that the faithful would often have heard in their churches, which now appears in the prologue to the Second Nun's Tale. Idleness, we are told, is a sin, through which the Devil might seize us, using his thousand sly cords, initially so lightly that we scarcely recognize it, but then ever more forcefully. The word used for "seize" is *hente*, which is related to our word "hunt." The Fiend continually waits to *biclappe* (grab) us.[55]

Although this sermon concerns idleness, a typical preacher could apply the same lesson to any sin, large or small. The believer who failed in watchfulness could and would be grabbed and hunted. The mistranslation of the psalm's lines had the incidental effect of making many clerical writers deeply hostile to the practice of hunting, given that the hunter was so explicitly identified with Satan, and that concern was expressed in emerging canon law. Without fail, those texts and canons traced their condemnation back to Psalm 91.[56]

So much of the demonic literature, Jewish or Christian, concerns threats to entrap and destroy human beings, and individuals fight back on a strictly localized basis, defending themselves, their families, and their households. But particularly for Christians, warfare against evil forces had a cosmic dimension, which was central to the church's concept of its very being, and 91 supplied the imagery and vocabulary. As long as the state remained closely bound to the church, the psalm shaped ideas of governance as much as worship. It became the warrant for expressions of triumph and power, worldly as well as religious, and, on occasion, of real arrogance.

5

Tread upon the Lion and Adder

The Psalm as a Manifesto of Christendom

> When the martyrs were being slain, it was the raging lion: when heretics are plotting, it is the dragon creeping beneath us. You have conquered the lion; conquer also the dragon: the lion has not crushed you, let not the dragon deceive you.[1]
>
> —Augustine of Hippo, c. 410 CE

The city of Ravenna is celebrated for its Roman (Byzantine) mosaics, which mainly date from the sixth century CE. In the Archbishop's Chapel in the bishops' palace, Christ is spectacularly depicted as a Roman emperor in military garb, who tramples underfoot a lion and a serpent. Such an invocation of Psalm 91 was a standard feature of ordinary life across the Christian world around this time, but this was no mere call to spiritual defense, no attempt to protect the palace from demonic assaults. The image offered powerful lessons in theology of the most sophisticated kind, for the enlightenment and instruction of Christian cultural elites. Throughout the early Christian and medieval centuries, Psalm 91 taught multiple lessons about Christology and the resurrection, about temptation and faithfulness, about the Trinity and the divine nature, and, scarcely less significant, about the dangers of heresy and the defense of orthodoxy.[2]

The promise to tread or trample evil forces continued to fascinate. The range of enemies that could be comprehended under that label was broad to the point of limitlessness, and frequently included foes we would think of as secular rather than spiritual. Throughout late antiquity and the Middle Ages, Psalm 91 was a mainstay of political ideology, a means of asserting strength and literally demonizing enemies, who became serpents to be crushed.[3]

He Will Save You from the Deadly Pestilence. Philip Jenkins, Oxford University Press. © Oxford University Press 2023.
DOI: 10.1093/oso/9780197605646.003.0005

Persecutors

Immersed as they were in 91, Christian leaders readily applied its swaggering language and imagery to combating the church's enemies. During the pagan persecutions, the churches naturally turned to the psalm for its promises of victory, but they did face one practical limitation in exactly how it might be deployed. The natural text to use to prophesy the destruction of paganism would be v. 13, and it is at first sight puzzling that the psalm does not appear much in the portions of the so-called Apostolic Fathers attributed to great second-century figures such as Ignatius and Polycarp. But then we recall that most of what we know from or concerning these early leaders has to do with their martyrdom, texts in which they often write of upcoming confrontations with literal lions and other wild beasts. Using something like v. 13 would be embarrassingly inappropriate for those about to confront very real and material wild beasts in the arena, which they would conspicuously not defeat in any physical sense. Sometimes, the texts that people do not cite are as suggestive as those they actually do.[4]

Nevertheless, 91 does emerge in some key martyrdom narratives. One of the most memorable is that of Perpetua and Felicity, who suffered death in the city of Carthage in the early years of the third century. The Christian who reported the events stressed their staunch resistance to their persecutors, and subtly used 91 to indicate their moral and spiritual triumph. (Some think the author in question might have been Tertullian himself.) Perpetua has a vision of an Egyptian gladiator who is to fight and kill her. However, we are told, she maintains her resistance in the only way possible: *Perpetua psallebat caput iam Aegyptii calcans*, that is, "Perpetua sang psalms, already treading under foot the head of the Egyptian." In the context, that combination of *caput* and *calcans*, of head and treading, must be a reference to 91. Although the two women were destined to fight beasts, the specific story imagines a conflict with a human fighter, which allows the use of that otherwise troublesome line about conquering and overcoming.[5]

Heretics

If indeed the Church inherited the promises and blessings specified in the text, then those powers could properly be deployed against those who tried to subvert and discredit truth and orthodoxy.

Psalm 91 became a standard feature of polemical denunciations of heretics. It offered multiple attractions, particularly when the correct interpretation of scripture was so central to these debates. The fact that Satan himself had quoted the psalm to Jesus proved beyond doubt that accurate biblical quotation did not automatically establish authority. In the early third century, Origen used that argument to combat the influence of his formidably learned heretical rivals, using the wilderness story as an object lesson in how not to read and value scripture. Unlike Satan, the true Christian should eschew literalism removed from true faith. "Marcion reads the scriptures as the Devil does. So do Basilides and Valentinus. . . . When an opportune moment arises, the Devil cites the Scriptures."[6]

Commonly, it was v. 13 that was targeted against the "serpents" who subverted the authority of the true Christian community. I have already quoted the verse from the Epistle to the Romans in which Paul imagines God crushing "those who spread dissension and place obstacles [skandala]," contrary to the orthodox teachings the church has learned. In later terms, Paul is describing heretics who are to be silenced and destroyed. Outsiders, of course, would often view such conflicts more impartially as feuds between rival church factions, and might differ on the proper allocation of the Satanic designation.[7]

Later Patristic writings raided the psalm's text to find ammunition against heretics. In the late fourth century, Jerome suggested that by the psalm's "destroying word," "we may comprehend this word of destruction to be the teaching of heretics, of philosophers, of Jews." In fact, Jerome knew the actual meaning of the verse in question and the erroneous derivation of the "word," but that false translation fitted his rhetorical purposes at that moment.

He continued:

> The flying arrow of the devil, if you ask me, is the disputation of heretics and philosophers, for they promise the light of knowledge and claim that they have the light of day.[8]

That "light" metaphor drew Jerome to the psalm's image of the noonday demon. He mocked the *simplices* who believed that a pernicious demon was likely to strike at a particular time of day, and focused instead on the bright light that heretical false believers claimed to shed on spiritual matters. In doing so, they served their master, Satan or Lucifer, who was originally an angel of light. "When some heretics promise quasi-mysteries, such as the kingdom of heaven, continence, abstinence, holiness, renunciation of the world, they promise the noon. But because it is not the light of Christ, it is not the noon, but the noonday demon." Jerome's approach influenced anti-heretical writing over the next millennium, as that noonday imagery resurfaced to describe each new perceived threat to orthodoxy. As we saw in Chapter 4, Walter Hilton was still deploying that rhetorical strategy against the Free Spirit heresy in 1390.[9]

Augustine

The greatest figure of the Latin Christian West was Augustine, whose works shaped church readings of scripture for centuries to come. Augustine had a long-standing love for 91, citing it in the account of his conversion in the *Confessions*. Describing his changing beliefs, he contrasted the writings of the Platonists with Christian scripture. Only the latter gave believers a way to advance through all the obstacles they faced in the world. Just as worldly travelers faced the constant menace of plundering deserters and bandits, so the spiritual path was under threat from demons who were "deserters" from the heavenly army, rebels against God. These demons were symbolized by the lion and the serpent, as described in the psalm. But the Christian would advance on the main road, "guarded by the host of the heavenly general"—that is, the angels.[10]

Augustine continued to be fascinated by the Psalms—we might say obsessed—and his *Expositions on the Psalms* engaged his attention for much of his career, from 391 through 418. In the process, he created one of the lengthiest works of Christian antiquity, twice the length of the already substantial *City of God*. He treated Psalm 91 very respectfully. That reflected its importance in popular Christian thought, but also the number of lessons that could be extracted from it, not least for the use of preachers. Augustine stressed above all the theme of temptation in the psalm:

> This psalm is that from which the Devil dared to tempt our Lord Jesus Christ: let us therefore attend to it, that thus armed, we may be enabled to resist the tempter, not presuming in ourselves, but in Him who before us was tempted, that we might not be overcome when tempted.[11]

Throughout, his emphasis is less on individual temptations than on the collective menaces of heresy and persecution. He takes familiar texts about demons as lone tempters and applies them in a political context, to the threats to faith that Christians suffer in times of persecution. Expounding the terror by night and the arrow by day, he offers a psychologically subtle analysis of Christian responses to persecution, and how such threats affect believers differently depending on the maturity of their faith. Again, persecution is the noonday demon, so called because "the persecution is very hot; and thus the noon signifies the excessive heat." At such times, the persecuted could only endure to the end if they placed absolute faith in God:

> But what is said to Christ? You shall tread on the lion and the dragon. Lion, for open rage; dragon, for hidden treachery. The dragon cast Adam out of Paradise; as a lion, the same persecuted the Church.

The lion and dragon represented two faces of the same evil, each subject to the Devil, and each a different strategy for overthrowing the church. The lion signified the persecution leading to martyrdom; the dragon was the subtler but no less lethal face of heresy.[12]

Christians Against Christians

Similar themes emerge in the sixth-century writings of Cassiodorus, another author of widely read commentaries on all the psalms. Like Augustine, he confronted the immediate reality of heresy, which he naturally interpreted through our psalm.

To understand his writings, we need to appreciate the dire political and religious situation in which he lived. From 493, Italy was under the control of the Ostrogoth people, who held to the Arian form of Christianity, which traced its origins to the early fourth-century thinker Arius. It differed from the Orthodox or Catholic form of the faith held by the Roman Empire, in placing Christ as subordinate to God the Father, rather than a fully equal member of the Trinity. Each side saw its opponents as driven by outright evil, and Jerome had applied his familiar argument to characterize Arius simply as *daemonium meridianum*, a noonday demon.[13]

This religious difference created a gulf between the Arian Gothic rulers of Italy and the Catholic and Roman populations they governed. In Ravenna, an Arian cathedral and baptistery stood uncomfortably near the Catholic versions of those same structures. When the great mosaic we have encountered was constructed in the Archbishop's Chapel in the early sixth century, it was intended as an assertion of Catholic resilience over Arian heretics, who are symbolized as the lion and serpent. Reinforcing the core Catholic teaching, the Christ figure bears a book asserting his unique role as "the way, the truth and the life." It is thus a gesture of defiance against the Gothic regime. In the 530s, a revived Roman Empire invaded Italy and ultimately drove out the Ostrogoths, following a series of wars that devastated the country.[14]

Cassiodorus was a Catholic who nevertheless served the Arian Gothic court. He knew Ravenna well, and must have known that mosaic: he may have seen it when it was newly unveiled. The bloody collapse of the Gothic regime in the 540s sent him into retirement, where he undertook his work on the Psalms. Like Augustine, he held 91 in high esteem, and framed it in exalted terms. Using the Septuagint numbering, the psalm was 90, which represented for him "thrice three tens," and pointed infallibly to the Trinity.[15]

Like most Christian writers, Cassiodorus believed that the psalm could defeat evil, but such struggles went beyond spiritual warfare. If demons were indeed active in the world, which they assuredly were, then their activities manifested in large-scale physical attacks on the church and its members, which in the context of the time implied different forms of persecution, often amounting to martyrdom. In the early centuries, such demonic assaults were attributed to pagan forces, but after the imperial conversion to Christianity, heretical rivals were commonly blamed. Given the religious struggles that Cassiodorus himself knew in Italy between Catholic and Arian Christians, it is not surprising that he read the psalm chiefly in those terms:

> *The terror of the night*, then, is the cloudy persuasion of heretics. *The arrow that flieth by day* is open persecution by tyrants. *The business in the dark* is the debased study by which the mental eye of right believers is blinded. *The noonday devil* is the massive danger ignited by the heat of persecution, in which destruction is often feared, and human weakness overcome.[16]

The Psalm of Triumph

Cassiodorus, like Augustine or Jerome, would have been perplexed by modern complaints that their readings were political rather than spiritual, and would indeed have rejected any such distinction. The spiritual was political, and vice versa, and both were integral parts of the new Christendom. Once empires and kingdoms were Christian, those states became integrated into the Christian worldview, and they acquired the powers and promises offered to the church in Psalm 91. This transformation ushered in a long period when the psalm served to assert worldly power and hegemony. The first Christian emperor, Constantine, himself symbolized his defeated rival, Licinius, as a dragon, pierced in combat. That image draws on multiple biblical texts, but increasingly our psalm became the explicit foundation of imperial iconography. Those lions and serpents symbolized hostile rulers or nations, and enemy attacks were readily portrayed as arrows, terrors, or plagues.[17]

Even before the rise of Christianity, such crushing or trampling references were well established in Roman imperial culture and iconography, and were manifested in ceremonial parades as well as the visual arts. So common was the theme of treading on the neck that it has its own technical term in art history, *calcatio colli*. Christian rulers reproduced many aspects of this theme, exalting Christ the Conqueror in a way that we might think gruesomely unsuited to the New Testament's core messages of forgiveness and turning the other cheek. Following legends surrounding Constantine's conversion, medieval Latin Christians knew unquestioningly that the abbreviated form of Jesus's name, IHS, also signified *in hoc signo*—"In this sign [the cross], conquer." That triumphal tradition continued into the Renaissance and beyond, and at every stage, Psalm 91 provided a goldmine of imagery. Both in Eastern and Western Europe, the theme of a conquering imperial Christ figure subordinating demonic animals often appeared in royal iconography, in paintings, in mosaics, and on coins.[18]

The psalm proved useful when a king or lord defeated his enemies and wanted to exhibit a public triumph, often in bloody or sadistic ways. In 695, the tyrannical East Roman emperor Justinian II was deposed by one of his generals, who had Justinian mutilated—cutting off his nose—before sending him into exile. Several years of turmoil followed in the empire, as two consecutive military usurpers enjoyed brief reigns. In 705, Justinian returned and subjected those two interlopers to public torture and humiliation. Fortuitously, the two men's names were Leontius and Apsimarus, which sounded close enough to the lion and asp destined to be trodden down. Justinian used their living bodies as his footstool at Constantinople's Hippodrome, as his followers led the crowds in chanting the psalm.[19]

Into the West

In the emerging barbarian nations of Western Europe, the treading motif appeared in sculptures and stone crosses, paintings and manuscripts. That imagery seemed all the more appropriate as those newly Christian kings were combatting actual pagan peoples, rather than just rival Christian rulers. In Britain, the mighty Anglo-Saxon kingdom of Northumbria was converted in the 630s, and over the following decades stone crosses were erected to commemorate that triumph. This region is home to some of the greatest surviving examples of the kind, at Bewcastle and Ruthwell, and presumably many other now-lost crosses once existed. Each depicts a range of images drawn from the Bible. At Ruthwell, the most imposing panel depicts Christ treading the beasts, with the explanatory Latin inscription "Jesus Christ: the judge of righteousness: the beasts and dragons [*bestiae et dracones*] recognized in the desert the Savior of the world." Apart from the obvious psalmic reference, some scholars believe the figure is drawn from an Egyptian monastic original. A similar scene occupies center stage at Bewcastle. The image of the treading was a proclamation of victory over paganism, and probably served as a visual aid in preaching and evangelization.[20]

The most important Western state was that of the Franks, who from the 750s were ruled by the dynasty that became famous as the Carolingians, the house of successive rulers named Charles (Carolus in Latin). As the Franks extended their power into Italy, they interacted with the Byzantine Empire, and saw and envied symbols of imperial power, above all in Ravenna. In 800, the greatest Frankish ruler, Charles the Great (Charlemagne), received the imperial title in Rome from the hands of the pope. Over the next century, the Carolingians enthusiastically appropriated imperial imagery, especially as derived from Psalm 91. Charlemagne himself not only knew Ravenna, but tried to reproduce many of its features at his own court, in Aachen. Further contributing to those scriptural themes, the empire's intellectual and religious life was under powerful Northumbrian influence. Like those Northumbrians before him, Charlemagne saw himself as a Christian warrior against pagan enemies, and oversaw forcible mass conversions in Germany. Naturally, the psalm's vision of suppressing dangerous beasts appealed to him.[21]

Those motifs permeated the religious art of the period, the so-called Carolingian Renaissance, and they shaped contemporary interpretations of Christ. As the emperors became more Christlike, so Christ became ever more Carolingian. We see this in several of the magnificent artworks of the period.

In the great Stuttgart Psalter, which was originally made in the royal abbey of St. Denis, Psalm 91 is illustrated by a military image that directly recalls the Ravenna mosaic, albeit in cruder terms. Again, a cloaked and armed warrior treads down a ferocious lion and serpent. The cross surrounding his head indicates his identity as Christ, as does the divine hand reaching from the cloud above him. He is attended and supported by an angel. But however clearly the Christ figure is identified, his armor and clothing unmistakably portray him as an elite Carolingian warrior, and hint at the emperor himself. The great king's adviser and biographer was Einhard, and around 820, the famous reliquary known as Einhard's Arch (originally in Maastricht) depicted the triumph of a very military-looking Christ and his saints, who tread down serpents.[22]

The same theme occurred in works of art that are among the great surviving treasures of the age. One was the Douce Ivory (which I have already cited), with its convenient acronym SUP ASP, and which was set in the binding of a gospel lectionary. The ivory was commissioned by the renowned abbey of Chelles, which was headed by the emperor's sister Gisela, and the piece may have been made at his flourishing court in Aachen. Christ again tramples the beasts on the carved ivory panel that forms the back cover of the spectacular Lorsch gospel book, another Carolingian work of the early ninth century. In the Genoels-Elderen ivory, a book cover from the same era, Christ tramples four beasts, among which are a serpent and lion. That *super aspidem* motif appears prominently in the ninth-century Utrecht Psalter, one of the finest manuscripts of the period.[23]

Liturgy

The psalm was equally familiar to believers who had no access to such elite treasures, as it was widely used in Christian prayer and liturgy. Monastics and clergy so appreciated 91 because it mentions various times of day, specifically the four broad divisions into day, noonday, twilight (*tenebris*), and night. That feature has made it appropriate for the daytime cycle that we find in various traditions. It has featured in Christian daily offices for noonday and especially for night prayer. To put that development in context, the origins of compline in the West owed much to Benedict and Cassiodorus, who belonged to the same era as the Ravenna mosaic. In the ninth century, Charlemagne's close ally Amalarius of Metz stressed the lesson that "because our sleep has some likeness to the sleep of those who have left this world under the Lord's protection, the same psalm also recalls the intention of those who are in difficulty and nevertheless pass from this difficulty to peace."[24]

From early Christian times, 91 featured in liturgical settings to announce the triumph of Christ over evil, and how those powers were conferred on the faithful. It had a special resonance during ceremonies of baptism and initiation. In 381, the great archbishop of Constantinople, Gregory of Nazianzus, preached his famous oration on baptism. He urged believers to seal themselves with baptism, with all the protections that offered: "And listen to David giving thee the good news, 'Thou shalt not be afraid for the terror by night, for mischance or noonday demon.'" In another Eastern Rite service of the same era, the celebrant prays:

> Thou whom none can deceive, deliver them from every sickness, and every disease, and every offence, every injury and deceit, *"from fear of the enemy, from the dart that flieth in the day, from the mischief that walketh about in darkness."*[25]

The psalm's language and imagery permeated the Christmas liturgy of the Byzantine world, which imagined the clash between the Christ child and the forces of evil seeking to assail him. As the child grew, we are told, he would humble the asp and the basilisk.[26]

Among their other attempts at centralization and standardization, the Carolingians undertook extensive liturgical reforms, whose impact would be felt for centuries to come. Probably from this Carolingian era stems the "Old Roman" tradition of liturgical chant. The setting of Psalm 91 is known by its opening verse in Latin, *Qui habitat in adjutorio Altissimi*, and it often features in medieval chant collections, as well as the Old Roman and Gregorian.[27]

We have already encountered Amalarius of Metz, who became a key activist in the Carolingian reform. His writings show how 91 was incorporated into the liturgy, and in contexts that we might find surprising. On Good Friday, the most solemn day of the liturgical calendar, churches were to read the psalm alongside the third chapter of John, which includes a much-quoted dialogue between Jesus and his secret follower, Nicodemus. The linkage between the two texts, psalm and gospel, is puzzling, until we realize the shared symbol of serpents and snake venom. In John 3, Jesus refers to an Old Testament episode in which a brazen serpent was raised in the wilderness for the healing of those assailed by snakebite. The gospel interprets this as prefiguring Christ, who was raised on the cross for the healing and salvation of humanity. Juxtaposing those Johannine words with Psalm 91 reinforces the idea of the triumph over sin, and the winning of lasting spiritual benefits.[28]

The West favored the psalm in services that were mournful or penitential. Its use at the start of Lent was singularly appropriate because in Christian tradition that season commemorates Jesus's time in the wilderness, and the temptations. Homilies show that Anglo-Saxon clerics used 91 to interpret the crucifixion, and also the Harrowing of Hell that in legend immediately followed that event. Drawing on apocryphal gospels, they taught that Jesus visited the underworld to free the souls of those holy people who had died before his time. In so doing, he subjugated and bound the powers of evil, making the 91 citation vitally relevant.[29]

While appreciating its theology, believers found other attractions in the psalm, and the sermons derived from it. Preachers often used v. 13 to elaborate on the beasts, real and imaginary, giving their perorations a sensational or fantastic quality. One of the most esteemed teachers of the twelfth century was Honorius of Autun, whose sermon on 91 includes lengthy disquisitions on dragons, lions, and basilisks. The basilisk is

> a deadly four-footed animal, whose breath instantly kills all who breathe it. Even the birds flying overhead choke and drop dead from the sky, shedding feathers withered as if by some flame. This noxious beast spreads death all about him, and yet when defeated by a small weasel it wastes away and dies.

Such sermons appealed to what we might term a *Wild Kingdom* fascination with the exotic natural world.[30]

From late antiquity through the early modern period, the Psalter was so central to Christian practice because of its role in monastic life and the daily offices that were also followed by better-off laypeople. The Psalter became the inescapable foundation of devotional life. The Psalms were central to the spiritual lives of mystics and contemplatives, who were inspired by the assurances that 91 offered about the subjugation of demons, whether these were conceived as literal or metaphorical. Probably around 1390, one of the flourishing English school of Christian mystics used our psalm, the *Qui habitat*, as the basis for an elaborate treatise on spiritual contemplation, the narrow paths that led to authentic spiritual exaltation. That tract is almost certainly the work of Walter Hilton, one of the most revered of that widely read circle. The fact that it is written in the English vernacular means that such ideas were now being offered to laypeople as well as clergy and monastics.[31]

Naturally, the Psalter was the single book that was most often illustrated and commented on, and it appeared in deluxe editions. We have encountered the use of 91 in such works as the Stuttgart and Utrecht Psalters, and the English were if anything even more enthusiastic about such depictions than their Frankish neighbors. The superb Crowland Psalter (eleventh century) has a full-page illustration of Christ trampling the beasts, appropriately next to another of the archangel Michael fighting a dragon. The Odbert Psalter, from around 1000, elaborately cross-references the trampling imagery with scenes of Christ's temptations in the desert. One of the finest English examples is the St. Albans Psalter, probably from around 1120, with a full-page illustration of Christ trampling a large and threatening dragon.[32]

Psalm 91 tended to appeal to the creative imagination of scribes, and often their grotesque side. Just as the rabbis had let their imaginations run wild in portraying the psalm's monstrous beasts in words, so Christian artists gave them visual form. In the 1330s, England's wealthy Luttrell family commissioned a magnificent Psalter, in which 91 is appropriately illustrated with a warrior defending himself, while a man seeks to club a nonspecific demonic monster that is a hybrid of lion, lynx, and (perhaps) giant toad. A scholarly commentary characterizes this beast aptly as "nondescript." The pictures here and elsewhere in the volume are so bizarre that they have a strong humorous touch.[33]

The Papal Revolution

The Carolingians and their successors worked closely with the churches and often exercised great authority over church affairs, including the choice of bishops and higher clergy. In turn, churches happily enabled royal and imperial iconographies of triumph. But those uses shifted together with the balance of sacred and secular forces. In the 1070s, Pope Gregory VII made a far-reaching bid to establish the power and independence of his office and that of the church at large, sparking a long series of ideological and military struggles against the Western emperors, who claimed the heritage of Charlemagne. Central to the struggle was control over the right that kings claimed to install or invest bishops—hence the term for this momentous conflict, the Investiture Contest. In the course of these battles, the church appropriated the themes of triumph and trampling for its own ends. Just as the Frankish rulers had snatched the psalm from the Byzantine Empire, so the papacy now claimed it from their successors.[34]

The papalist militants, followers of Pope Gregory, drew special inspiration from Augustine's preaching on the psalm and his belief in the church's victory over spiritual temptations. In this view, the four beasts represented multiple evils, including the Devil, heresy, and resistance against church authority. Symbols derived from such interpretations became common in the visual arts of twelfth-century Rome, proclaiming the glory of the city and the papacy.[35]

That emphasis on the psalm was evident during the great rebuilding of Italian cathedrals over the next two centuries, in the splendid tympana under which believers entered the building. Looking up at images of the defeated and trampled beasts—serpents, lions, and basilisks—the faithful knew that they were witnessing the victory of the church and its popes over all enemies. They could if they chose identify those creatures with the unfaithful secular kings who wantonly defied the authority of the popes. Such depictions of triumph over evil were a signature of the work of the most influential Italian sculptor of the early twelfth century, known only as Nicholaus, and they appear in superb work at Ferrara and Verona. Nicholaus was explicitly recalling late antique and Carolingian examples, which now enjoyed a renewed vogue in church architecture, repurposed for papalist propaganda.[36]

The pro-papal message was reinforced by the mosaics or paintings that the faithful saw within the buildings. The cathedral at Trieste includes a thirteenth-century mosaic of Christ bearing a book and treading down mysterious reptiles. The inscription reads, *Maiestate deum liquet hunc regnare per aevum / ambulat en Christus super aspidem et basiliscum* (Now God can rule forever in majesty: Christ treads on the snake and the basilisk). Bishops' tombs likewise showed the deceased trampling threatening beasts. Such imagery was not confined to embattled Italy. In France and elsewhere, Gothic cathedrals situated snakes and dragons in the piers supporting cathedral doors, to show the church's triumph over the forces of Hell. Curiously, such imagery even had its impact on Jewish thought and iconography. Already in the eleventh century, a synagogue in Cologne was divided over the decision to add windows with churchlike lion and serpent imagery. Meanwhile, as the dragons of v. 13 increasingly came to be understood as evil or Satanic, they were regularly portrayed in synagogue decoration.[37]

Long after the titanic struggle between empire and papacy, the popes laid claim to what had once been this key component of imperial iconography. In 1458, Pope Pius II celebrated his victory over anti-papal conspirators by forcing them to carry his litter during a triumphal entry into Rome. Quoting v. 13, he commented, "This prophecy has often been fulfilled before now and shall be fulfilled today. For what beast is more savage than man?" The papal throne in St. John Lateran includes at its base the four beasts from the psalm, upon which the pope would sit. Contemporary foes of papal excesses made much of such arrogant assertions, and one legend, of a pope treading on the neck of an emperor, would become a mainstay of anti-papal polemic for centuries to come (see Chapter 6).[38]

Beyond Christendom

Other enemies to be subjected in the name of the psalm were all too obvious. As we have seen, Patristic writers freely included Jews among the enemies to be trodden down, and such references occurred often in medieval polemic. Much more systematic was the use of the psalm to frame Muslims as the key danger, as obvious serpents and basilisks. The psalm's military character again came to the fore, and it proved invaluable for justifying Crusades and holy wars. It featured prominently in liturgies designed to support and inspire Crusaders.[39]

That popularity continued long after what we often think of as the peak of the Crusader phenomenon. In 1389, Serbian Christian forces fought the Ottoman Turks of Sultan Murad at the extraordinarily bloody Battle of Kosovo, which became a venerated moment in Serbian history. Although the Serbs were all but annihilated, survivors recalled the battle in heroic terms. In 1404, a marble column erected at the site recounted the conflict in mythological terms, in which Christians slaughtered so many Turks. These included

> the great Murad and his son, the offspring of the asp and the adder,
> the pup of the lion and the basilisk, and along with them quite a many
> others.[40]

Also around this time, in 1402, the French Duc de Berry acquired some recently cast gold medallions depicting Roman emperors. (One of the finest connoisseurs of the age, the duke is associated with some of its most splendid illuminated manuscripts.) One image depicted the seventh-century Byzantine emperor Heraclius, who had defeated the rival Zoroastrian Empire of Persia, and in the process recaptured Jerusalem and reclaimed the True Cross. This proto-Crusader was depicted surrounded by our psalm's v. 13, celebrating his trampling of those pagan foes.[41]

As we will see in Chapter 6, that crusading role continued long after the end of the gravest confrontations with Islam. When Christian kingdoms encountered the New World a century later, many saw the struggle against those pagan natives as a continuation of older Crusader efforts against Muslims, and they used the mighty psalm in their cause. Aggressive and triumphalist, this was a worldview that would have made perfect sense to the Roman authorities who commissioned that mosaic at Ravenna almost exactly a millennium previously.

Throughout the Middle Ages, the psalm continued to be an unavoidable presence in politics, theology, culture, and science. That role did not diminish with the early modern period, which began around the year 1500, and many of its uses and functions remained unchanged. What was new, however, was that the work of translation radically changed understandings of the psalm for some Christians, though by no means all. In effect, Christendom now read not just one version of the psalm, but two very different ones, and each interpreted their own text accordingly.

6

My Refuge and My Fortress

The Psalm Divides Christendom

> Would that we truly understood and impressed on our hearts the
> divine promises, namely, that our sins have been forgiven us, that
> death and the Devil have been conquered, and that hell has been
> destroyed, as this is gloriously proclaimed in Ps. 91:13 *You will tread
> on the lion and adder, the young lion and the serpent you will trample
> underfoot!* He who firmly believes this imbibes these promises, feeds
> most pleasantly on these vines, and is lord over death.[1]
>
> —Martin Luther, 1545

In the seventeenth century, the Catholic duchy of Bavaria was a thriving
center of European culture and art, as well as a key player in the political
and military affairs of the day. During the Thirty Years' War, Bavaria faced a
deadly threat from the forces of Protestant Sweden, which occupied its capital city, Munich, in 1632: plague struck the city in 1634 and again in 1636.
When the grueling crisis had passed, Bavaria's duke erected a monument
in the heart of Munich to thank the Virgin Mary for the city's deliverance.
Dedicated in 1638, that "Mary Column," the Mariensäule, is still a proud
Munich landmark, and one of the glories of European Baroque sculpture.
It gave its name to the Marienplatz, the historic square in the city's center.
The Mariensäule is also an explicit invocation of Psalm 91. Surrounding the
column on which now stands a golden statue of Mary are four figures of armored putti, each fighting and trampling a monstrous symbolic beast: the
lion, dragon, basilisk, and serpent. These probably represent the evils of, respectively, paganism, heresy, schism, and Judaism, although a case can be
made for the figures representing other menaces, such as war, hunger, pestilence, and heresy. Lest any observer be so religiously obtuse as to miss the
scriptural origin, the putti's shields each bear a phrase from the psalm—*et*

He Will Save You from the Deadly Pestilence. Philip Jenkins, Oxford University Press. © Oxford University Press 2023.
DOI: 10.1093/oso/9780197605646.003.0006

basiliscum, et leonem, and so on. The Munich column, with its attendant warriors, inspired other spectacular examples in Vienna and Prague, and many lesser imitators.[2]

At first sight, such a monument seems to show how little had changed from the medieval world. Psalm 91 still asserted the triumph of the church and of faithful monarchs against their enemies. Nor was there anything new about depicting fellow Christians as monstrous beasts to be subjugated. The wars and religious struggles following the Reformation produced such confrontations in abundance, with neither side having a monopoly on such depictions. In crucial ways, however, interpretations of the psalm now changed fundamentally, and in fact became so divided that we are almost reading two distinct histories. As Protestants rediscovered the original Hebrew text, 91 began a whole new career in terms of its functions and uses. Catholic and Orthodox Christians, meanwhile, clung to the meanings that had been standard since the earliest Christian times, and going back to the Septuagint translation. The text marked a religious frontier, as the Protestant Psalm 91, with its "noisome pestilence," confronted the Catholic Psalm 90, with its "bitter word." Martin Luther himself began his career by devoutly praying what he called Psalm 90, before embarking on his discovery of Psalm 91. The builders of that Munich column were assuredly thinking in terms of Psalm 90, but differences of interpretation went far beyond numerical trivia. Whichever version prevailed, 91 continued to fascinate reformers and conservatives alike.

Luther's Psalm

Martin Luther loved 91, which he called "a most distinguished jewel among all the psalms of consolation."[3] He wrote about it extensively, and those commentaries and opinions were widely read across the emerging Protestant Europe.

As a late medieval monastic, Luther knew the psalms intimately through the daily services, but this text above all was deeply relevant to his fundamental insight about redemption and justification, and how the redeemed person could trust absolutely in God. The psalm's first two verses represented something like a credal statement about that assurance. He took the "trampling" verse to apply to the faithful Christian believer, rather than exclusively to Christ himself, and held that such triumphing over evil was a central part of Christian spiritual life:

If I believe the promise of God, I am certain my life is pleasing to God and is superior to all the orders, since it makes a heavenly man, a conqueror of death, an heir of eternal life, and one who tramples the devil underfoot, as is stated in Ps 91.13.

Giving force to that view was the sense that true Christians were an embattled minority, constantly under assault by the forces of evil, and in constant need of spiritual defense. Luther had no hesitation in placing himself as the hero of the psalm, one who would receive its blessings.[4]

But every other portion of the psalm also had its relevance, following from and building upon that initial declaration. Luther's vision of the self-reliant believer holding fast to faith in a faithless world chimed with the promise that a thousand would fall by one's side. The psalm also prophesied the scriptures on which Christians would rely for their resolute faith. In one of his last great sermons, in 1544 Luther preached on 91:

> This faith alone lasts; it is protected from all peril and destruction of false teachings, from the assaults of the devils on both sides, physical and spiritual, so that all other faiths must fall and suffer ruin. This happens because he shelters himself under Christ's wings and shoulders, where he places his refuge and confidence . . . his two wings are the two testaments of Holy Scripture which spread over us his righteousness and take us under him.

The psalm was an epitome of the Protestant worldview, in a strongly individualistic form. It features very frequently in Luther's voluminous writings. Whatever the topic—say, a lengthy and learned commentary on the Book of Genesis—91 will infallibly appear to support and illustrate arguments.[5]

The psalm even contributed to Luther's hymn "Ein feste Burg ist unser Gott," "A Mighty Fortress Is Our God." This was arguably the greatest work of its kind from the Reformation era, and long the anthem of German Protestantism. In the nineteenth and twentieth centuries, it became almost an alternative German national anthem, and a hymn to nationalism. Accounts of the hymn's origins rightly stress the influence of other scriptures, notably Psalm 46, which supplies the reference to the Lord of Hosts, "der Herr Zebaoth." But "Ein feste Burg" lacks some key themes of that text, while its strongly demonic emphases closely echo Psalm 91. The hymn speaks of a "world with devils filled" (*die Welt voll Teufel*) and the power of the old enemy, the prince of this world. Even the word *Burg* occurs in Luther's version of 91, and not 46. If the hymn was primarily founded in Psalm 46, it often betrays the influence of that other text that Luther loved so fiercely. Scholar Hannibal Hamlin refers to the work simply as a "hymn paraphrase of Psalm 91."[6]

The Old-New Psalm

Luther brought the psalm to much wider awareness through his epic work of translation. From the start of the sixteenth century, Western European scholars became much more familiar with Greek and Hebrew, and realized the inadequacies of the Latin version they knew so well. Luther published his new German translation of the New Testament in 1522 and the Psalms in 1523–1524; a complete Bible followed in 1534. In Psalm 91 particularly, Luther acknowledged the weakness of the Vulgate, and used both the original Hebrew and Jerome's "Hebrew Psalter."[7]

That allowed him to rediscover the psalm's central emphasis on plague and disease. He abandoned the use of the harmful "word" in v. 3, correctly speaking instead of a plague, "der schädlichen Pestilenz." Likewise, he exorcised the "noonday demon" from the text, so that v. 5 now referred both to a *Pestilenz* and a *Seuche*, "epidemic." At v. 10, Luther abandoned the metaphorical "scourge" in order to revive the plague element, preferring *Plage*. As we will see, that shift transformed the ways in which the psalm was read and understood across Protestant Europe. Luther also returned to the Hebrew original for the order in which the four beasts appeared in v. 13. More substantially, he toned down the supernatural qualities of the creatures, changing the basilisk to the more mundane *Ottern*, cognate to the English "adders." (Despite the image this might summon up for an English-speaker, Luther's version did not actually promise the ability to suppress dangerous otters.) He did keep *Drachen*, "dragons," however, rather than a more generic word for snakes.[8]

Luther minimized the demonic themes that had so long dominated interpretations of 91. Obviously, he believed passionately in Satan and in the earthly works of the Devil and his minions. However, removing the familiar Latin words about demons changed the psalm's emphasis, and Luther wrote remarkably little about the text in the context of spiritual warfare or exorcism. He did, however, address himself to the angelic protections on which the faithful could rely, for which 91 offered such explicit warrant: "There is a ministry of the angels for our benefit, and this must always be preached." Our failure to comprehend just how near angels are to us, and how active on our behalf, resulted from the blindness caused by original sin. He was well aware of that reality in his own life, and he believed that angelic protection was the only thing that had allowed him to live and preach for so many years in Wittenberg, despite the lethal fury of the pope and his cohorts.[9]

Luther's appreciation of the original Hebrew meaning did not totally change his citations of the psalm, which he had known so very well during his years as a monk. Accordingly, he often shifted between Hebrew-based and Vulgate readings. He freely cited the noonday demon or the bitter word as occasion presented, although in another part of his scholarly brain he must have recognized those phrases as the linguistic errors they were. When assailed by crises and criticisms in the mid-1520s, he invoked the "basilisk" as one of the four creatures he was empowered to trample. Apart from the long habit of usage, the older translation made his references intelligible to his less sophisticated readers. Luther treasured not just one Psalm 91, but multiple versions of it.[10]

Luther's Wars

In Luther's time, the psalm's multiple references to evils and menaces made it a common currency of polemic. When Luther was defending his views at the Diet of Worms in 1521, his Catholic antagonist Dr. Vehus of Baden cautioned him with the psalm's vv. 5–6, with its images of destruction and arrows. In turn, Luther made the psalm a standard weapon in the controversies and debates that so dominated his life from his revolutionary actions in 1517 until his death in 1546. Already in 1521, the satirical book *Murnarus Leviathan* depicted Luther as a (seemingly) humble monk standing over a monstrous demon, accompanied by several biblical texts concerning dragons and monsters, and, inevitably, v. 13 of our psalm is quoted. In 1526, the same verse supplied the text for the earliest French engravings and cartoons attacking Luther, with the Lutherans as the animals, the trampled rather than the tramplers.[11]

Luther had a signal talent for making enemies, and his polemics were bitter and often violent. When attacked for being too closely allied with ruthless kings, Luther responded:

For what are these [enemies] but the voices of Satan, by which he tries to disgrace me and the gospel? He, who has thus far so often beaten Satan under my feet, and has broken to pieces the lion and the dragon, will not allow the basilisk to tread on me.[12]

Such words were commonly directed against the pope and his "papist" followers, whom Luther saw as simply serving the Devil. In baptism, the Christian believer rejected the works of Satan and, by extension, the pope, so therefore, "he is commanded to avoid, flee, and trample the Pope, the Devil, and all his creatures, as Psalm 91 says."[13]

A like polemic dominated the commentary that he specifically devoted to 91 in 1530, which wholly focused on the errors of his rivals, of those who rejected his assertion of salvation through faith in Christ alone. In this view, "this entire psalm is an exhortation to the right faith against those who choose their own ways and set up their own righteousnesses, in which they look for God's help and grace, yea, rather tempt Him." Guilty of such offenses were Jews, heretics, and more generally, the proud and superstitious, who "[reject] all forms of His aid and protection, with which they ought to have been directed by Him." Luther used 91 to support his anti-Judaism. He believed the catalog of evils and dangers in vv. 5–8 could be "explained in a literal sense as referring to the Jews." For example:

The terror of the night is that which is experienced in the night. This is the slavish fear which is in the Law, a fear which Christ took away through faith and for which He bestowed love, and with this He gave the daytime fear, which is holy, enduring forever and ever.

The "snare of the hunter" referred to "the ungodly teachings [which] are the nets of the Jews, Pharisees, and heretics, cast out to catch souls."[14]

Through all these confessional wars, Luther took confidence from the promise of 91 that the righteous would see the punishment of the wicked. Throughout history, God's people had repeatedly seen and rejoiced over the destruction of enemies and persecutors, and the present age would be no exception. Luther, together with the rest of the righteous, would mock his defeated foes. The prime example of this ultimate reversal was Jan Hus, the Bohemian reformer who had foreshadowed many of Luther's views, and who had been executed in 1415. Now, Luther's success avenged Hus, as the wicked were put to shame.[15]

Protestant Reformers

Other reformers of the era likewise found in 91 a stark affirmation of core ideas of the new theology, and absolute trust in God. The text had a transformative effect on Theodore Beza, who heard it sung when he first attended Geneva's Reformed Assembly in 1548. He attributed many of his later achievements to the spiritual power he received from that experience. Ultimately, he succeeded John Calvin himself in Geneva. Through the lethal religious civil wars of the following decades, Beza set his hope on the psalm's final verse, "I will show him my salvation." Beza, like Luther and Calvin, was a prolific writer, and through their works, the psalm became a potent theme in later Protestantism. Published commentaries on the psalms proliferated.[16]

Like Luther, the other reformers diverged from their medieval predecessors in downplaying the demonic to a degree we may find surprising. Obviously, they were anything but "secular" or rationalist. However, they preferred to stress what the psalm could teach about lived Christian experience, and the Christian life as they understood it. In his 1557 *Commentary on the Psalms*, Calvin's substantial discussion of Psalm 91 stresses above all the trust that God's people should have in his power and protection against all dangers:

> God watches over the safety of his people, and never fails them in the hour of danger. They are exhorted to advance through all perils, secure in the confidence of his protection. The truth inculcated is one of great use, for though many talk much of God's providence, and profess to believe that he exercises a special guardianship over his own children, few are found actually willing to intrust their safety to him.[17]

He mentions Satan and temptation, but says virtually nothing about the demons and devils who would once have been so prominent. For Calvin, the lion, serpent, and the rest are merely "the obstacles which Satan throws in our course." With respect to "the terror by night," Calvin offered readings that were psychological rather than supernatural, pointing to the role of exaggerated fear: "Mention is made of *the fear of the night*, because men are naturally apprehensive in the dark, or because the night exposes us to dangers of different kinds, and our fears are apt at such a season to magnify any sound or disturbance."[18]

That metaphorical approach reflected Calvin's broader attitude to the supernatural. Calvin held that authentic miracles abounded in the New

Testament as God's means of establishing the truth of his new revelation, but those wonders had ceased when they were no longer needed. True miracles were thus neither necessary nor appropriate in subsequent ages; the wonders claimed by the Catholic church were either fraudulent or actually diabolical. Calvin is thus credited as the founder of the Protestant doctrine known as cessationism. Accordingly, he does not ascribe any miraculous or healing quality to the psalm, despite its great value in fortifying and encouraging Christians. "Troubles, it is true, of various kinds assail the believer as well as others, but the Psalmist means that God stands between him and the violence of every assault, so as to preserve him from being overwhelmed." Troubles come, but the true Christian is granted strength to bear them.[19] Calvin's prestige as a political and spiritual leader naturally gave special weight to his writings on the psalms, which were very widely read through the Calvinist or Reformed churches.

Believers at War

Calvin, Beza, and the rest were venerated as towering figures in the Protestant movement, and their writings achieved canonical status. The widespread grassroots use of our psalm is also well documented. The rise of printing and new forms of popular media vastly increased the number of religious texts available to ordinary believers. That included a torrent of devotional material, advising families and individuals how to lead lives of piety and holiness. We can see from those works just how common Psalm 91 was in everyday life. Luther himself had commended 91 as the psalm that "is particularly good to be read by all who are sick," and by no means only because of a severe plague. One popular English work was Lewis Bayly's *Practice of Piety* (1611), which taught Anglican readers how angels watched and guarded their actions. Psalm 91 reinforced the injunction to "do all things, therefore, as in the awful presence of God, and in the sight of his holy angels."[20]

Because the psalm was such a mainstay, it could be invoked with the assurance that an audience would know it intimately. For 150 years after Luther launched his revolution, Protestants and Catholics fought each other across Europe and their overseas possessions. The encounters were often bloody. Some two million died in the French Wars of Religion between 1562 and 1598, and another several million in the Thirty Years' War between 1618 and 1648. Through all these conflicts, both sides resorted to their religious and scriptural resources, as psalms became battle hymns. If Psalm 91 was not the most popular among Protestants—that dubious honor belonged to Psalm 68—it was one of a select group of such texts that were frequently deployed. In an age when sudden death was such a likely prospect, 91 was an obvious and recurring refuge. In 1628, France's Protestant leader Henri de Rohan stood in imminent danger of assassination but, as he wrote to his mother, he had no fear: he quoted the psalm's two opening verses. The psalm was much used by historians, clerical and lay, to interpret the horrible consequences of the ongoing wars.[21]

Sometimes contemporary events lent themselves almost too easily to framing through the psalm text. One of the most feared enemies of Catholic Spain was the English pirate (or naval hero) Sir Francis Drake, who was finally defeated and killed in the Caribbean in 1596. Based on his name—Drake resembles *draque*, "dragon"—Spaniards often applied serpent imagery to this lethal Protestant foe. In 1598, the great poet Lope de Vega published an epic work on Drake's defeat, under the title of *La Dragontea*, dedicated to the new Spanish king, Philip III. Serpentine imagery pervades the piece. The title page shows the dragon's fall and ruin, surrounded by the words of our psalm's thirteenth verse, telling how "you"—that is, King Philip—will trample the serpent and the dragon.[22]

Resorting to the psalm for protection did not necessarily imply staunch faith, and as in modern conflicts, many soldiers just used it as a spiritual insurance policy. Lest we imagine the warriors of these holy struggles as fanatics for their cause, it helps to recall a curious incident that occurred in the Battle of Poitiers in 1569, when French Protestants were besieging the Catholic-held city. A German cavalryman fighting on the Protestant side was shot and killed. Hanging around his neck were found two taffeta purses, one of which contained a parchment folded in four, written in Hebrew letters organized in ritualistic geometric style. These letters contained the whole of Psalm 67 and some key verses of 91, namely, vv. 1, 11, and 13. The other bag contained small roots and bones. The amulet might conceivably have been the work of an erudite Christian occultist, but it so closely resembles Jewish and Qabalistic amulets of the time that it probably originated as one. The Protestant soldier might have bought the manuscript from a Jewish source, to protect him in this internecine Christian conflict.[23]

In an age when religious conflicts were likely to land dissidents in prison, the psalm gave strength and solace. A celebrated victim of official persecution was Thomas More, whom England's Henry VIII imprisoned in 1533 for his refusal to recognize the king's marriage to Anne Boleyn and his ensuing break with the papacy. While in the Tower of London awaiting execution, More composed his tract *A Dialogue of Comfort Against Tribulation*, which was at once a work of devotion and political philosophy. The *Dialogue* included a lengthy disquisition on Psalm 91, drawing heavily on Augustine, who had focused so sharply on the theme of temptation. That had immediate relevance for More, who had the option of saving his life, but at the cost of betraying what he understood as the true church and of losing his eternal salvation. In his solitude, he meditated at length on the verse about the terror by night, and the inner fears that could drive a person to cowardly actions.[24]

The psalm featured regularly in struggles against deviant religious beliefs, and learned church leaders often invoked Jerome's interpretation of the "noonday demon" as referring to heresy, or heretical leaders. To take one example of many, in 1655, English Presbyterian cleric Christopher Fowler exposed an allegedly heretical mystical sect in a tract impressively titled *Dæmonium Meridianum. Satan at Noon. Or, Antichristian Blasphemies, Anti-Scripturall Divelismes, Anti-Morall Uncleanness*. Yet the same psalm gave strength and encouragement to those humble believers who found themselves at odds with political and religious authorities, the fowlers of the world, and their snares.[25]

Throughout the sixteenth century, the much-persecuted Anabaptists commonly turned to 91 as they faced imprisonment or death at the hands of political and religious forces they regarded as allied with the Devil. In 1551, a married couple imprisoned at Antwerp faced the prospect of being burned alive. The man encouraged his wife, "Yea, we must fight and contend against ferocious lions, dragons, and bears, yea, against the wicked and perverse generations of vipers and serpent rulers, and against the subtle serpents of this world." Another martyr in 1564 warned his fellow believers that the clergy would quote scripture against them, just as the Devil had quoted the psalm to Jesus in the wilderness. Others warned family and friends to resist the temptation to conform, that they may be preserved from "the pestilence that walketh in darkness." This is exactly the same language that the Catholic church itself had long directed against heretics and dissidents, now appropriated by those very grassroots believers for their own purposes.[26]

The Pope and the Emperor

The psalm's fame was further spread by stories that circulated as folktales, without being associated with any particular sage or scholar, and some endured for centuries. One of the best-known such tales concerned a monstrous abuse of papal power, and the fact that it had never occurred did nothing to diminish its visceral power. In its day, it was central to religious polemic.

We have already noted the long series of wars between popes and emperors, the Investiture Contest. In the 1170s, the German emperor Frederick Barbarossa was engaged in renewed wars with Pope Alexander III. In 1177, following a series of military and diplomatic defeats, the emperor was forced to submit to humiliating terms. That (historically factual) submission in Venice became the basis of an enduring legend according to which Alexander placed his foot on the emperor's neck. In the words of the sixteenth-century English Protestant polemicist John Foxe:

> The proud pope setting his foot upon the Emperor's neck, said the verse of the Psalm: *Super aspidem & basiliscum ambulabis & conculabis leonem & draconeum*: That is: Thou shalt walk upon the adder and the basilisk: and shalt tread down the lion and the dragon, &c. To whom the Emperor answering again, said: *Non tibi sed Petro*, that is, not to thee but to Peter. The pope again, *Et mihi, & Petro*. Both to me & to Peter. The Emperor fearing to give any occasion of farther quarrelling, held his peace & so was absolved, & peace made between them.

The pope's fault was in grounding his power in himself and his pagan-derived office, rather than in God the Most High. (A similar story was told of the submission of an earlier king to a pope, in the notorious confrontation at Canossa in 1077.)[27]

The legend spread among late medieval humanists, and in the sixteenth century it became for the reformers a potent symbol of papal arrogance and overreach; moreover, it asserted the impropriety of clerical hegemony over secular monarchies. Adding to the story's power for the biblically literate was the echo of Jesus's temptations. Then, too, a wholly evil power had cited the very same psalm, even though it was commonly known to work against demons. How dare the pope cite v. 13 when, as every good Protestant knew, he was himself one of those evil beasts to be trampled? The contrast with the original St. Peter was pointed. In the Book of Acts, we hear how the Gentile Cornelius falls at the feet of the apostle Peter, who is appalled: he "took him up, saying, Stand up; I myself also am a man."[28]

The medieval legend was a potent weapon for any reformer, such as Luther himself, seeking to enlist the aid of a king or lord. The story made for a powerful visual illustration and featured commonly in anti-Catholic tracts, such as Foxe's best-selling *Book of Martyrs*. When a patriotic English Protestant wished to denounce Catholic Spain after the Spanish Armada of 1588, this was an obvious resource. As Robert Greene wrote:

> Peter was humble and spent his time in prayer and preaching, these are proud and meddle with states, empires, kingdoms and monarchies, pulling down one and creating another, having emperors kneeling at his feet, and casting off their crowns with his toe, treading on their backs, and blasphemously applying the text to himself, *Calcabo super aspidem, & leonem.*

For Greene, the popes were "professed Antichrists."[29]

The legend of Alexander III features frequently in later travel literature, as North European Protestant visitors through the nineteenth century felt obliged to recount this horrifying tale of supposed papal excess. William Wordsworth told the tale in one of his *Ecclesiastical Sonnets*. The poem "Scene in Venice" begins with a description of Alexander, with "Black Demons hovering o'er his mitred head." (This follows on from the previous sonnet, which is entitled "Papal Abuses.")[30]

Translations

Probably the most important aspect of the Reformation was the translation of the Bible into vernacular languages, with all that implied for the status of the laity and the need to promote literacy. Luther's work inspired translations in most European languages. Of course, such translations varied somewhat according to the whims of individual translators, but comparisons with the Hebrew text revealed the errors in the Vulgate reading of 91 that we have already noted. One involved the several references to plague and sickness; the other concerned the dangerous beasts to be subdued in v. 13.

As early as the 1380s, long before Luther's time, the daring English scholar John Wycliffe had produced a pathbreaking vernacular translation of the

Bible. Miraculously, the proto-Protestant Wycliffe died in his bed rather than at the stake, but his Lollard followers were much persecuted into the early sixteenth century, when they merged into the new Protestant movement. In the eyes of the church hierarchy, Wycliffe's sin lay not in any specific aspects of his translation, but rather his decision to offer the vernacular at all. In fact, his version of our psalm followed the Vulgate closely, including numbering it as the nineteenth. Accordingly, we still find here "the sharp word" in v. 3, and the lively rendering of v. 6 as "Of an arrow flying in the day, of a goblin going in darknesses [*a gobelyn goynge in derknessis*]; of assailing, and a Midday Fiend." In v. 13, the four beasts listed are "a snake, and a cockatrice . . . a lion and a dragon."[31]

Interpretations of the psalm changed fundamentally with the new Hebrew-derived versions of the 1530s. The first complete English translation of the Bible was Miles Coverdale's rendering of 1535, which became the basis of most later Protestant readings in that language. This relied in part on the pioneering work of William Tyndale, but Coverdale himself translated much of the Old Testament, with much assistance from Luther's recent German versions. At our psalm's v. 3, Coverdale restored the ancient plague reference with a plea for protection from the "noysome pestilence," a phrase that continued in later English translations. In vv. 5–6, the Coverdale version offered:

> So yt thou shalt not nede to be afrayed for eny bugges by night, ner for arowe that flyeth by daye. For the pestilece that crepeth in ye darcknesse, ner for the sicknesse yt destroyeth in the noone daye.[32]

Following Luther, the English definitively restored the disease ("sicknesse") reading, and removed the more egregious demonic references, including (sadly) Wycliffe's fiends and goblins. At v. 10, Coverdale adopted Luther's plague reading, and he was followed in that by most later English translations. Oddly to modern eyes, the terror by night now became "bugges," which at the time implied fears rather than vermin. (A subsequent 1551 translation that used the same word became known as the Bug Bible.) In the list of creatures, Coverdale followed the Hebrew order rather than the Greek or Latin. He also echoed Luther's *Ottern*: "Thou shalt go upon the Lyon and Adder, the yonge Lyon and the Dragon shalt thou treade vnder thy fete." The use of "tread" again echoes Luther's choice of words, in this instance *treten*.[33]

That Coverdale version was largely followed by the much superior, widely used Geneva Bible, which sounds far more like the later biblical versions that

English-speakers would come to know so intimately. To take one example, this renders vv. 5–6 as "Thou shalt not be afraid of the fear of the night: *nor* of the arrow that flieth by day: *Nor* of the pestilence that walketh in the darkness: *nor* of the plague that destroyeth at noon day." The "fear" of the night echoes Calvin's reading of a psychological threat, and does not lend itself easily to a supernatural or demonic interpretation. The famous King James version of 1611 generally followed the Geneva, although with a few subtle variants. At vv. 5–6, the KJV offers "Thou shalt not be afraid for the terror by night; nor for the arrow that flieth by day; Nor for the pestilence that walketh in darkness; nor for the destruction that wasteth at noonday." Like the Geneva, the KJV is explicit in marshaling the various "plague" references.[34]

Preserving the Old Ways

In considering the role of translations in Christian understandings of the psalm, it is important to note the resistance of those who resolutely refused to accept the new insights and revisions. Far from accepting change, the Catholic church now doubled down on older readings stemming from the Septuagint and the Vulgate. Although the Catholic church certainly had excellent Hebrew scholars, their insights were not allowed to revise the commonplace use of the cherished Vulgate. In 1546, the Council of Trent listed the canonical books of the Bible (including a number not found in the Protestant selection), and further

> ordains and declares that the old Latin Vulgate Edition, which, in use for so many hundred years, has been approved by the Church, be in public lectures, disputations, sermons and expositions held as authentic, and that no one dare or presume under any pretext whatsoever to reject it.[35]

That decision shaped Catholic readings of 91. In the key instance of v. 3, Catholics until modern times continued to read not about pestilence but rather the harm wrought by the bitter word. In v. 6, likewise, the noonday demon stubbornly persisted, as did the basilisk in v. 13. That deep conservatism shaped the English translations that were eventually approved by the church, such as the Douay-Rheims of the early seventeenth century, where the "noonday devil" duly appears in English guise. This version likewise avoids the "pestilence that walketh in darkness" for the mysterious and

Vulgate-derived "business that walketh about in the dark." In ways great and small, Catholics and Protestants were literally reading different psalms.[36]

Older readings of 91 continued to dominate even commentaries by such erudite figures as Cardinal Robert Bellarmine, who rooted himself firmly in the Septuagint and Vulgate translations. In a lengthy commentary on Psalm 91 in the early seventeenth century, he entirely avoided discussion of plague, disease, or pestilence, in a way that would have astonished his Protestant contemporaries. Like his fellow Catholics, he continued to enumerate the harms caused by ill-chosen words. Such influential writings made it ever harder for the church to accept the new textual reality. If they accepted something like Luther's rendering, they were rendering obsolete not just the efforts of Bellarmine but also most of the early Fathers, including Augustine himself. Not until 1943 did a papal encyclical allow Catholics to use translations not based on the Vulgate.[37]

Pagans and Heretics

As the case of the Mariensäule shows, Catholics continued to use the psalm in religious commemoration and controversy, which is not surprising given its common use in the offices and liturgies of religious orders old and new. Catholic clergy and writers knew its words very well, and it naturally came to their minds in the struggles of the time. Also, as we have seen, the "trampling" verse was intimately associated with the pope and papal ideology: it was a symbol of the church's triumph over all its foes, and ideally at some future date over Protestant heresy.

The church continued to engage its enemies with weaponry both material and spiritual. The papacy of Paul V (1605–1621) marked new heights in the Catholic Reformation, and in the final years of his reign, Catholic victories in the Thirty Years' War augured very well for the papal cause. Among other achievements, the pope issued a new version of the *Rituale Romanorum* (1614), which systematized and formalized the church's approved ceremonies. This included standardized forms of exorcism. Any mature, experienced demon possessing a faithful Catholic would be wearily familiar with the words with which he was challenged, hearing the priest call on him to depart by the power of the immaculate Lamb, *qui ambulavit super aspidem et basiliscum, qui conculavit leonem et draconem.* In 1608, the Italian witch-hunter's manual *Compendium Maleficarum* declared that cases of possession could be proved if the individuals in question refused to cite a core body of scriptural texts, including Psalm 91 and the opening verses of John's Gospel. Presumably, these words were simply too holy and potent for the demons involved (although that principle had not prevented Satan himself using verses of 91 in Jesus's time).[38]

Adding to the psalm's relevance to these conflicts was its association with the Virgin Mary, a linkage that might not seem immediately obvious. But as we have seen, the depiction of Mary treading down a snake was well established, and finds warrant in at least two key scriptures apart from 91. Genesis 3:15 tells how Eve, or her descendant, was promised the right to tread down the serpent who had tempted her, and later readings understood that descendant as female (the Vulgate specified the ultimate victor as "she"). In the second century, Irenaeus argued that Mary's obedience to God negated Eve's disobedience, allowing Mary to defeat the serpent. Meanwhile, the Book of Revelation portrays "a woman clothed with the Sun," menaced by a fearsome red dragon who was defeated by Michael and his angels. Michael, the warrior archangel, appeared alongside Mary in scenes depicting the casting down— or treading down—of the dragon or serpent. The most celebrated artistic representation of that scene is found at Bavaria's Freising Cathedral, in Peter Paul Rubens's 1625 altarpiece "The Virgin as the Woman of the Apocalypse." Freising stands just a few miles from Munich, where the Mariensäule would be erected in the following decade.[39]

During the spiritual and intellectual upsurge of the Catholic Reformation, pious scholars searched the scriptures for any and all possible allusions to Mary, partly to prove to upstart Protestants that Marian devotion was firmly rooted in scripture. Any text portraying an exalted or noble female figure was seized upon, and whole "Marian Bibles" circulated. At first sight, Psalm 91 offered little material for such a feminine reading, but the parallels to the Genesis verse were obvious. In the psalm's v. 13, a long tradition had imagined Christ himself treading down serpents and other evil forces, but the text does not demand that: it only makes the promise to "you." Mary was already being portrayed in that role in the late Middle Ages, as sculptures in Italian churches showed the Virgin trampling the customary four beasts. The idea gained popularity in the early modern period, most dramatically in figures like the Mariensäule. The Marian association was made explicit in statuary, engravings, and prints. In 1632, the celebrated printmaker Jacques Callot produced a magnificent etching, "La bienheureuse Vierge Marie triumphant des demons" ("The Blessed Virgin Mary Triumphing over

Demons"). Despite the demons of the title, the accompanying text is our v. 13, *super aspidem*, with a French translation added. To a degree that would have appalled Protestants, Psalm 91 became a Marian text.[40]

The Psalm of Catholic Empire

The psalm found a new lease on life in the church's ambitious global ventures. During the sixteenth and seventeenth centuries, the Spanish and Portuguese expanded their empires widely across Africa, Asia, and Latin America, and Catholic missionaries followed closely in their path. In these new territories, the church encountered many very different religious traditions that the clergy found suspect or indeed loathsome, from the pagan and animist faiths of Central and South America to the great world faiths of Asia. As the church readied its spiritual arsenal to confront such foes, it turned to the resources of 91. The church's exorcism rituals were widely used in the global arena, as 91 reclaimed the role it had possessed a millennium previously, as a vital weapon for missionaries challenging paganism.

When the Spanish announced their imperial discoveries in the 1520s, their manifesto included a portrait of the reigning pope, Clement VII (1517–1534), who is flanked by the words of the psalm's v. 13. By this point, these words had become firmly associated with the papal office, but in the context of the document, more is certainly intended. In Mexico, we are to believe, Catholic Christians were finding new heresies and idol worshipers to suppress, new asps and lions: did not the pagan Mexicans even venerate a feathered serpent deity?[41]

In the face of paganism, Psalm 91 served missionaries as a standard weapon of both defense and offense. Although the psalm was not the exclusive preserve of the Jesuits, it played a special role in their history. In dangerous settings like the Native societies of French Canada, where martyrdom was a constant prospect, the French Jesuit missionaries knew they had little realistic hope except in divine protection. In 1634, one brother was warned that Native warriors were wandering the countryside seeking to kill any Frenchman they might encounter. However, he wrote, we should always remember the words of *Qui habitat in adjutorio Altissimi, in protectione Dei cœli commorabitur*, quoting the opening of our psalm. In fact, reliance on the psalm only postponed the inevitable, and several Jesuits were indeed slaughtered a few years later.[42]

In other regions, the psalm proved a triumphant weapon in the annals of conquest and Christianization. One legendary Catholic figure was the Jesuit Antonio Ruiz de Montoya, who in the 1630s led what he termed the "spiritual conquest" of the Upper Amazon, of "Paraguay, Paraná, Uruguay, and Tape." (This was very much the time of the triumphalist declarations of Catholic faith in Munich's Mariensäule and the Callot engraving.) This spiritual conquistador often used the language of demons to describe the pagan societies with which he had to contend, where shamans gave special veneration to snakes. His biographer, a fellow Jesuit, reported the means by which Montoya defeated demons and possessions. Of course, 91 featured regularly. In one possession story, the victim takes the form of a writhing snake, terrifying the spectators, but not the Jesuit father. In order to humiliate the demon, he places his foot upon the victim's neck, duly and inevitably reciting the *super aspidem* of v. 13.[43]

The same verse served as a motif for one of the most remarkable saints of the era, the Asian-born slave who in Mexico became known as St. Catarina de San Juan, or La China Poblana. Her Jesuit biographer wrote at pious length of the fierce spiritual assaults that she endured every day in the city of Puebla, the terrifying monsters and demons that threatened to surround and overcome her if she left the house even to go to her church. But she placed herself wholly under God's protection, "treading down serpents and basilisks, breaking the spears and stepping over the hosts of Hell," and that alone prevented her from being terrified or even torn apart. The author often returns to those demonic "serpents and basilisks," who were so jealous of the saint's holiness and prophetic gifts and were so ubiquitous in this hazardous New World.[44]

That trampling imagery appealed to the colonial clergy of the time, and shaped their attitude to enemies and dissidents of all kinds. One sensational story of the era concerned William Lamport, an Irish adventurer in Mexico, who in the 1640s plotted a multiracial rising to create an independent state. This naturally aroused the fury of the Spanish government and of the Inquisition. During Lamport's long imprisonment, an aggressive friar who was interrogating him made him lie down so that he could place his foot on the prisoner's neck while reciting the familiar *super aspidem*. Presumably, the friar saw Lamport as not just radical but possessed, and he had apparently gone native. Although the Inquisition in Spain itself was capable of many atrocities, the particular form of this humiliation was very characteristic of the New World and the mission fields. (Lamport later earned indirect fame as an inspiration for the fictional Zorro.)[45]

In addition to "paganism," these global ventures brought the Catholic church into contact with other hitherto unsuspected forms of "heresy." As clergy and missionaries spread across the world, they encountered Christians long separated from the European churches. For those who sought to understand these believers and to bring them under papal authority, our psalm naturally offered an ideological justification. In the first millennium, the Syriac-speaking church of the East had been a very large component of the global Christian picture, but Islamic expansion across the Middle East reduced that group to a pitiable remnant. In the 1550s, that church split, as one faction sought alliance with the papacy and founded what still survives as the Chaldean Catholic church, which accepted Western interpretations of disputed points of Christology.

That context explains the publication in Vienna in 1555 of an innovative volume titled *Liber Sacrosancti Evangelii*, a Syriac-language version of the New Testament, the first of its kind to be printed. The book featured an imposing woodcut of the crucifixion, which stands over a lion and a reptile, and the inscription *In hoc signo vinces, et conculcabis leonem et draconem*, which is also translated into Syriac. Psalm 91 here celebrated yet another papal and Catholic triumph, and the incorporation of one of the world's most ancient Christian communities into a new globalized church firmly directed from Rome. The psalm became the manifesto of global Catholicism.[46]

Secret Faith

So central was the psalm to that missionary ideology that church leaders found it shocking when its words were thrown back in their collective faces. In the sixteenth century, the Spanish realm had attempted to expel the whole of its Jewish population. Many Jews, however, accepted notional conversion, while continuing their religious and ritual life as best they could, often recalling beloved portions of Jewish prayer and liturgy. Over the next two centuries, the Inquisition tried to detect and uproot the usages of those crypto-Jews, and official records show the extraordinary persistence of a vernacular adaptation of Psalm 91, which was known as Oração da Formosura (Prayer of Exaltation). As they spread through the larger imperial world, those crypto-Jews (*Anussim*) took their customs and prayers with them. Historian Moshe Lazar notes that the Oração "is found with slight variations in a great number of specimens preserved for centuries among the *Anussim* of Portugal, Spain, Brazil, Mexico, and elsewhere."[47]

The psalm featured in a crypto-Jewish context in a case that is celebrated in Mexican history. The affair in question involved a Guatemalan cleric named Rafael Crisanto Gil Rodríguez, who in the early 1790s incurred the rage of the Inquisition for his explicit affirmation of Judaism. Gil Rodríguez was the not-so-crypto Jewish descendant of Sephardic refugees from Spain, who developed an impressive religious synthesis that drew on Qabalism as well as Spanish chivalric romance, with a heavy dose of messianism. As a would-be warrior knight of the imminent (Jewish) messianic age, he stood firm against the Inquisitors. He grounded himself in the psalms, but above all in Psalm 91, which he quoted to them in full as a perfect epitome of his views. At once, the psalm was an affirmation in the God of the Hebrew Bible, and a plea for protection in struggle. Even more provocatively, he explicitly identified it as number 91, using the Hebrew numbering, the usage among the Jews, *apud Hebreos*. In a remarkable reversal, Catholic authorities found their prized psalm cited as the bulwark of another very confident religious tradition firmly rooted in scripture. Gil Rodríguez endured lengthy imprisonment, and in 1820 earned fame as the very last prisoner of the Inquisition to be released in Mexico, and indeed in the whole of the Americas. In so many ways, his career spanned ages and cultures.[48]

Music

That divergence of Protestant and Catholic interpretations naturally affected their respective musical treatments of the psalm, which included some spectacular manifestations in these years. Catholic composers used its common Latin descriptor, "Qui habitat in adjutorio Altissimi," and produced numerous versions for liturgical use. These were of course faithful settings of the Vulgate text. In the early sixteenth century, Josquin des Prez wrote motet settings for many psalms, in a style that proved very influential on Renaissance composers, and his "Qui habitat" became one of the best-known.[49]

Protestants differed not just in the general musical styles of their homelands, but also in the purposes for which they used music. Having eliminated much traditional liturgical music, Protestant cultures reconstructed their practices on the basis of the psalms, which had the noble precedent of

Temple worship. In Scotland, Calvinists made the metrical psalms the centerpiece of their worship, and their Psalter hewed closely to the standard English translations. For 91, their Psalter of 1650 offered:

> Thou shalt not need to be afraid
>> for terrors of the night;
> Nor for the arrow that doth fly
>> by day, while it is light;

> Nor for the pestilence, that walks
>> in darkness secretly;
> Nor for destruction, that doth waste
>> at noon-day openly.

Those psalms, repeated week by week, became as familiar to the lay public as they had previously been to monastics. Beza was by no means untypical in his musical encounter with 91.[50]

From the mid-sixteenth century, German Protestant composers produced metrical versions of the psalms that used or paraphrased Luther's translation. Some evolved into elaborate choral compositions, and in the process produced hymns that would have a lasting appeal in German culture. A striking number used or adapted Psalm 91, and the popular "Wer heimlich seine Wohnestatt" (1587) took its title from the opening verse. Reflecting the religious turmoil of the age, this vernacular triumph was the work of a Protestant who converted to Catholicism, and who became a priest. Whatever its specific origins, hymnody—as sung by the congregation as much as a church choir—became a hallmark of Protestant worship, and a fixture of the larger cultural world. When people remembered or quoted the psalm, it was often in the paraphrase they heard as hymns.[51]

The greatest achievement was that of Heinrich Schütz (1585–1672), a prolific composer commonly regarded as the leading figure in German music before J. S. Bach. Although a staunch Lutheran, he was responsible for importing cutting-edge Italian and Catholic styles, and in the process he did much to create the early Baroque. Schütz's 1619 *Psalms of David* (*Psalmen Davids*), which mainly used Luther's translations, became one of his most popular works. In another collection published in 1628, he took inspiration from the popular 1602 Psalter of Cornelius Becker, and this too attracted great praise. The treatment of 91 was a highlight, under the title "Wer sich des

Höchsten Schirm vertraut" ("Who Trusts in the Protection of the Highest").
The Thirty Years' War was a disastrous time for Germany, and great cities like
Munich thanked God for their preservation. So did Schütz's city, Dresden,
which was the capital of Saxony. This city too was deeply affected by the wars
and plagues of the time, although it never actually fell to the enemy. While
the Catholic city erected a column, the Protestants marked their struggles
with those musical treatments of the Psalter, and in both cases, the combative
and defiant Psalm 91 took pride of place.[52]

Although Becker's lyrics are not an exact quotation of Luther's translation, they follow it closely. Like Luther, Becker specifically refers to the threat
of the *Pestilenz* and the *Plage*. The roster of creatures to be trodden down
(v. 13) also follows Luther's canonical list, including his *Ottern*: "Auf Ottern
wirst du gehn herein, Auf Löwn und Drachen treten." Lions and *Drachen*
also featured in another famous rendering of the psalm from this era, the
1653 paraphrase of Paul Gerhardt, "Wer unterm Schirm des Höchsten sitzt."
A confessional or religious map of Europe delineated which Bible was used
in each realm, and (among many other things) which beasts constituted the
menagerie of Psalm 91.[53]

English poets and hymn-writers too devised their own versions of psalms,
often with the intention of bringing the biblical language more into con-
formity with the poetic standards then prevailing. In some cases, these were
thinly disguised attempts to modernize what had become the antiquated language of the King James Version, and to make the Bible more fit for polite
society. Some versions were very well suited for use as hymns. In the early
eighteenth century, Isaac Watts managed to give the psalm a much more
Classical tone, straying from the biblical language. Here is Watts's treatment
of "the destruction that wasteth at noonday":

> If burning beams of noon conspire
> To dart a pestilential fire,
> God is their life; his wings are spread
> To shield them with a healthful shade.
>
> If vapors with malignant breath
> Rise thick, and scatter midnight death,
> Isr'el is safe; the poisoned air
> Grows pure, if Isr'el's God be there.[54]

One of the most quoted English writers of this or indeed any century was Alexander Pope, whose version of Psalm 91, "The Believer's Hope" (1710), was so uncompromisingly Classical as to raise suspicions among some scholars that he was offering a deliberate pastiche. A typical heroic couplet promised that:

> By day no perils shall the just affright,
> No dismal dreams or groaning ghosts by night.

Pope's version includes a number of phrases that may puzzle until we realize that, as a stubborn Roman Catholic, he was adapting the Vulgate. That explains his version of "the bitter word" as "the sharp arrow of censorious tongues." Meanwhile, the creatures to be trodden down include "the fiery basilisk," "the huge dragon," and "the swelling aspick's head." Like Pope's other works, this psalm version reached a wide and enthusiastic audience mainly composed of Protestants. It would be intriguing to know how many recognized the Catholic origins, or if they simply assumed that the "basilisk" and its like just represented flowery poetic language.[55]

Counting Christians

The point about diversity of readings raises questions about just who was interpreting the psalm in particular ways during the early modern period. Alexander Pope's work represented a rare outlier in the England of that time, and a deviation from the norm of Protestant Europe. But we should query exactly what the Christian norm was in this era. When we write the history of Christianity, we naturally pay great attention to the Reformation and to the subsequent history of Protestant nations and cultures. But Catholics remained a very numerous contingent in the Christian world, and even in Germany they constituted perhaps half the population. As we have seen, the global Catholic presence grew substantially in the seventeenth and eighteenth centuries with the expansion of Catholic empires overseas. If Protestants were significantly more likely than Catholics to have read their Bibles personally, all Catholics had heard the texts in their churches and encountered them through sermons or liturgy. The same was true of Orthodox Christians, who relied on the Septuagint and translations that drew heavily on it.

Although exact figures are not easy to come by, a reasonable estimate suggests that in 1900, Protestants and Anglicans combined represented around a quarter of the world's Christian population, Catholics a half, and Orthodox just over 20 percent. In the case of our psalm, then, some three-quarters of the world's Christians knew it as 90, and still read or heard references to the harmful word, the noonday demon, and the basilisk. Two centuries earlier, the proportion would have been even higher. Those 1900 figures measure a world built by the Industrial Revolution, after the explosive growth of populations that had transformed mainly Protestant nations such as Britain, Germany, and the United States. Each of these societies had grown enormously in absolute terms over the previous century, but also in their relative position in a demographic league table. In 1700, say, in the time of Alexander Pope and Isaac Watts, those who read the Protestant 91 rather than the Catholic or Orthodox 90 might have constituted as few as one-fifth of the world's Christian readers and hearers.[56]

Some of the differences between the two versions had little theological relevance and virtually no application to ordinary lived reality. But the overall divergence of interpretation really did matter. As we have seen, Protestant 91 was loaded with disease references, with the "noisome pestilence," *schädlichen Pestilenz*, or whatever the vernacular equivalent might be. From the time of the Reformation, this revived understanding of the psalm and its original intent made it powerfully relevant to the plagues and maladies that were so pressing an issue in the contemporary world. Psalm 91 now acquired a whole new life, or rather, a life in the midst of death.

7

Neither Shall Any Plague Come Nigh Thy Dwelling

The Plague Psalm, Once More

> A German physician was wont to speak of [Psalm 91] as the best pre-
> servative in times of cholera, and in truth, it is a heavenly medicine
> against plague and pest. He who can live in its spirit will be fearless,
> even if once again London should become a lazar-house, and the
> grave be gorged with carcasses.[1]
>
> —Charles H. Spurgeon, 1874

In 1874, the legendary Baptist pastor Charles H. Spurgeon, the "Prince of Preachers," published a commentary on Psalm 91 that is still much used by evangelicals. Spurgeon praised the psalm as uniquely cheering, and quoted the "German physician" for the material protections it could offer. (A lazar house or *lazaretto* is a place of quarantine, originally reserved for lepers.) Such a declaration of faith in the practical value of prayer would be remarkable in any period, but Spurgeon was writing in an era of the telegraph, trains, and Gatling guns, not to mention extensive scientific discoveries about the physical causes of disease. Did the preacher really and literally believe that praying Psalm 91 would be an effective safeguard against epidemics? But read carefully: what Spurgeon actually says is that the believer who prayed 91 would be fearless in the face of cholera, not that the person would necessarily survive it. (I will return to his mysterious "physician" in Chapter 8.)[2]

The great preacher was wrestling with issues that had agonized religious thinkers for centuries, and which were often discussed in the precise context of 91. Once the Reformation translators had restored the text's central role as a plague psalm—as *the* plague psalm par excellence—those discussions became the arena for bitter conflicts over such core religious concepts as

He Will Save You from the Deadly Pestilence. Philip Jenkins, Oxford University Press. © Oxford University Press 2023.
DOI: 10.1093/oso/9780197605646.003.0007

the workings of providence, direct divine intervention in human affairs, the proper limits of human science and endeavor, and the possible efficacy of prayer in changing divine intentions. These debates charted a real intellectual revolution.

Deadly Beasts

As we have seen, the Vulgate translation of the psalm greatly underplayed its explicit emphasis on epidemic disease. Even so, Christians never ceased to resort to 91 to appeal for good health, and they often understood its various metaphors as referring to disease, however obliquely. Already in the Middle Ages, it played a major role in natural science and medicine.

The psalm's promises concerning the flying arrow were suggestive. In the later Middle Ages, arrows served as an image for the assaults of the plague, reflecting the seemingly random outcomes that struck one household but left another unharmed. Prayers, sermons, and learned tracts often juxtaposed the words *sagitta* and *pestilentia*, "arrows" and "plague," with the suggestion that the supernatural archers were angelic figures implementing God's angry judgments. In times of plague, that association with archery led to a special interest in St. Sebastian, the early Roman martyr who was shot with arrows, and who was thus invoked to urge God to withhold his wrath. That cult in turn involved frequent allusions to our psalm, and especially v. 5.[3]

The ever-popular v. 13 also featured prominently in medical and pseudo-scientific accounts of diseases, and possible means of combating them. Medieval bestiaries, a sizable subset of the medical literature, commonly studied the four beasts found in the verse, using them as chapter titles to structure books. The verse was inevitably cited in accounts of basilisks, a creature that long intrigued would-be natural scientists. The basilisk occupied a whole niche in bestiaries, as well as in alchemical tracts. Contemporaries were intrigued by the creature's reputed power to kill at a distance, even to bring down birds in flight, and that idea inspired an entire literature about the projection of energies or forces, including disease and plague. In this wildly speculative literature, the basilisk's powers were connected to evil influences exercised by women, particularly during menstruation. However bizarre these notions might be, they at least represented an attempt to comprehend the mechanisms by which infections might spread.[4]

In the sixteenth century, these ideas intrigued the esoteric school associated with the brilliant but erratic polymath Paracelsus, who exercised an inordinate influence on medical thought. As syphilis ran wild across Europe during the sixteenth century, the disease was known as "the venom of the basilisk." Against such a threat, any prospect of supernatural protection was welcome, leading believers to turn to the psalm to protect against the ills that were visited on humanity.[5]

Re-Plaguing

But the explicit plague emphasis in the new Protestant translations marked a real division in the psalm's reading and interpretation. While Catholics retained the older emphases on arrows and basilisks, Protestants focused on the implications for disease and divine providence. They were supported in this by the leading commentaries of the time. The Lutheran Heinrich Möller (1530–1589), the much-cited "Molerus," was the author of the *Enarratio Psalmorum Davidis*, which had a huge impact on European Protestants. For Molerus, disease was evidently the core theme of 91.[6]

Whenever plague struck Protestant societies from the 1520s onward, we can dependably rely on an outpouring of sermons and tracts on 91, and we can predict the major themes of debate. Protestants were deeply committed to the Old Testament worldview, in which plague and other afflictions were visitations sent from God to chide or punish a sinful people. The account of David's plague in 2 Samuel 24 was especially influential. Yet disease did not have to afflict everyone, virtuous and evil alike. Psalm 91 seemingly taught that the truly faithful believer would be delivered from pestilence, even as thousands perished around him. And drawing the explicit analogy to David's curse, this protection would be the work of angels, who on this occasion would safeguard rather than curse. So plain were the psalm's words as almost to defy a believer to doubt or contradict them. If scripture had any literal truth whatever, how could anyone possibly doubt the assurance that "neither shall any plague come nigh thy dwelling"? That scarcely left room for a more nuanced reading: it would or it wouldn't.[7]

The implications were both troubling and counterintuitive. If plague was indeed a divine visitation, why should faithful Christians seek to escape this manifestation of God's will, except by prayer and penitence? If an angel was pointing a lethal arrow at one's heart, was it proper to flinch and turn away? Godly believers might properly resort to 91, but should they go beyond such spiritual defenses to take practical and worldly steps against plague, such as quarantine or simply fleeing? Some Christians held that God would deliver believers if that was his pleasure, regardless of any worldly efforts they might make. In that light, a plague outbreak was a paramount test of faith. Others agreed that, certainly, God was ultimately responsible for all worldly events, but that even so, plague was an infectious disease, an objective material reality, and Christians were allowed and even required to minimize its harm, as a matter of prudence.

The Gruesome Plague of the Pestilence

Giving urgency to such debates was the near-constant menace of devastating diseases in early modern times. Bubonic plague was endemic in Europe from the mid-fourteenth century until 1720, and that was only one of the grave diseases of the time. Other lethal epidemics involved influenza and some severe infections that still remain unidentified. When disease struck, the psalm might be chanted or recited in churches or public processions as penitential liturgies, and it often formed the subject of sermons. In hindsight, we realize that gathering people together for large communal events was not the optimal strategy to limit the spread of a surging epidemic.

The beginning of the Reformation coincided precisely with a renewed outbreak of plague in Germany. Martin Luther's legendary confrontation with imperial authorities at Worms occurred where it did only because the disease threat had ruled out the originally planned venue, Nürnberg. The Reformers could not fail to address the theological implications of these disasters. Two works in particular sketched the agenda for later controversies. In 1527, Luther preached on "Whether One May Flee from a Deadly Plague." He challenged those who condemned flight or escape. While acknowledging that God might send a plague as a visitation or judgment, human beings should not respond by inaction or despair, but should take proper means to preserve life and health. If holy figures in the Bible had fled from war, famine, or massacre, why should modern people not try to evade the curse of plague? The indispensable need throughout was to maintain true faith, and Christians should never forget the psalm's declaration of divine power. As Luther asked, "Do you not know that you are surrounded as by thousands of angels who watch over you in such a way that you can indeed trample upon the plague, as it is written in Psalm 91?"[8]

In 1533, Lutheran theologian Andreas Osiander preached a famous and much-reprinted sermon in response to another plague outbreak in Nürnberg, under the title "How and Whither a Christian Man Ought to Fly the Horrible Plague of the Pestilence" (*die grausamen plag der Pestilentz*). He took as his text "the Psalm, *Qui habitat*," that is, 91.[9]

The plague in Nürnberg produced a variety of very different responses. Some people fled the city, naturally enough, and a great many absolutely refused to have anything to do with anyone they believed might have been exposed, even close relatives. Osiander condemned such behavior for its lack of charity. At the other extreme, some contemporaries so relied on the psalm's promises that they refused any medical help and did not even avoid places where the sickness raged most fiercely. For these pious believers, the plague was a matter of punishing sin, and as they declared, "Such plague toucheth no man, but those that be ordained of God thereunto" (I am quoting Miles Coverdale's English translation, which appeared in 1537). Osiander admitted the possibility of some natural causation of the disease, whether it originated in the stars or the earthly elements. But his main emphasis was on the divine plan, as God expressed his wrath against human sinfulness. Abandoning and atoning for such sins was the only reliable way of halting or reversing the plague.[10]

Most of Osiander's sermon builds on these principles, through a detailed exposition of the psalm, which proved that God can and will protect his faithful from all evils in this life. Osiander addressed the agonizing dilemma that, yes, despite the psalm's explicit words, the plague would indeed come near the godly: "We ought not to doubt but that there die thereof many virtuous men, and leave many ungodly." But Osiander offered a solution to this theological and scriptural dilemma, stressing that the faithful dead faced the confident prospect of heaven. In a simple worldly sense, evil would indeed befall the believer, in the form of physical death, but that was by no means the most important consideration. That heavenly salvation fully satisfied God's promises of protection. "Whether good men die or live, it is done for their wealth [i.e., well-being]. But whether the wicked die or live, it is done for their punishment, and always shall they be plagued, and their wickedness shall be rewarded them." This would be a frequent theme of later responses to 91.[11]

While emphasizing the psalm's message of reliance on God, Osiander urged practical medical responses as he understood them, together with loving care for neighbors and the assertion of mutual care and benevolence. Of course, he said, the psalm was a precious resource and protection, but it could not replace or supersede larger Christian principles. The psalm taught Christians to cast out fear, to empower them to act in love. Yet however humane and charitable they may sound, Osiander's opinions must raise problems for a modern reader, who would be much more sympathetic to those callous folk who staunchly avoided any contact with infected people, even for charitable ends. Their "inordinate fear," their "fond childish fear," does not sound unreasonable to us, while any advice to visit and keep companionship with plague sufferers is problematic. At the same time, the issue of accepting or avoiding medicine looks rather different when we know that no medical treatments available at the time did the slightest good in combatting pestilence.[12]

When to Flee?

Throughout the early modern period, a surprisingly persistent view held that, to adapt a modern phrase, bad things really did not happen to truly good people, and that only sinners suffered. This opinion was sometimes justified through Seneca's Classical maxim, *Nihil accidere bono viro mali potest*, "No evil can befall a good man," but the idea also had Patristic warrant. The fourth-century Christian Father Lactantius was credited with the opinion "that no just man can perish by war, or by tempest," and plague was surely a logical extension of such perils. Why, then, should the righteous fear epidemics?[13]

When a new series of plague outbreaks ravaged Europe after 1568, it coincided with an intensification of theological controversy within the rising Calvinist movement. The Swiss pastor Christoph Lüthardt warned the faithful against seeking to avoid divine punishments, which were inflicted by angels. If that was the actual source of the plague, then the malady could not even be viewed as a regular disease and was not actually infectious. Even if the plague did have some natural elements, God governed and guided those causes, so he ultimately decided who would or would not suffer from pestilence, and he could protect whomever he wished. Was that not the obvious promise of Psalm 91? Whatever the fact reveals about the quality of his argument, Lüthardt himself died of the plague in 1577.[14]

Lüthardt's work drew a riposte from Theodore Beza, the Protestant leader we have already encountered, and who owed his conversion to 91. In 1579, he published his *De Peste*, translated as *A Learned Treatise of the Plague*, with what seems to us a startling subtitle questioning whether the plague was in fact infectious (*contagiosa*) and, moreover, "whether, and how far it may be shunned of Christians, by going aside [fleeing]?" He answered both questions in the affirmative. As to the first point, "who can deny that many diseases are gotten by handling and touching? of the which some are deadly, and other some are less dangerous; unless they will also contend that the Sun shineth not at noon day?" These were natural realities, through which God worked his will. As to fleeing, Beza turned to biblical precedent to show that holy figures of the Bible had fled to escape dangers, including King David himself.[15]

1603: Angels and Arrows

Despite such weighty authorities, contrary views about plague and illness continued to surface in a genuinely open debate that persisted well into the seventeenth century. The range of arguments directly stemming from our psalm became sharply apparent in England in 1603, when London faced one of the worst outbreaks of plague in the era. In a deeply religious and literate society, the epidemic could not fail to call forth abundant commentary and speculation. Although the disaster was only one of many, it encapsulates a much broader European debate.

The year 1603 is a landmark in British history: the Scottish king James replaced Queen Elizabeth, and the Tudor dynasty gave way to the Stuarts, as James became the first king of the new nation of Great Britain. The plague presented the incoming king with a grave crisis. To modern eyes, the admixture of religious and secular responses seems baffling. The new king's government promptly issued a strictly practical medical guide to means of preventing infection, a text that is completely free of any religious allusions or scriptural references. Given the time and place, it is almost stunningly secular in tone. Yet when the king addressed parliament shortly afterward, he cited God's decision "to lighten his hand, and relent the violence of his devouring angel against the poor people of this city." As so often in such instances, it is not obvious when the language about the angel directing plague should be taken literally and when it begins to have a more metaphorical quality. When clergyman James Balmford produced a sane practical guide to controlling infection, he naturally introduced his *Dialogue* with a quote from 91: "He shall give his angel charge over thee."[16]

The crisis produced the usual crop of sermons on the psalm. "T.C." published his *Godly and Learned Sermon upon the 91 Psalm*, addressing the familiar question of whether a faithful Christian should seek to flee the afflicted city. (The author saw no problem in such flight.) But such citations of 91 were not just lip service. Another response to the crisis called forth a serious and systematic reading of the psalm, which in turn ignited a real public controversy.[17]

The culprit was Henoch Clapham, a puritanical pastor who in 1603 published *An Epistle Discoursing upon the Present Pestilence*. At least as he was understood, Clapham was making some quite outrageous statements—namely, that the plague was not infectious, and that only egregious sinners fell prey to it. Those who died from the plague did so because of their lack of faith. Although he would have rejected any such analogy, Clapham was harking back to the biblical figure of Eliphaz, in the Book of Job, and he was also returning to a theme that Beza had combatted in his day. In the English setting, infuriated clergy demanded that the bishop of London intervene against Clapham. He was thrown into prison, where he remained for two years: at the time, conditions in jails made such a lengthy incarceration a likely death sentence. From his cell, Clapham issued a new pamphlet to clarify his views, without much improving his reputation.[18]

However reckless Clapham's ideas may sound, he was asking some good theological questions. In an erudite history of the psalm and its readings, he showed how the Septuagint and Vulgate had misinterpreted the Hebrew original and underplayed its original role as a plague text. Throughout, Clapham interprets the plague entirely in terms of the "angel's stroke," which "appeareth to be deadly, from the epithets given to it in Psalm 91, where it is termed a lion, an asp, a dragon, who naturally devour and poison to the death." In his view, there was a simple choice: either plague arose from the stroke of an angel, or it was a natural phenomenon, and the scriptural evidence clearly proved the former: "That stroke which the angel inflicteth, is supernatural, and not within the compass of physical causes: but infection is natural and within the compass of physical causes: therefore the angel's stroke not infectious." Hence, plague was not infectious. If the conclusion is shocking, the logic is solid, according to the assumptions of the time.[19]

Clapham argued that the psalm did indeed promise deliverance to the faithful, and he could adduce a number of prestigious authorities to support that stance. Had not king James himself referred to the "devouring angel"? Psalm 91 thus became a test of scriptural reliability and infallibility. The argument foreshadows those later believers who would take literally the promise that faithful Christians would be able to handle poisonous snakes without being harmed. When such enthusiasts were nevertheless bitten, they resorted to the same solution as had Clapham before them: it was not that divine promises had failed, but rather that their individual faith was not strong enough.[20]

Such an accepting and submissive attitude to God's anger with his people long persisted, and repeatedly found a focus in the debate over fleeing an epidemic. In 1625, Anglican scholar Robert Horne preached on the psalm during a renewed plague outbreak in London. He declared, "If God send any trouble, his children shall (either) be delivered from it, or preserved in it: if he send an arrow, and that of the pestilence, he will send his shield before it." Plague had to be seen primarily in a supernatural context, requiring the spiritual protections of prayer and penitence. The real danger was the infection of sin, the spiritual pestilence. When literal plague strikes a city, that sin must be purged before society returns to true health. Believers should not rely on worldly means of protection, including fleeing: "to use any means of help, and not in a subordination to God's work and blessing, is to make ourselves idolaters, and them gods."[21]

Plague as Metaphor

The idea of protection through faith alone had been attacked repeatedly since Luther's time, and Henoch Clapham was regarded as being sufficiently extreme to find himself in prison. During the seventeenth century, such supernaturalist ideas were challenged on two fronts, both of which involved moving away from strict literalism. One tactic was to spiritualize the meanings of plague, so that the psalm's promises applied more generically to misfortunes than to literal medical ailments. The other was to examine more closely and subtly the promise that "no evil shall befall thee," and (commonly) to project the promised benefits into the heavenly or otherworldly dimension. Any real physical harm that believers would suffer should be understood in the context of a larger divine plan, which might not be comprehensible to mere mortals. Either way, the psalm still promised enviable spiritual advantages, even though an individual believer might indeed suffer physical harm or death. Such ideas gained the status of mainstream Protestant orthodoxy during the first half of the seventeenth century.

From early times, commentators had read at least some of the menaces outlined in the psalm in metaphorical or psychological terms. That was a common interpretation of the "terror by night." After the translations of the Reformation era, many writers extended that approach to the references to plague and pestilence. Luther himself remarked on the

> pestilence or fever, which stalks in darkness; these are the secret intrigues, devices, stratagems, tricks, and pacts whereby the adversaries take counsel together in their rooms and closets (which no one is supposed to notice or understand) and agree on how they will suppress the word of God and exterminate the righteous.

That did not mean that readers should not also view the psalm as a prophylactic against real and worldly diseases, but it helped reduce the impression that the Psalter contained an infallible mystical medicine against plagues, available to anyone who sought it.[22]

Such spiritual readings spanned the denominational spectrum. Among the most influential Bible commentators in the English-speaking world was Matthew Henry, author of the six-volume *Exposition of the Old and New Testaments* (1708–1710), which still today finds faithful readers. Henry himself was a Calvinist and Nonconformist, the son of a militant Puritan critic of the established English church. Yet in his writings on the psalms, including 91, he was very open to symbolic or metaphorical readings. He felt, for instance, that "the noisome pestilence" was not literal disease, but rather "the contagion of sin."[23] In 1779, the *Olney Hymns* of the Anglican evangelical John Newton offered new renderings of our psalm, which thoroughly spiritualized the plague danger:

> When like a baneful pestilence,
> Sin mows its thousands down
> On every side, without defence,
> Thy grace secures thine own.
> No midnight terrors haunt their bed,
> No arrow wounds by day;
> Unhurt on serpents they shall tread,
> If found in duty's way.
> Sin was *like a* baneful pestilence.[24]

Bad Things and Good People

Another insurmountable problem for Henoch Clapham's reading of the psalm involved what we might term the inconvenient intrusions of hard reality. The plain promise of its tenth verse meshed poorly with observations of actual disease. Anyone with the grim opportunity to observe the workings of a plague readily observed that the disease spread according to a reasonably predictable progress of infection, whatever the precise vehicle for that diffusion might be. Very holy and innocent people died alongside egregious sinners, and some of those godly must have invoked Psalm 91. Many religious writers accepted that reality, and they used different strategies to adapt and accommodate what appeared to be an explicit scriptural promise.

Luther himself had been familiar with these potential difficulties of interpretation. Like Osiander, he acknowledged the danger that believers could rely so totally on the promises of angelic protection that they would ignore obvious forms of self-preservation. He mocked those who misunderstood 91, and who exclaimed, "Ah, it must happen, for I have God's promise! Therefore, I will hurl myself into the midst of lions and wolves, since God has promised that He wants to save me. I will not eat, for God will feed me!" In fact, Luther explained, bad things might happen to true believers, "because of a special purpose that is hidden from us and especially from our adversaries." "The godly should comfort themselves in this manner: 'I know that I have guardian angels; but that I have to bear some misfortune, this I leave to the will of God. For I am in the camp of the angels. God is not a liar. Therefore, He will not forsake me.'" Christians could not and must not wait upon miraculous intervention.[25]

One of Luther's friends and theological allies was Hieronymus Weller, who further explicated the blessings offered in 91, and somewhat diluted them. As Weller noted, it was obvious that good and holy people did die suddenly and, apparently, without reason. But perhaps God was showing them mercy by taking them so unexpectedly from the earth. Such a removal saved them from multiple evils, including having to face the terror of death and to suffer Satanic temptations and accusations during a prolonged process of dying. Viewed properly, "we should consider it a great blessing that God sometimes takes righteous people away out of this disastrous life by means of a sudden death." Such opinions shaped readings of 91.[26]

English theologians offered some of the most nuanced statements of that view. During that nation's Civil War of the 1640s, the revolutionary

Parliament summoned a prestigious group of Puritan divines to supervise the reform of the church. The group commissioned a series of biblical commentaries and studies, which maintained their impact long after the Puritan political cause had collapsed. On popular understandings of 91, the authors were scathing. Following Calvin, they declared that the promised blessings were infallibly true, but must be read correctly:

> Not that we are always actually delivered out of every particular danger or grievance, but because all will turn (such is our confidence in God) to our greater good; and the more we suffer, the greater shall our reward and our glory be . . . And therefore here is no ground, if the words be rightly understood, for any man absolutely to presume or conclude that he shall actually be delivered out of any particular danger; much less upon such a presumption willfully to run into dangers.

The idea of absolute and unqualified protection should be regarded as a kind of literary hyperbole, which readers were quite familiar with in secular writings, so why not in religious settings as well? For the Puritan commentators, "most dangerous then and erroneous is the inference of some men, yea, of some expositors, here, upon these words of the psalmist, that no godly man can suffer by the plague, or pestilence."[27] Although here applied narrowly to the question of pestilence, the idea of reading Bible texts in a metaphorical sense would have powerful consequences for later debates over biblical literalism, and the idea of divine inspiration.

An ingenious scriptural solution to the various theological dilemmas was offered in a 1661 commentary on the psalms by Anglican deacon Abraham Wright. He sagely observed that "there is no sickness befalls any man that might not befall the best man. . . . It may befall a saint to share in a calamity; as the good corn and weeds are cut down together, but for a different end and purpose." The reference to corn and weeds recalls Jesus's parable of the wheat and tares, as reported in Matthew's Gospel. As Jesus explains to his disciples, good and evil people grow and develop together in this present world, but at the final judgment the angels will sort them, and send some to salvation and some to destruction. In this present life, human eyes might see no difference between the worldly fates of the two, but their eternal destinies will be utterly different. The enormous advantage of that verse over Psalm 91 is its source: David might have been a great king and prophet, but the parable came from Christ himself. Wright's implication is that one scripture might overrule another, that the New Testament overrules the Old.[28]

The Righteous Man's Habitation

The last major English encounter with plague occurred in 1665, and preachers and pamphleteers again used 91 to understand the calamity. One of the sanest and widest-ranging interpretations of the psalm came from the uncompromising Puritan William Bridge in his *The Righteous Man's Habitation in the Time of Plague and Pestilence*, which serves as a capstone to the Protestant literature on these debates. (The "habitation" recalls the psalm's v. 9.) Besides centrally addressing 91 itself, Bridge offers a lengthy and learned survey of the many biblical texts concerning plague, and that comprehensive quality added to the book's value. It was still being reprinted two centuries later, when the main pandemic danger facing the West came from cholera rather than plague.[29]

Even in the 1660s, Bridge walked a delicate path between claiming special protection for believers and acknowledging that they would indeed suffer in worldly or physical terms. On the one hand, "though the danger, evil, and misery of the pestilence be exceeding great, yet God will in an especial manner protect and deliver those that do trust in him in the time of a plague." But, more ambiguously, "the scope of it is not, that every particular believer shall not die; but the drift and scope of the psalm is, to hold forth a speciality of protection for believers in the time of a plague." That is a nuanced promise, framed quite legalistically, and one that would represent cold comfort even to a stalwart believer caught in the midst of a pandemic. To the question "May a believer die of the Plague?" Bridge answered unequivocally: "Without all doubt he may. Seventy thousand died in David's time; do you think there was not a good man among them? 'Tis recorded of several good men, that they died of the plague." A person might be very holy through his life, yet may sin at the end, leading him to an untoward death. But whatever the exact circumstances, plague could indeed claim the pious.[30]

By this point the question of fleeing a plague site was far less controversial. Was it right for a man to flee? "Yes," says Bridge, "without all doubt it is, so you carry God along with you for your habitation, so you make God your habitation still; a man may lawfully seek the preservation of his life and the life of his family." Nobody seriously disputed a family's right and duty to flee from famine, so why not plague?[31]

Evil Shall Befall Thee

Similar opinions were expressed by Matthew Henry at the start of the eighteenth century. Henry certainly knew the long religious debates over the problem of evil befalling the good person, but he was working in a world that was ever more skeptical of explicitly supernatural claims. He was writing in the age of the Deists, who questioned divine revelation and rejected the idea of divine or miraculous intervention in human affairs. While Henry is duty-bound to assert the special divine protection of the righteous, he does so in such a qualified way as to undermine its popular interpretations. The good person certainly would suffer from sickness or old age or death, but would also realize that such things were not necessarily evil of themselves:

> *There shall no evil befall thee;* though trouble or affliction befall thee, yet there shall be no real evil in it, for it shall come from the love of God and shall be sanctified; it shall come, not for thy hurt, but for thy good; and though, for *the present, it be not joyous but grievous,* yet, in the end, it shall yield so well that thou thyself shalt own *no evil befell thee.* It is not an evil, an only evil, but there is a mixture of good in it and a product of good by it.

Henry seems to be recommending that sufferers from any such evils simply refuse to acknowledge them as such. But however you framed them, trouble or affliction would indeed strike.[32]

He also suggests that at least some of the protection that we are promised comes without our noticing it. A bird might not know that it is escaping the snare of the fowler. Similarly, "We owe it, more than we are sensible, to the care of the divine Providence that we have been kept from infectious diseases and out of the hands of the wicked and unreasonable." He concludes, "Whatever happens, nothing shall hurt the believer; though trouble and affliction befall, it shall come, not for his hurt, but for good, though for the present it be not joyous but grievous." Such reasoned accounts did not exclude all hope of miraculous preservation from plague or disaster, but they established more realistic expectations.[33]

Such frank realism left a lasting legacy in one of the best-known works on epidemics in the English language: Daniel Defoe's *Journal of the Plague Year* (1722), the account of the Great Plague of 1665. Defoe himself came from a Dissenting Presbyterian family, from the same Puritan tradition as commentators such as William Bridge and Matthew Henry. As the plague danger grows, the narrator reports his agonized internal debate over whether to flee blighted London. Praying for guidance, he opens the Bible providentially at Psalm 91, which he quotes at length:

> I scarce need tell the reader that from that moment I resolved that I would stay in the town, and casting myself entirely upon the goodness and protection of the Almighty, would not seek any other shelter whatever; and that, as my times were in His hands, He was as able to keep me in a time of the infection as in a time of health; and if He did not think fit to deliver me, still I was in His hands, and it was meet He should do with me as should seem good to Him.

The story involves a compromise of approaches very characteristic of the time. Yes, the author believes that he will be protected, but even if he is not and loses his life, he still remains in God's hands. He may die, but will not suffer evil.[34]

Spurgeon's Dilemma

By the nineteenth century, scientific advances severely limited the range of natural calamities that were inexplicable except in terms of the divine will or demonic intervention. In the case of disease, vaccination was extensively deployed against smallpox from the 1790s, and the germ theory of causation swiftly gained acceptance from the 1850s, with the work of Louis Pasteur. In 1884, Robert Koch isolated the bacterium that caused cholera. By midcentury, no credible scientist doubted that diseases were the result of material causes, even if they struggled to find an exact source. The question then obviously arose: what, if any, room did that leave for traditional theories of supernatural causation and intervention, and of self-defense? As so often in the past, 91 was at the heart of controversy.

Somewhat disguising the cultural shift was the extensive use of religious metaphors to characterize epidemics and disease, and language borrowed from 91 continued to frame Western discourse in these matters. Psalm 91 supplied the images and metaphors that were regularly used for cholera, while yellow fever was the "yellow demon," with appropriate citations of the "noonday demon." When a yellow fever epidemic struck Mobile, Alabama, in 1853, Methodist minister John Wesley Starr wrote, "The pestilence walketh in the darkness, and the destruction wasteth at noonday. Day and night, more or less, I am visiting the victims of the plague." (The disease killed Starr shortly thereafter.) Similar words, with the same verse quoted, featured regularly across the U.S. South over the following decades. When yellow fever ravaged Shreveport, Louisiana, in 1873, one preacher "faced the pestilence that walketh in darkness and wasteth at noonday, until his exhausted strength succumbed to the deadly miasm [*sic* for miasma]." The same language also thoroughly permeated secular accounts. Very few of those who used the psalm in this "biblical" way were seriously attributing a given epidemic to supernatural forces. Rather, the words were attractive because they were so well known and offered an effective rhetorical tool for stressing the potential threat of a particular ailment. The Rev. Starr knew very well that he was not dealing with literal "plague," but the word carried so much Old Testament freight.[35]

It can be difficult to know just how literally religious thinkers were using such biblical language. It is not hard to find what appear to be quite unequivocal proclamations that 91 will safeguard from evil and plague, but serious caveats do exist. We have encountered the nineteenth-century account by Charles Spurgeon, whose career coincided closely with that of medical researcher Robert Koch. Spurgeon was deeply interested in the use of 91 through the centuries, and in particular its use against plagues and pandemics. But despite his story of the "German physician," it is not entirely clear whether Spurgeon himself literally believed that the psalm would defend Christians against diseases, and he chooses his words deftly. On occasion he suggests that "such as this Psalm speaks of [will] survive the scythe of death," even if the death statistics, the "bills of mortality," should soar. That seems plain enough, and at least some believers have continued to cite his argument as authoritative through the decades. But he also speaks of triumph over metaphorical diseases, "of the plague of moral evil, of heresy, and of backsliding." "*In a measure* [my emphasis] this also is true of physical evil; the Lord still puts a difference between Israel and Egypt in the day of his plagues."[36]

One giant step in the scientific study of epidemics was realized in 1854, when English physician John Snow famously traced a London cholera outbreak to one particular street pump. That story has often been told, but it deserves a footnote for its impact on Spurgeon. The young minister was a recent arrival in London, and he spent much time and effort visiting the sick, to the point of facing despair. As he was returning from yet another funeral, he noticed "a paper which was wafered up in a shoemaker's window in the Dover Road," which included words from Psalm 91 "in a good bold hand-writing." The words were somewhat jumbled together in a manner that we often witness in popular amulets: "Because thou hast made the Lord, which is my refuge, even the Most High, thy habitation; there shall no evil befall thee, neither shall any plague come nigh thy dwelling." As Spurgeon remarks:

> The effect upon my heart was immediate. Faith appropriated the passage as her own. I felt secure, refreshed, girt with immortality. I went on with my visitation of the dying in a calm and peaceful spirit; I felt no fear of evil, and I suffered no harm. The providence which moved the tradesman to place those verses in his window I gratefully acknowledge, and in the remembrance of its marvelous power I adore the Lord my God.

He was at once stirred and shamed by the knowledge that an ordinary lay-person would have more faith than he himself, a trained clergyman. It was the affirmation of faith that so transformed him, and not the promise of safety from disease. Someone, at least, was not speaking in terms of mere metaphor. For Spurgeon, that was a life-changing moment.[37]

Spurgeon certainly knew that cholera and other diseases are natural events that will kill many, including many faithful Christians, and yet he wanted to preserve at least some space for asserting the possibility of protection by means of faith and prayer. The reader has to pay close attention to see how limited that space is, just "in a measure."

As a literal and efficacious defense against disease, the psalm had already lost much of its power before the end of the seventeenth century. But that statement should be qualified; a growing gulf separated educated opinion, which drew on scientific insights, and a very extensive vernacular usage, which retained attitudes that would have been instantly recognizable a millennium before. During and after the Enlightenment, the psalm acquired multiple audiences, which differed widely on its interpretation and its efficacy in preventing harm. For many believers, providential doctrines were by no means extinct.

8

There Shall No Evil Befall Thee?

Modernity and Reaction

> When faith in an ultimate security is couched in symbolic expressions which suggest protection from all immediate perils, it is easy to be tempted to the illusion that the child of God will be accorded special protection from the capricious forces of the natural world, or special immunity from the vindictive passions of angry men. Any such faith is bound to suffer disillusionment. Nor does it deserve moral respect.[1]
>
> —Reinhold Niebuhr, 1937

In 1844, a disturbed politician attempted to murder the king of Prussia, Friedrich Wilhelm IV, in Berlin. Public reaction to the sensational event was somewhat mixed, as some dissidents circulated scurrilous rhymes and prints hostile to the monarchy. But for anyone with the slightest establishment sympathies, the crime was a singular atrocity, and the king's escape demanded commemoration. The greatest and most enduring response came from Felix Mendelssohn, who composed an eight-part motet that was performed in the Berlin Cathedral and was subsequently included in his oratorio *Elijah*. The work, *Denn er hat seinen Engeln befohlen*, was a setting of vv. 11–12 of Psalm 91, the words spoken by the Devil in the wilderness. In the context of 1844, the piece suggested that angels had miraculously safeguarded the king, who was at least obliquely compared to Christ. (At least one other composer of the time also used 91 to celebrate the king's survival.) Such an allusion was justified by the fact that Friedrich Wilhelm was not only an anointed king, but also the head and supreme governor of the Prussian Church, claiming the authority of its highest bishop.[2]

He Will Save You from the Deadly Pestilence. Philip Jenkins, Oxford University Press. © Oxford University Press 2023.
DOI: 10.1093/oso/9780197605646.003.0008

This use of the psalm would not have been surprising in reference to any anointed Christian monarch over the previous fifteen hundred years, but in 1844, it seems distinctly old-fashioned. In a post-Enlightenment world, attitudes to the psalm, and the worldview it epitomized, were changing rapidly. Educated people interpreted the psalm in ways that scorned or rejected what had long been the popular approach to its meaning and uses. As they did so, they found themselves challenging not just vernacular religious practice, but the most basic assumptions of the Bible itself. At the same time, older understandings remained very much alive, and not just among the poor and humble. The two worlds of high and low culture coexisted in often surprisingly close proximity and repeatedly clashed. In this as in so much else, the triumph of modernity had its limits.

Games of Thrones

In using the psalm to laud kings and damn enemies, kings and states in the early nineteenth century continued to do much what they had always done, and that remained true during the great conflicts following the French Revolution. Among the deadliest enemies of that Revolution was the Russian emperor Alexander I. In 1828, a Swiss Protestant author published a near hagiography of Alexander, presenting him as a devout Christian warrior who owed his conversion to Psalm 91. According to this account, Alexander first learned of the psalm from an aristocratic friend, but shortly afterward he heard its thirteenth verse in a church service. The experience seemed to go beyond mere coincidence, pointing to the workings of providence. Alexander was inspired to struggle against the lions and serpents that required trampling in his own day, Napoleon being the obvious candidate. The tsar's forces occupied Paris in 1814. Not for the first time, 91 offered a justification for holy war. When the Allies again defeated Napoleon at Waterloo the following year, the psalm featured prominently in the services of thanksgiving that followed.[3]

In the nineteenth-century world, kings held no monopoly on symbolism. Napoleon himself had restored church structures after the chaos of the French Revolution, and sermons and tracts used the Bible in imperial propaganda. Naturally, they applied to him the scriptural language that had previously belonged to legitimate monarchs. In 1809, the sermon greeting Napoleon's fortieth birthday presented him as a man under divine protection, so "a thousand fall beside him and ten thousand at his right side."[4]

Radicals too drew on the psalm, using its evil beasts to represent their own oppressors. In 1830, another French king was overthrown in a popular revolt, an event that called forth one of the most celebrated paintings in European history, *Liberty Leading the People*, by Eugène Delacroix. At first sight, the painting seems to have no connection to the familiar iconography of 91; however, in a daring but convincing argument, scholar Marijke Jonker shows that the painting draws precisely on older images of triumphant kings. In this view, the goddess Liberty advances over two corpses that do indeed resemble a lion and a serpent. Delacroix was thus subverting a tradition of royal iconography that dates back to the famous Ravenna mosaic and beyond. Further celebrating the new post-1830 revolutionary regime was a celebrated and much-reproduced sculpture by Antoine-Louis Barye, which depicted the victory of a lion crushing a serpent. Louis-Philippe, the monarch who took power during that insurrection, made the work a centerpiece of his campaign to promote his legitimacy.[5]

Quite diverse revolutionary iconographies emerged in the Bible-obsessed United States. One radical departure appeared as the insurgent colonies were moving apart from British traditions and were increasingly prepared to reject the monarchy. After a millennium in which kings had been portrayed trampling serpents and noxious beasts, radical Americans identified their own emerging nation with the stubborn and defiant rattlesnake. This image achieved canonical status with the revolutionary Gadsden Flag of 1778, with its slogan "Don't tread on me!" In the context of the time, the conjunction of "treading" with the snake image naturally suggested 91, but now that age-old tradition of royal propaganda was inverted.

As the new nation consolidated, some Americans appropriated that trampling imagery for their own purposes. When the American Anti-Slavery Society was founded in 1833, its commemorative declaration included a potent image of a warrior defeating threatening creatures, with the psalm's v. 13 quoted underneath. In the American Civil War, a cartoon depicted a rebel being hanged by a python around his neck. This might be a reference to the strategy of containment and blockade that the Union used to isolate and then crush its enemy, which became known as the "Python" strategy, and which was much reported under that name in the press. A happy Black observer comments on Confederate failure, "De fowler caught in his own snare!" In 1864, Frederick Douglass drew on the familiar rhetorical arsenal when he declared that the Confederacy and its cause "rivaled the earthquake, the whirlwind, the pestilence that walketh in darkness, and wasteth at noonday." As we will see, variants of those words became very common during the Civil War years.[6]

The Psalm as History

As the psalm was democratized, so it was increasingly subjected to secular scrutiny, to be reintegrated into worldly history. That process of historicizing involved stripping away many of its outright supernatural aspects.

Critical biblical scholarship was a centerpiece of the intellectual enterprise of the Enlightenment, and scholarly analysis of both Old and New Testaments was well advanced by the time of that attempted assassination in Berlin. During the nineteenth century, European—and especially German—scholars became increasingly skeptical of the authorship traditionally ascribed to various psalms, and tried instead to place them in the context of the political and religious needs of Israel at various eras. Among the most erudite interpreters were August Tholuck and Ernst Wilhelm Hengstenberg, whose works profoundly shaped the thought of biblical scholars in the English-speaking world. However reactionary the political regime of Prussia might have been, the nation was a center of cutting-edge scholarship. In the 1840s, Tholuck was the principal adviser to King Frederick William IV on all matters religious.[7]

Living as they were in a time of surging skepticism and religious liberalism, such authors sought to downplay the apotropaic or demonic elements of a text like 91, in order to minimize what could otherwise be seen as its primitive or superstitious quality. These were difficult years for conservative believers, with the explosive success of David Friedrich Strauss's radical study of Christian origins in his *Das Leben Jesu* (1835) and the outright atheism of philosophers like Ludwig Feuerbach. Demons were not just out of fashion; they were actively embarrassing. Just as nineteenth-century writers strove to deemphasize the miraculous and healing elements of the story of Jesus, so it was important to make other biblical texts respectable for a modern world. Although the word "demythologize" would not gain currency for another century, the idea prevailed strongly in the 1840s. Accordingly, critical scholars were concerned to understand the psalms as historical texts, which were just as firmly located in their time as a poem of the European Middle Ages, or indeed a Luther hymn. Tholuck convincingly imagined the psalm's original setting in antiphonal performances in the Jerusalem Temple, in a choral dialogue that he frames exactly on the model of Lutheran cathedral practice in the 1840s.[8]

That anti-supernatural quality was evident in Hengstenberg's writings. He firmly stresses the psalm's collective quality: it is addressed to the community rather than the individual. "The character of the Psalm is entirely general; for it applies to the whole church, at all events, no less than it does to its individual believing members." It is also a response to war, rather than to plague, and emphatically not to demonic assault. That applied to the terror by night; Hengstenberg cites other biblical examples in which warriors remain armed at night for fear of sudden attack. As to spiritual assaults, "It is not the Psalmist, but merely a part of his expositors, that lead us here into 'an unsafe spiritual region.' The Old Testament knows nothing of specters." (That last comment invites debate.) For Hengstenberg, the arrow by day was precisely that, an enemy arrow.[9]

Anglophone scholars adopted similar strategies. The *Notes* on the psalm by American scholar Albert Barnes began with a then-surprising remark that it was not intended to apply to Christ. He also spoke of the evils enumerated in the psalm as strictly material in nature. The terror by night might be "a sudden attack; an unexpected incursion of enemies; sudden disease coming on by night; or the pestilence which seems to love night."[10] In 1894, the oft-reprinted commentary of celebrity Baptist scholar Alexander MacLaren systematically rejected any hint of the demonic in 91:

> "The terror of the night" seems best understood as parallel with the "arrow that flies by day," in so far as both refer to actual attacks by enemies. Nocturnal surprises were favorite methods of assault in early warfare. Such an explanation is worthier than the supposition that the psalmist means demons that haunt the night.

The word "worthier" is notable, suggesting "more credible to modern sensibilities."[11] The relevant volume of the hugely influential *Preacher's Complete Homiletical Commentary* (1879) wholly reduced the once-dominant theme of demonic threats to metaphor:

> The good man finds that in himself there are "fleshly lusts which war against the soul." His life is a great moral battle. Numerous and powerful forces are arrayed against him. Seductive influences also are brought to bear upon

him to lead him astray. His life is one of peril. He needs a "fortress" from which he may hurl defiance at his foes.[12]

The Psalm and Empire

Authors were naturally shaped by the conditions and insights of their own age, which were often imperial or Orientalizing in tone, so they presented ancient Israelites as parallel to the nomadic peoples of a later Middle East. It is not clear whether, in his commentary of 1857, Charles Spurgeon was referring to the "Indians" of contemporary South Asia or the Wild West:

> There is not a place beneath which a believer walks that is free from snares. Behind every tree there is the Indian with his barbed arrow; behind every bush there is the lion seeking to devour; under every piece of grass there lieth the adder.[13]

Given their ever-expanding empire, British scholars were especially prone to "Oriental" rethinking. One of the most popular English-language works on psalms was the Commentary (1864–1868) by the Anglican bishop John Perowne. Perowne offered his own explanation of the terror by night as an "allusion, probably, to night attacks like those of Gideon (Judges 7), a favorite artifice of Oriental warfare." The *Preacher's Complete Homiletic Commentary* offered this globally informed, and indeed pith-helmeted, interpretation of the psalm's various allusions to disease:

> The diseases of all hot climates, and especially where vegetation is highly luxuriant, and marshes and miry swamps are abundant, proceed from the accumulating vapors of the night, or from the violence of the sun's rays at mid-day. The beriberi of Ceylon, the spasmodic cholera and jungle-fever of India, and the greater part of the fevers of intertropical climates, especially that called the yellow-fever, chiefly originate from the first of these— "the pestilence that walketh in darkness"; while sunstrokes, apoplexies, inflammations of the brain, and liver complaints of most kinds, proceed from the second, "the destruction that wasteth at noonday."[14]

To explain that "destruction that wasteth at noonday," other nineteenth-century scholars turned gratefully to the deadly simoom wind that had been invoked by early Syriac translators. That offered another opportunity to de-supernaturalize this and other psalms. Another demon down.

The Facts of Life

Even if preachers purged their Satanic images, they still faced a central problem in the psalm—namely, the biblical worldview that attributed worldly evils to supernatural causes and imagined a God whose anger had to be appeased. In light of the scientific discoveries of the nineteenth century, the tendency to blame calamities on divine anger or retribution became ever more implausible, and for many, morally repulsive. Religious thinkers had to contend with these insights, and more broadly with the implications for the effectiveness of prayer. The idea that God might dispatch literal angels to safeguard a beloved absolute monarch had fallen into disrepute among all but the most reactionary. More generally, was it reasonable to believe that God might change the course of human events in response to a pious plea? Might that extend to averting disease, changing weather, or deflecting a sword or bullet? Such ideas were of course found throughout the Bible, but the psalm epitomized them in what appeared to be their crudest and most naive form.

From the mid-nineteenth century, commentators shied away from miraculous interpretations and their accompanying promises, stressing instead the psalm's importance for inner and moral struggles. That must be highlighted, as sometimes it is easy to misinterpret comments in a simplistic way. As we have already seen with respect to plague and pestilence, we need to read such remarks carefully, and strictly in context. Witness, for instance, August Tholuck, who offered an inspiring if flawed analogy in his discussion of "a thousand shall fall":

> As a general, conscious of having a great work to perform, stands with a calm look and firm foot, while the balls whiz past him on the right hand and on the left, saying, I know that the ball which is to touch me is not yet cast; so stands a prophetic believer in danger's hour, conscious that the lightning will go past his head, that the waters will dry up at his feet, and the arrow fall back from his chest, because the Lord willeth it thus.[15]

The objections are obvious. Generals actually do get shot on the battlefield, however firm their convictions; witness Stonewall Jackson. And even men (and women) of prophetic faith really do fall to arrows that fly by day, no matter how fervently they pray the psalm. But Tholuck's remarks were preceded by a sentence that made it clear he was speaking in a spiritual context, and the weapons were those that "the tempter may use against the children of God." Tholuck was in fact quite realistic about any worldly benefits that the psalm might appear to confer, even in achieving a longer life. As he said, condescendingly, this was a Jewish concern: "Long life being mentioned among the promised goods, corresponds to the character of the old covenant, which referred a sensuous people to temporal reward." Christians, he believed, should know better.[16]

The 1869 edition of Albert Barnes's *Notes* offered a strikingly material foundation to the psalm's promises of material blessings, suggesting that placing faith in God in and of itself really did improve one's defenses against so many worldly threats. But to make his case, he presented arguments that to modern eyes demonstrate glaring prejudices of class and ethnicity. As Barnes declared:

> It is to be remembered that in times of pestilence (as was the case during the prevalence of the Asiatic cholera in 1832 and 1848), very many of the victims are the intemperate, the sensual, the debased, and that a life of this kind is a predisposing cause of death in such visitations of judgment. A large part of those who die are of that number. From the danger arising from this cause, of course the virtuous, the temperate, the pious are exempt; and this is one of the methods by which God saves those who trust in him from the "noisome pestilence." . . . [T]he tendency of religion is to lengthen our life; since virtue, temperance, regular industry, calmness of mind, moderation in all things, freedom from excesses in eating and in drinking—to all of which religion prompts—contribute to health, and to length of days.

Barnes argued that faith in God led to good moral habits, which helped one evade many perils that befell the impious, with alcohol abuse and sexual promiscuity as obvious examples. The more purely one lived, the greater the sense of safety and protection at a time when an epidemic was sweeping the nation: "The general course of the divine dealings is such as to show that God is favorable to virtue, and is opposed to vice."[17]

To this argument, it might properly be countered that Barnes was neglecting the effects of class and poverty. In reality, the "vicious" people who died in the American outbreaks Barnes describes would be the urban poor and immigrants, mainly Catholics, who lived in densely overcrowded and unhygienic conditions, and who were more likely to live in ways not to the liking of a Presbyterian cleric. But his larger point was well taken, in that lifestyle choices can indeed promote better health, a point now thoroughly substantiated by abundant research. To that extent, the psalm's statements were literally and demonstrably correct, without recourse to any supernatural activity.

Barnes admitted that his model was not perfect, in that some virtuous people really did die in untimely and seemingly unjust ways. But those anomalies only raised theological difficulties "if the present world were all, and if there were no future state: but the course of events indicates the general character of the divine administration, and what is the tendency of things. The completion—the actual and perfect adjustment—is reserved for a future state." All would ultimately come out right in the afterlife.[18]

Most leading commentators were similarly skeptical of claims of miraculous protection or preservation. The psalm did not mean that evils would not come; rather, it meant that God would allow believers the strength to resist them. Alternatively, the promise of deliverance might well apply to salvation in the next life, rather than security in this present world. Alexander MacLaren believed that, read properly, the words about "no evil befalling" could readily be reconciled with what he termed "the facts of life": "Evil may be experienced. Sorrows will come. But they will not touch the central core of the true life, and from them God will deliver, not only by causing them to cease, but by fitting us to bear." In understanding worldly matters, commentators regularly turned to Jesus's statement that God "makes his sun to rise on the evil and on the good, and sends rain on the just and on the unjust." In this present world, personal piety or godliness had little to do with one's vulnerability to natural conditions, and even disasters.[19]

Metaphorical and spiritual readings of the psalm transformed the "trampling" v. 13. Taking demons out of the picture left the creatures to be subjected as straightforward symbols of human sins or temptations. In 1882, the critic John Ruskin wrote what at first sight appears to be a thoroughly archaic interpretation of the medieval imagery at Reims Cathedral, which he duly described using the psalm's Vulgate text of v. 13. But even this determined Romantic reads the iconography in strictly modern and non-demonic style. The lion and dragon symbolize "the distinctively human sins, anger and lust, seeds in our race of their perpetual sorrow—Christ in His own humanity, conquered; and conquers in His disciples." In lesser churches too, artists felt free to use neo-medieval imagery without any of the demonic baggage. In a church in the English village of Swaffham Prior, a splendid series of stained-glass windows created at the end of the nineteenth century offered several images from 91, appearing alongside an abundance of other angelic themes and characters. The representation of v. 13 shows a medieval knight (albeit with an anachronistic Victorian mustache) who spears a writhing dragon as a lion slinks away. But as with Ruskin, the viewer is meant to read here the victory of virtue and manly courage, rather than a defeat of demonic forces.[20]

Against the Current

Learned writers, including theological conservatives, presented 91 in ways far removed from its traditional role. But such interpretations did not destroy or discredit older views. We have already encountered Charles Spurgeon as a visible (and prolific) exponent of the psalm, although even he had to acknowledge that literal belief in demons had to be adapted for a modern audience. In his 1857 sermon on 91 entitled "The Snare of the Fowler," he mocked crude medieval concepts of Satan as "a black and grimy thing." The modern reality was quite different in style if not in substance:

> The devil of this day is a well-spoken gentleman: he does not persecute— he rather attempts to persuade and to beguile. He is not now the furious Romanist, so much as the insinuating unbeliever, attempting to overturn our religion, while at the same time he pretends he would make it more rational, and so more triumphant. He would only link worldliness with religion; and so he would really make religion void, under the cover of developing the great power of the gospel, and bringing out secrets which our forefathers had never discovered. Satan is always a fowler.

The new Satan was a well-dressed liberal Protestant, an advocate of Higher Criticism.[21]

The desire to counter such liberal views inspired Spurgeon to write his commentaries on psalms in *The Treasury of David*, which appeared over two decades. As for Augustine many centuries before, 91 attracted Spurgeon's special attention and zeal. This volume was a monument of its kind, a detailed discussion of the psalm, but also an extensive anthology of remarks on it by authors through the centuries, from the Early Fathers to such key advocates as St. Bernard and William Bridge, as well as many obscurer preachers. The whole runs to some 24,000 words. The cumulative impact is to present an overwhelming case for the importance of the psalm, and also its protective properties in the real material world.[22]

Legends

The persistence of older beliefs is suggested by the extraordinary continuity of stories claiming that individuals or groups who prayed 91 had received literal and direct protection against plague and other evils. Throughout its history, the psalm has attracted a sizable body of folklore and myth-making, which we occasionally glimpse in homilies and sermons. Such tales suggest what people wanted to believe.

Some stories persisted through the centuries. In 1720, the city of Marseille suffered one of the last major outbreaks of bubonic plague in the West. The city's clergy, under the leadership of its bishop, worked heroically to relieve the victims. The account of this Christian heroism was widely admired and reported by Catholics and Protestants alike. Soon, however, it became associated with Psalm 91 and its promise about invulnerability to plague and misfortune. In 1771, Anglican bishop George Horne published his popular *Commentary on the Psalms*, in which he explained the verse about a thousand falling at thy side:

> This promise has oftentimes, in a wonderful manner, been verified to those faithful servants of God, whom the pestilence itself hath not deterred from doing the duties of their station. The bishop and some of the intendants of Marseilles, who continued to perform their respective offices, during the whole time of the plague there in 1720, are signal and well-known instances.[23]

Such an exemplar was powerful at a time when ideas of science and Enlightenment were becoming widely established, and it was helpful to claim a "verified" precedent, even if the process of verification was not explicit. That Marseille story became a commonplace of the literature on the psalm through the nineteenth century and beyond, usually with a citation of Horne's work. Of course, Spurgeon quotes it in the context of 91. The claims duly escalated, from the clergy receiving general protection to a total immunity from plague.

In the 1840s, a learned Scottish commentator recalled "the good Bishop of Marseilles, who, during the plague in that city in 1720, when nature sickened, and each gale was death, though in constant attendance on the infected and dying thousands, entirely escaped the contagion." (The bishop did survive, but the diocese actually lost some 250 of its clergy to the disaster.)[24]

Another example was that of the learned "German physician" cited by Spurgeon, who supposedly described Psalm 91 as "the best preservative in times of cholera." On closer examination, the story looks more like a folktale than an actual event. The tale goes back to the midcentury German biblical scholar and mystic Rudolf Ewald Stier, who located the supposed doctor in St. Petersburg. As such, it probably dates from the 1830s, when the new menace of cholera first appeared in Europe, but any closer pinpointing is impossible. Nor, of course, is there any suggestion that the "physician" had the slightest empirical evidence on which to base his claim. Yet through frequent reprintings of Spurgeon, the tale lives on today, and it can easily be found on the Internet.[25]

Another *ben trovato* story tells of evangelist Dwight Moody, who certainly preached on 91, as well as a great many other scriptures. We still possess two recordings of Moody's voice; in one he recites Jesus's Beatitudes from the gospels, while in the other he is reading 91. One story in particular would link his name inextricably with 91, which he especially commended to travelers. In 1892, Moody was sailing on the steamship *Spree*, which encountered such fierce storms that it seemed sure to sink. As he reports, he led his fellow passengers in prayer, taking as his text the highly appropriate Psalm 107, with its lines "They that go down to the sea in ships, that do business in great waters." So perfectly suited was it for the occasion, indeed, that "a lady came to me afterwards and said I made it up to suit the occasion." But he makes no mention of 91. Regardless of the text, the ship was duly saved.[26]

Early on, the story circulated that Moody had actually used 91, and especially the promise of angelic protection in v. 11 (or, alternatively, in vv. 14–16; accounts differ). This was the story told by one of his fellow passengers, the distinguished Civil War general Oliver Otis Howard, a faithful and biblically literate evangelical. Yet it is hard to believe that Moody would have missed an opportunity to laud 91 if it had actually been the text in question. Presumably, Howard remembered 91 because that was what he had expected to hear. Whatever the story's origins, modern commentators often feature the Moody story in their laudatory accounts of 91 and its practical value, and it is now firmly part of the psalm's lore.[27]

The Limits of Superstition

Any sense of popular religious belief is of necessity limited by the nature of our evidence. It is not difficult to find out how educated people coped with the new environment of intellectual modernity, but the attitudes of humbler believers are a different matter. As we have seen, Spurgeon reported seeing 91 referenced on that paper "wafered up in a shoemaker's window in the Dover Road," which gave him an opportunity to make a comment on his own faith. Had he not written about it, we would have no idea of the shoemaker's invocation, nor can we say how common such practices were in times of crisis. Nor did Spurgeon inquire into the motives of the psalm's users. Presumably, the residents were seeking protection strictly in the old style scorned by the learned commentators. They were not merely seeking courage to bear illness, or asserting hope in the afterlife; rather, they wanted the disease to pass by. We have no way to identify the religious affiliations of the residents, but there is no reason to believe that they were anything other than mainstream Protestants, whether Anglican or Dissenting. Such vernacular beliefs are rarely preserved in published form. It is surely fair to assume, however, that a great many ordinary believers retained their belief in the power of evil and the psalm's protective abilities.[28]

Beyond the approved bounds of mainstream Christianity, 91 occupied a key role in a substantial body of magical and occult lore, which became more readily available with the coming of cheap printing during the eighteenth century. Through the early modern period, Jewish communities in Central and Eastern Europe had a lively tradition of occult practice and demonic belief, which among other things sustained the use of 91 in exorcism. A sizable number of Jewish writings summarized mystical and magical teachings that claimed at least some foundation in Qabalistic literature. At the end of the eighteenth century, many such products were translated into German and other languages, and these circulated very widely. One of the most popular was *Sefer Shimmush Tehillim* or *Use of the Psalms*, which was translated into German by Gottfried Selig (1722–1795), a Jewish convert to Christianity. This work was incorporated into a magical manual called the *Sixth and Seventh Books of Moses*, which enjoyed great fame through occult and esoteric circles, high and low, on both sides of the Atlantic. That often-reprinted manual or grimoire was a mainstay of the magical traditions of German Americans, in areas such as rural Pennsylvania.[29]

Psalm 91 is held in special reverence in this literature. Indeed, the modern editor of the *Sefer Shimmush Tehillim* remarks that "it is without doubt the classic psalm in Jewish and Christian magic. The documentary proofs for its magical uses are extremely numerous both in Judaism and Christianity." The *Sixth and Seventh Books of Moses* tells us that 91 is to be prayed "over a person tormented by an evil spirit, or one afflicted by an incurable disease." More generally,

> if anyone should be in danger of his life, or become distressed, be it what it may, such as being attacked by an incurable disease, pestilence, fire, or water, overwhelmed by enemies or murderers, in battles, sieges, robberies, close imprisonment, etc., let him confess his sins first of all, and then speak the *Vihi Noam* prayer (the name by which the 91st Psalm with the aforesaid verse is usually known), ninety-nine times, according to the number of the two holiest names of God, Jehovah Adonai.

The text closely follows Jewish practice in its readings of the psalm:

> Each time when he comes to the fourteenth verse, "Because he hath set his love upon me," etc., he shall keep in mind the Holy Name, and then pray devoutly.... Again write this Psalm in connection with the last verse of the previous Psalm upon clean parchment, and conceal it behind the door of your house, and you will be secure from all evil accidents.[30]

In the transformed world of science and modern media, Qabalism enjoyed a new birth.

The Occult Psalm

Alongside the Jewish and Qabalistic tradition, and sometimes intersecting with it, there was a lively school of intellectual Christian occultism, which also drew on ancient and Classical ideas such as the Hermetic literature. As in the Jewish works, the spells and formulae offered in this literature often draw on 91, and the psalm's v. 13 was a natural favorite. This tradition found a monument in Francis Barrett's astonishing treatise *The Magus* (1801), which brought these occult ideas in all their variety and ornate complexity to an English-speaking public who lacked access to Latin or Hebrew.[31]

Some commentators on 91 are hard to categorize because they straddle the frontiers separating Christian mysticism from the occult. One brilliant polymath of the Enlightenment era was Sweden's Emanuel Swedenborg, who claimed visionary and angelic revelations that fascinated followers for centuries. Among his extensive writings on scripture, he reasserted the special powers granted by 91, and particularly its v. 13, which empowers the believer to tread down dark forces. This reading depended on Swedenborg's idiosyncratic cosmology, in which dangerous exhalations issue from multiple material hells. These sinister forces

> continually breathe forth through the lands that are over these hells, or by which these hells are covered; so that to walk upon such places is dangerous to those who are only natural, and still more to those who are corporeal-sensual; for an exhalation arises therefrom, and a contagion affects those who walk there. But those who are led by the Lord may safely tread upon that earth without infection or infestation.

Widely circulated among his devoted followers, such passages are not far removed from occult and demonic belief.[32]

Occult ideas, together with the practice of ritual magic, actually became far more common and voguish as the nineteenth century progressed. A general reaction against materialistic science and modernity led to a surging occult revival among European intellectuals and avant-garde cultural figures. Although this was a general European phenomenon, the date conventionally cited for the start of the boom in the English-speaking nations is 1887, with the foundation of the Hermetic Order of the Golden Dawn. Its members explored the traditions of medieval magic and Qabala, often in bastardized form, and republished ancient grimoires, with all their scriptural references. One highly valued text was the *Clavicula Salomonis*, the Key of Solomon, published in 1889. Among many other magic sigils offered in the work was "the fifth pentacle of Mars," which included the *super aspidem* verse surrounding a scorpion. The would-be sorcerer is instructed to "write thou this pentacle upon virgin parchment or paper, because it is terrible unto the demons, and at its sight and aspect they will obey thee, for they cannot resist its presence." Well into the twentieth century, such spells and talismans exercised a powerful attraction for aspiring aesthetes and decadents. Hard-core devotees might wear something like that sigil on a robe as they performed invocations or exorcisms.[33]

The Gothic Psalm

Educated elites drew sharp distinctions between their own supposedly rational views and the superstitions of the masses. But that high-low distinction blurred considerably with this upsurge of interest in the esoteric. Prominent thinkers who would have been the first to condemn vulgar and simplistic beliefs about (for instance) invoking biblical texts to defend against plague were themselves entranced with medieval lore. Meanwhile, occult and esoteric ideas acquired a different kind of popularity among ordinary literary consumers. The more populations became concentrated in urban centers, the easier it became to treat rural areas and their archaic customs as mysterious or even romantic. From the end of the nineteenth century, urban dwellers on both sides of the Atlantic used rural areas with their beliefs in magic and witchcraft as literary inspiration, or even tourist attractions. That cultural distancing abetted the rise of a Gothic sensibility that allowed moderns to explore the realms of medieval superstition.

As overt demons were expelled from many (if not all) churches, so they became a standard feature of Gothic and horror fiction, which proved very hospitable to what Spurgeon had dismissively termed "the devil of five hundred years ago." As a symbol or epitome of those older demonic beliefs, Psalm 91 began a thriving new career as a Gothic motif.

One early example was "The Botathen Ghost" (1867), by the once-famous English author R. S. Hawker. In his tale, a seventeenth-century clergyman who encounters the ghost of a woman is alarmed because she "might be a *daemonium meridianum*, the most stubborn spirit to govern and guide that any man can meet and the most perilous withal." He duly exorcizes the presence, but not before she has fulfilled another task closely linked to the psalm, prophesying the great plague that would assail London in 1665. The cleric's citation of Psalm 91—and in the outdated Latin—deliberately consigns the tale to a rural and superstitious past, impossibly remote from modernity. Like many successors, Hawker used the Vulgate to medievalize the psalm and its thought-world. In 1895, the celebrated writer of supernatural tales M. R. James published the story "Canon Alberic's Scrap Book," one of his most popular creations. It imagines a seventeenth-century French cleric who records his encounters with the terrifying night demon that will soon claim his life. As Alberic approaches doom, he tries to invoke the powers of holiness, which naturally involves the psalm that he refers to as "Qui habitat."[34]

Particularly evocative was the idea that those older demonic forces could somehow, mysteriously, manifest into the modern world of science and reason. One of James's rivals in the world of horror and fantastic fiction was E. F. Benson, scion of a great Anglican clerical dynasty. In 1912, he used "The Terror by Night" as the title for a horror story, but his finest achievement came a decade later with his classic "Negotium Perambulans." Benson's story involves sinister paintings on the panels in an ancient church, which depicted a priest confronting a hideous monster:

> Below ran the legend "Negotium perambulans in tenebris" from the ninety-first Psalm. We should find it translated there, "the pestilence that walketh in darkness," which but feebly rendered the Latin. It was more deadly to the soul than any pestilence that can only kill the body: it was the Thing, the Creature, the Business that trafficked in the outer Darkness, a minister of God's wrath on the unrighteous.

The psalm is used to suggest spiritual warfare in medieval times, the surprise being that those evil forces might in fact be dormant rather than dead. "Negotium Perambulans" is still a staple of vampire fiction anthologies.[35] Benson was far from alone in his use of such consciously archaic references. When in 1929 Montague Summers published *The Vampire: His Kith and Kin*, which affected to take all such medieval lore with deadly literalism, the book's epigraph was our psalm's vv. 4–5, in the Vulgate.[36]

The psalm featured prominently in one of the metaphysical thrillers of the English mystic Charles Williams, who exercised such influence over C. S. Lewis and the other Inklings. Those faithfully orthodox Christians did not necessarily appreciate just how deeply Williams was immersed in the ongoing occult revival with its ritual magic practices: he knew his grimoires. Not surprisingly, Williams uses the psalm in his descriptions of spiritual warfare. In his *War in Heaven* (1930), an evil sorcerer laments his failure to overcome one woman character, and quotes the line "He shall give His angels charge over her." What the reader knows, and the sorcerer will soon discover to his great cost, is that in this instance, the statement is literally correct: she really is guarded by angels.[37]

The psalm pervades the imagery of Williams's novel *The Place of the Lion* (1931) and actually frames the plot. As with Benson and Summers, the plot concerns ancient and long-forgotten forces spilling over into an unsuspecting modern world. In this case, they take the form of overwhelmingly mighty angelic beings, as described in the writings of a Byzantine mystic of the twelfth century. Against such primal menaces, the book's characters must seek the protection of 91, and v. 13 is referenced on several occasions. At first, the hero, Anthony, speaks flippantly of the danger: "Goodnight, my dear, don't worry—the young lion and the dragon will we tread under-foot." But soon, he and his friends face literal and deadly combats against archetypal figures representing the Lion and the Serpent. In 91, he finds a medieval solution to a medieval assault.[38]

Such invocations of the archaic past were by no means confined to the Gothic, strictly defined. In 1934, F. Scott Fitzgerald wrote a much-anthologized essay, "Sleeping and Waking," for *Esquire*. He addressed the wakeful hours in the middle of the night, "a sinister, ever widening interval" between the early and later spells of comfortable sleep. "This is the time of which it is written in the Psalms: *Scuto circumdabit te veritas eius: non timebis a timore nocturno, a sagitta volante in die, a negotio perambulante in tenebris* [91:5–6]." He recalled the Vulgate text from his Catholic upbringing, but here he is offering it (untranslated) to a magazine audience that would find it exotic and even exciting, and that is the point. At these darkest tines of night, he suggests, we enter a realm of fantasy and unrest that had traditionally been understood as sinister and demonic. He represents that not just by quoting the Bible, but by using the form in which it would have been quoted in the superstitious Middle Ages—although obviously we moderns understand these terms in completely non-supernatural ways. However humorous and self-deprecating the tone of the essay, the psalm offers an ideal way to discuss those primitive concepts in a rational modern world. By this point, many of his readers may have recognized the Latin words from their frequent invocation in horror and Gothic fiction.[39]

"Demonic" words taken directly from 91 entered the vernacular to signify general threat or evil, with no necessary supernatural implications. Such metaphorical language appealed to authors who disdained any connection with the Gothic. When France went to war in 1914, the best-selling novel of the day was Paul Bourget's *Le Démon de midi* (*The Noonday Demon*), about a faithful Catholic man succumbing to sexual temptation during a midlife crisis. In 1946, Basil Rathbone reprised his popular role as Sherlock Holmes in a film titled *The Terror by Night*.[40]

Such appropriations had their effect in the mainstream religious context. The more demons were associated with the world of horror and the Gothic, literary or cinematic, the more difficult it became for mainline preachers or commentators to discuss them as part of a religious system that wished to be taken seriously. If 91 was a wonderful asset for fiction writers, it was a questionable basis for religion.

The Psalm at War

However much "superstition" seemed to have been consigned to irrelevance and mockery, it was above all the experience of war that kept bringing those older ideas back into the world of serious debate.

Psalm 91 is often called the Soldier's Psalm. Ever since the Reformation brought the scriptures to a general readership, soldiers have resorted to the psalm's words, and as we will see in Chapter 9, the psalm has never lost its popularity. The pious British officer Sir Harry Smith spoke for a great many other soldiers before and since when he recorded his experiences of the battle of Waterloo in 1815: "I repeated to myself a verse from the Psalms of that day, 91st Psalm, 7th verse: A thousand shall fall beside thee, and ten thousand at thy right hand, but it shall not come nigh thee." The reasons for the psalm's popularity are obvious enough, as soldiers throughout history have sought amulets and talismans, and 91 has the virtue of being found clearly in the officially approved Bible, rather than in any form of folk magic.[41]

One was likely to hear a great many stories of the psalm's effectiveness, and indeed its miraculous qualities. A soldier who prayed the psalm and survived the battle would gratefully recount his experience, which might well be reported in print. Of course, we have no records from those who were equally faithful in praying those same words but perished on the battlefield. Many of those thousands falling at one's side might well have been praying the psalm but never lived to tell the tale: We recall the German soldier who fell at Poitiers in 1569, despite the protection of a Qabalistic amulet. As a cynical soldier wrote from the bloody battlefront of the Ypres Salient in 1917, "'A thousand shall fall beside thee, and ten thousand at thy right hand, but it shall not come nigh thee' (Ps. 91). Very comforting that one, so long as you are sure you won't be among the unlucky 10,000! But David was obviously whistling to keep his courage up."[42]

The psalm has its history in famous conflicts since Napoleonic times. During the American Civil War, 91 features regularly in accounts of heroic and dying soldiers—not by any means as the only scripture so employed, but as a deeply valued text. One of the many soldiers to leave his recollections was John Beatty, later a prominent figure in Ohio politics. In January 1863, he noted how his unit's morale was rising: "I draw closer to the camp-fire, and, pushing the brands together, take out my little Bible, and as I open it my eyes fall on the XCI [91st] Psalm," which he then quotes in full. His experience was common in these years. In 1861, a Mississippi cavalry commander submitted an official report of his unit's actions in the day's battle: "And first allow me to record with gratitude the kind Providence which shielded us in the day of battle and saved so many from 'the destruction that wasteth at noonday.' "[43]

So commonly did both armies invoke the psalm during the American Civil War that its words and imagery inevitably framed their understandings of the larger conflict. Our psalm's v. 6 became a common metaphor for the war and its sufferings. It is hard to overstate how frequently this appears in accounts of individuals and events, whether we are looking at memoirs, regimental histories, or obituaries. The words had a special relevance because of the "pestilence" element: as soldiers knew from grim experience, disease was almost as effective a killer during the war as was actual combat. A Union veteran recorded the hideous conditions in the notorious Confederate prison camp at Andersonville: "Making that prison pen a very breeding place for disease and death, where 'the pestilence that walketh in darkness and the destruction that walketh at noonday' found no opposition." Such quotations and recollections could be multiplied almost endlessly.[44]

The Great War and After

It was in the First World War that the psalm's military uses became most visible, and when it attracted unprecedented controversy. Partly, this was because of the staggering scale of the conflict and the vast numbers of people involved directly in combat: ten million perished in combat, not to mention civilian fatalities. Service in those great armies brought together people from very disparate worlds who in other circumstances might never have encountered each other—rich and poor, educated and humble. Millions of those who served came from rural or peasant backgrounds where modern and skeptical ideas had made little headway, or else they were only a generation or so removed from that background. Accordingly, they were well used to amulets, spells, and charms. A detailed ethnographic study of popular beliefs among German forces in this war suggests that many operated in a world of folk belief and magic that would not have been out of place in the 1640s.[45]

But it was by no means only peasants who sought spiritual protection, and many ordinary city dwellers sent their sons off to war with sage advice about seeking divine aid. One typical German mother in the war's opening days advised her son to "buy yourself a New Testament with the Psalms, and read the 91st Psalm, where it beautifully states how God protects his people in face of all dangers." Psalm 91 found few skeptics in foxholes or trenches, regardless of the social background of the soldiers involved.[46]

The psalm now attracted a whole new corpus of legends and myths supporting its protective value, and such tales found ready audiences. The British-based Bible Society tells of a young private at the deadly Battle of the Somme in 1916 who placed his Bible in his pocket. "Then he heard the words from Psalm 91 go through his mind. They say, 'A thousand may fall at your side, ten thousand at your right hand, but you will not be harmed.'" A massive explosion killed all his comrades nearby, but left him alive. Such stories circulated among soldiers themselves, and also among their loved ones at home, the mothers and wives, among whom 91 became exceedingly popular. Recording such mystical beliefs and practices and the legends surrounding them, historian Owen Davies speaks aptly of the conflict as a "supernatural war."[47]

But that same Great War also attracted skepticism about the psalm, which in some ways paralleled the impact of the scientific discoveries concerning pestilence in the previous century. The fact that the psalm failed to protect many of its most pious adherents made it a target for protest against both war and religion. Of course, opposition to war or to particular wars was nothing new in history, but as the Great War dragged on, it attracted swelling opposition in many countries, opposition that was variously rooted in religiously based pacifism, or active socialist and radical politics. Radicals denounced war and the religious beliefs that were used to justify it; activists found a focus in the Soldier's Psalm and the worldview it reflected.

One of Germany's leading pacifist writers was Leonhard Frank, who later earned fame as an Expressionist novelist. In 1918, his daring story *The Mother* told of a woman who was anxious to secure blessings on her son away at the front; she naturally turns to 91, which is quoted at length. Only thus can he be supplied with the spiritual armor to ward off enemy weaponry. When she learns her son is dead, she runs screaming to a church, where the priest is thanking God, who has blessed German forces and crowns them with victory. She assails him for these outrageous lies, and leads a street protest. For Frank, 91 is an integral part of the military-religious complex, which drives people into war and deludes them into thinking they might survive it.[48]

Military use of the psalm is described critically by Boris Pasternak in his *Dr. Zhivago*, a novel written from the 1920s onward but not published until 1957. Pasternak offers an almost anthropological view of 91, as if a visitor from an advanced society is sketching the practices of a primitive tribe. As the author explains, 91 had been a common amulet for Russian soldiers during the First World War. (As good Orthodox Christians, they knew it as Psalm 90, and commonly under the title of "In the shelter of Vyshnyago," the Most High.) That usage continued during the bloody civil war that ravaged Russia from 1919 through 1922, as Bolshevik Reds fought anti-Communist Whites.

The hero, Zhivago, encounters 91 twice as he fights in the Red cause. On the first occasion, he finds the body of a fellow soldier: "The dead man had an amulet on a string around his neck. . . . In it there turned out to be a piece of paper, decayed and worn at the edges, sewn into a scrap of cloth." The text is the psalm, quoted selectively in a way that suggested frequent recitation as a spell or incantation, with all the errors that creep in as a result. Fragments of the Church Slavonic text were rewritten in Russian. The opening, "He that dwelleth in the secret place of the Most High," was corrupted to the brief "Dwellers in Secret," while the verse "Thou shall not be afraid for the terror by night nor for the arrow that flieth by day" was simplified as "Have no fear of the arrow flying by thee." As Pasternak says, "The text of the psalm was considered miracle working, a protection against bullets."[49]

Shortly afterward, Zhivago encounters a similar object on a wounded enemy White soldier. "A little cross fell and hung outside on a chain with a medallion, and also some flat little gold case or snuff box with a damaged lid, as if pushed in by a nail." It contains the full text of 91, in the venerable, difficult, and therefore auspicious language of Church Slavonic, "typed and in all its Slavonic genuineness." Zhivago surmises that the charm had been put together by the young man's mother, to secure his survival in battle, and it actually does have that effect, as the amulet deflected a bullet. Moved by the find, Zhivago spares the White's life. Arguably, in this case the psalm in this instance really did protect from death, twice. The reader is left to consider whether the different outcomes in the two instances—death and life—reflected the varying quality and accuracy of the psalm text that the two hopeful soldiers deployed.[50]

Drawing Lines

Educated believers, Christian or Jewish, could despise popular uses of 91, with its easily debunked promises of miraculous intervention. But such critiques raised broader and deeply troubling questions about the nature of mainstream religious thought and practice, and the proper frontiers separating faith and superstition. It was far from clear what separated "superstitious" prayers—for instance, that a plague would pass by, leaving a family untouched—from more general pleas that God might intervene to safeguard or benefit his loyal followers. Was it reasonable to expect that prayer might actually have any impact in the material world? Moreover, without the support and confirmation of such interventions, of signs and wonders, what happened to faith? Just how much of the older worldview could be discarded without utterly abandoning religion in anything like the form it had been known for millennia?

That dilemma of faith and miracle was famously posed by Fyodor Dostoevsky in his legend of the Grand Inquisitor, which was published in 1879–1880 as part of *The Brothers Karamazov*, and exerted an enormous influence on later Christian thought. In his story, the Grand Inquisitor condemns Jesus for his refusal to resort to miracles and mysterious deeds to prove his claims, and in effect to force all human beings to accept his church and its faith. As so often in such discussions, Psalm 91 occupies center stage, and specifically the moment when Jesus refused to cast himself off the Temple. By rejecting such crude and ostentatious displays, he left ordinary people the freedom to choose or reject faith. But, says the Inquisitor, Jesus blundered, because he fails to understand human nature. He does not realize that

> no sooner did man reject the miracle than he would at once reject God also, for man does not seek God so much as miracles. And since man is not strong enough to get by without the miracle, he creates new miracles for himself, his own now, and bows down before the miracle of the quack and the witchcraft of the peasant woman, even though he is a mutineer, heretic and atheist a hundred times over.

Mature belief, we are meant to conclude, does not rely on such miracles, which must be scorned, but such belief is exceedingly difficult to sustain. In this vision, 91—as it is popularly understood—symbolizes that lower and ignorant approach to faith, which so easily lends itself to exploitation and abuse.[51]

Dostoevsky was writing of miracles, but his words could easily be extended to any sense that God would respond to prayers by direct involvement in the material world. One of the most celebrated Protestant theologians of modern times was Reinhold Niebuhr (1892–1971), who stood in the Reformed tradition. Growing up in Illinois at the start of the twentieth century, he thought regularly of 91 when he witnessed the terrible storms that swept the area, and like so many other people, he sought divine protection. But also like so many others, he witnessed the abuse of religious claims and language during the First World War. As an educated adult in the 1920s, he came to see the psalm's promises of safety and invulnerability as "a perfect illustration of all the illusions which may arise from an ultimate religious faith." He scorned "lobbying, with whining entreaties, in the courts of the Almighty, hoping for special favors which are not granted to ordinary mortals or to godless men." Niebuhr's position was challenged by more conservative thinkers, who were more open to the potential of prayer to achieve observable material results, but views like his came to occupy the theological mainstream.[52]

The Bible as Problem

Niebuhr's views on prayer and faith raised many unresolved questions, notably with respect to those many believers who prayed for such benefits in the material world as the psalm seemed to proffer. If the highly educated lived in a world that was free of "lobbying," a great many other Christians did not, and still do not. Should such vernacular believers be regarded as practicing a sub-Christian form of superstition, against which faithful Christians should protest? If that was the case, that left little room for the supernatural tenets that the great majority of Christians had held since apostolic times, and which were deeply rooted in the scriptures themselves.

The conflict between modern and pre-modern belief was agonizingly portrayed in a story told in the 1930s by Emanuel Hirsch, one of Germany's most erudite Protestant theologians, and a leading Luther scholar. During the First World War, Hirsch encountered a poor woman who was devoted to Psalm 91 in a way that was utterly typical of the time, but which he regarded as magical. Just like the mother described by Leonhard Frank, she fervently believed that the verse about surviving in the midst of thousands of casualties promised that her son would survive the war, while the sons of her neighbors would not. Hirsch gently tried to bring her to a more sophisticated faith, to realize "that this kind of trust in God was less than Christian." He failed, and the woman ended the pastoral relationship.[53]

But as Hirsch reflected on the encounter, he realized that the woman was to some extent correct in her understanding of the psalm, and the problem lay in the text itself. To return to Dostoevsky's fantasy, it was precisely the literal reading of that psalm that had produced "the witchcraft of the peasant woman," to the detriment of what Hirsch regarded as authentic Christianity. Hirsch continued:

> After that, I avoided this psalm in my Christian pastoral care and instruction. More, I became quite cautious about the use of the Old Testament Psalter at all, either at the sick bed or in instruction. Instead, I read from the New Testament and from our German evangelical psalm book, that is, the hymnal.[54]

Hirsch, a committed Nazi, urged the church to abandon the Old Testament, with what he viewed as its crude Jewish superstitions, and to stress instead a distinctively Aryan Christianity.

Obviously, such a total rejection of the psalm and indeed the Old Testament was a strategy of desperation. But in modern times too, a gulf separates vernacular uses of the psalm from established religious doctrines. Even as institutional faith has weakened, popular religiosity flourishes.

9

But It Shall Not Come Nigh Thee

Demons and Plagues Persist

So, dispatch angels around you, your family members, your home,
your vehicles and any building you walk into. Say, "Ministering
angels, I send you forth to protect my family according to Psalm 91."
Then, expect it![1]

—Kenneth Copeland Ministries, 2019

A story that circulates in multiple versions on the internet tells of

a Brigade commander in WWI who gave a little card with Psalm 91 on it to
his men who were in the Brigade of the same number—91st Brigade. They
agreed to recite this daily. The story goes that after they started praying
this prayer they were involved in three of the bloodiest battles in WWI yet
suffered no casualties in combat despite other brigades suffering as much
as 90%.

In the standard version of this tale, the soldiers were American, and the three
battles were Chateau Thierry, Belleau Wood, and the Argonne. The fact that
there never was a 91st Brigade in the US Army of the time does throw some
doubt on the pious tale, but that has not prevented its proliferation.[2]

At first sight, this story represents the kind of superstition that Reinhold
Niebuhr was denouncing a century ago, and which became so widespread
during and after the Great War. The daily recitation gives the story a ritualistic character and, moreover, assigns a fetishistic quality to the number 91.
For many believers, even in the post-Christendom West, the scripture still
exercises much the same appeal that it did centuries ago, and its appeal is
enhanced by contemporary means of marketing and promotion.

He Will Save You from the Deadly Pestilence. Philip Jenkins, Oxford University Press. © Oxford University Press 2023.
DOI: 10.1093/oso/9780197605646.003.0009

These manifestations may often seem worrying or even disreputable, but the psalm also continues to exercise its power in strictly mainstream and "approved" faith traditions, as it inspires believers with spiritual strength. In music and popular culture too, 91 still speaks to publics thirsty for its succor. To use a commercial analogy, the psalm operates in a complex and highly segmented market. If we think of the psalm's story as a biography, then in its most recent phase, it has become endlessly versatile, presenting very different faces to multiple audiences. It is a highly visible face of contemporary spirituality.

The Fortress

Modern scholarship has come to appreciate the significance of 91 within both Jewish and Christian traditions. Building on the foundation of nineteenth-century scholarship, studies of the Old Testament and the psalms in particular have achieved a remarkable sophistication. New generations of scholars have some resources not available to their predecessors with respect to recent archaeological and documentary finds, which we have already noted above, and especially newly discovered charms and amulets from various cultures. These allow 91 to be understood in the context of the larger Middle East of the first millennium BCE, and by no means only its Jewish setting. The most famous such find was the Dead Sea Scrolls, but 91 also featured in the vast trove of Jewish documents found in the Genizah, the storage collection, of an ancient Cairo synagogue. The spiritual worlds that produced 91 have come into sharp focus, making possible some splendid works of advanced scholarship. Other studies have described what is termed the reception of the psalms, the ways in which they have been read, interpreted, and depicted though Jewish and Christian history.[3]

These new insights transformed the use of the psalm in multiple ways, some trivial, others more substantial. From midcentury, Catholic scholars increasingly acknowledged the superiority of Hebrew readings and moved away from the Vulgate. In the 1950s, Thomas Merton was still citing the psalm as 90, but when in 1971 a distinguished German Benedictine scholar published his study of the psalm, he identified it as 91. At least in the West, and admittedly not in the Orthodox world, the phrase "Psalm 90" declined in use, and so did the distinctive readings with which it was associated: if they did not become quite extinct, basilisks were at least an endangered species.[4]

An Epitaph

Long after most learned readers had ceased to believe in the psalm's protective powers, they appreciated its core message of faith in God as ultimate refuge. For Karl Barth, the psalm was a perfect expression of absolute faith in Christ and in his victory. For the believer, that faith "rests upon the fact that the Lord Jesus Christ . . . is also his refuge, his fortress, his God: the secret place in which he dwells; the shadow under which he abides." The focus shifts from the promises of defense against diverse dangers to the staunch affirmation in the opening verses, from which every other detail follows. The one verse contains the whole in miniature.[5]

A surprising example of this theme came from the sociologist and philosopher Max Horkheimer, one of the most respected intellectuals of the twentieth century. He was a leading figure in the influential Frankfurt School, which drew heavily on Marxist theory, which is of its essence materialistic and atheist. Horkheimer had no sympathy for institutional religion, which was so often allied to repressive causes and regimes. He died in 1973, and it is striking that he chose the second verse of Psalm 91 to be inscribed upon his gravestone and that of his parents: "Denn Du Ewiger bist meine Zuversicht" (For you, Eternal One, are my refuge). Although he was anything but typical of the religious thought of his age, Max Horkheimer's connections with 91 were strong, if paradoxical. He lived through the horrors of Germany between the two world wars, and as a Jew, he was eager to escape from the new Nazi regime. Horkheimer prayed the psalm through the war and later in the grim circumstances of postwar Germany. He was also keenly aware of the experience of his mother, who faithfully prayed 91, and who successfully fled Germany for Switzerland at a time when such travel was extremely difficult for Jews. In other circumstances, that remarkable flight would undoubtedly have become part of the miraculous lore surrounding the psalm.[6]

But Horkheimer's use of the psalm did not invoke the concept of miracle. Instead, he offered a moving meditation on 91 as a perfect vision of justice, an absolute contrast with the heinous oppression and mass slaughter that characterized the twentieth century. For Horkheimer, the psalm epitomized the core message of monotheistic faith: relying totally on God and dwelling confidently within his promises. It was also a collective promise, in which "you" represented the whole body of the faithful. Somewhere, it promises, we have "a divine homeland in the face of the misery and the horror in reality." That was the refuge and the fortress. The verse he chose for the epitaph was not the very popular v. 13, which promised triumph over forces of evil and chaos. In the real world of the twentieth century, the era of Hitler, Stalin, and Mao, such a victory seemed beyond hope.[7]

Horkheimer strove to free the psalm of its traditional connotations. He made a significant choice of translation in the epitaph, with its use of *Ewiger*, "Eternal," rather than *Herr* or *Gott*, the words used in Martin Luther's translation, by far the best-known German version. In the Germany of the 1940s, Luther occupied a disturbing role as a patron saint of German nationalism and anti-Semitism. Horkheimer therefore turned to a German-Jewish translation, a tradition in which the word *Ewiger* dated back to the eighteenth century philosopher Moses Mendelssohn. Although Horkheimer did not scorn the hopes that believers place in the Christian gospels, his own citation of 91 was a reclamation of Jewish foundations, no less than a visionary assertion of faith in the future and of ultimate justice.[8]

Shadow of the Almighty

Others too found a dependable fortress in 91, without expecting immunity from harm in the present world. One influential story involved Jim Elliot, a young evangelical missionary killed in 1956, who subsequently became known as a martyr and role model who inspired generations of American Christians. In so many ways, Elliot represented an utterly different world from the sophisticated European intellectual Horkheimer, but their stories would cross in a surprising way. Elliot was one of five Americans who were attempting to evangelize the Huaorani Indians of Ecuador. The encounter proved disastrous, and all five perished. The incident was widely covered in magazines and books, the most important of which were written by Elliot's wife Elizabeth. The second of her books bore the title *Shadow of the Almighty*, which references the first verse of 91. Set against some popular interpretations of the psalm, the reference might be seen as grossly inappropriate. If Elliot and friends actively trusted in 91, placing themselves under that shadow, how could God possibly have let them suffer their fate? Where were the angels?[9]

But Elliot lived in the spirit of that psalm in another sense, letting God take absolute control of his life, wherever it might lead, even if that meant failure or death in an earthly sense. God, after all, did not spare his Son, Jesus, from a brutal death, but that in no sense meant that he abandoned him. In the words of prominent evangelical author John Piper, Elizabeth Elliot "was utterly convinced that the refuge of the people of God is not a refuge from suffering and death, but a refuge from final and ultimate defeat." The central truth of 91 was and remains God's absolute omnipotence and his overall plan, in which believers trust, even to an untimely death. Piper concludes that

> Psalm 91 means two things about the suffering of the saints. One is that *often* God amazingly delivers them physically when others around them are falling. The other is that God often wills for his children to suffer, but forbids that the suffering hurts them in the end. *Such* evil will never befall you.[10]

Other thinkers from across the religious spectrum love the psalm and preach its value but are likewise cautious about explicit promises of worldly benefit. Billy Graham, for example, was a great advocate of 91, which perfectly fitted his strong belief in angelic interventions, and he urged believers to "read and reread this beautiful Psalm." There they would find "genuine safety and security," but with no warrant that this might change their worldly circumstances or material conditions, still less their physical health.[11]

Hymning the Psalm

The psalm has inspired serious and reverent artistic compositions, some intended for cultured elites, while others have been wildly successful in reaching out to general audiences. On the elite side, in 1937, Benjamin Britten included a setting of "Whoso dwelleth under the defense of the Most High" in his sequence on angels and cosmic warfare in *The Company of Heaven*, which later evolved into a substantial cantata.[12]

Just how influential the psalm has been is camouflaged somewhat by the use of excerpts or thinly disguised adaptations not explicitly credited to the biblical source. One appears in C. S. Lewis's 1945 fantasy novel *The Great Divorce*, which like most of that author's writings has sold very widely through the decades, reaching readers who would not normally think of themselves as consumers of high theology. Lewis uses a free adaptation of the psalm in a heavenly context, as a hymn of praise. The narrator hears Bright Spirits escorting a holy Lady through the heavenly realms. They sing a hymn that is a version of our psalm, with some unsettling modernist touches:

A thousand fail to solve the problem, ten thousand choose the wrong turning: but she passes safely through. He details immortal gods to attend her: upon every road where she must travel. They take her hand at hard places: she will not stub her toes in the dark. She may walk among lions and rattlesnakes: among dinosaurs and nurseries of lionettes.

Lewis even harks back to the Bug Bible when the spirits promise that "bogies will not scare her in the dark: bullets will not frighten her in the day."[13]

The "hymn" displays multiple oddities, not least its jokey tone and its combination of high-flown rhetoric and chatty language: striking one's foot has an effect quite different from stubbing a toe. Some commentators have suggested that it is an effective pastiche of W. H. Auden. Lewis was greatly interested in the psalms in general but had little to say about 91 in his other writings, so it is curious to find it placed so significantly here. Lewis is probably harking back to Charles Williams's novel *The Place of the Lion*, which Lewis characterized as "one of the major literary events of my life": reading that book helped him decide to write fiction himself. *The Place of the Lion* not only gave special honor to 91, but even featured a modern-day dinosaur, in the form of a pterodactyl. The best explanation for Lewis's hymn is that the story in which it appears is a dream, with all the attendant inversions and distortions of reality. But it is striking to find even this odd version of a psalm in such a celestial setting, and its presence in such a popular work has exposed millions to the psalm, albeit in a strange guise.[14]

Lewis's poem has not (yet) found a place in actual church hymnals, but the psalm itself appears commonly in such contexts. In recent times, we find adaptations in hymns like "Within Your Shelter, Loving God" (1982). By far the most remarkable modern story of such a hymn is that of Fr. Michael Joncas's iconic 1976 setting, "On Eagle's Wings." The hymn was originally composed as an affirmation of faith to support a friend whose father had died suddenly. Although it draws on other sources, it is primarily a rendering of 91, and a strikingly faithful one, despite the intrusion of the extraneous "eagle" in the title:

> You need not fear the terror of the night,
> Nor the arrow that flies by day,
> Though thousands fall about you,
> Near you it shall not come.[15]

The hymn is an authentic landmark of contemporary American Christian devotion, almost an "Amazing Grace" of our own time. It is probably the most popular hymn of the post–Vatican II Catholic church in the United States, but Pentecostals have also adopted it widely, as have mainline Episcopalians and Lutherans. The "eagle" reference gives the hymn a special cachet among Native American believers. Part of its larger appeal is its lack of reference to any particular faith tradition. "On Eagle's Wings" offers a nondenominational spiritual exaltation that can be appreciated by the "spiritual but not religious." It has been translated into many languages.

The hymn is a commonly sung at Catholic funeral masses, and became associated with memorials for catastrophic events. It featured at the service following the Oklahoma City bombing of 1995. The following year, Islamist terrorists struck at U.S. personnel at Khobar, Saudi Arabia, killing nineteen and wounding many more. President Clinton attended that memorial service, which featured both a reading of 91 and a performance of "On Eagle's Wings," which was appropriate given that many of the victims were members of the U.S. Air Force. The hymn went on to become the standard anthem for the burial of victims of the September 11 terror attacks. It soon moved into general usage, which has made the words of Psalm 91 almost as familiar a feature of Catholic funerals as of Jewish events.[16] The hymn gained a still larger audience in 2020 when Joe Biden quoted it in his victory speech following the presidential election, to the delight of countless American Catholics. (He was specifically applying it in the context of victims of the coronavirus pandemic.) In turn, Biden's citation of the hymn sparked a new wave of recordings and renditions.[17]

Although "On Eagle's Wings" has few rivals in terms of mass popularity, other musical treatments have followed the psalm closely. One of the most influential is "My Sisters and Brothers (in Christ)," which was originally recorded by the African American gospel star Charles Johnson, of the Sensational Nightingales. It proclaims that "our Bible reads" that believers shall be safe against the familiar roster of perils listed in the psalm's vv. 5–6. In the 1970s, the song was often performed by the Jerry Garcia Band, as well as Maria Muldaur and other artists. The psalm has frequently proved attractive to creative musicians exploring faith and confidence in the divine, and not necessarily in a Christian context. In 1987, the first album by Sinéad O'Connor was The Lion and the Cobra, which took its title from 91. The album included an Irish-language rendering of the psalm by the vocalist

Enya. In her 2007 album *Theology*, O'Connor's "Whomsoever Dwells" was a straightforward English version of most of the psalm's text. The psalm features in Christian hip-hop, from artists such as the U.K.-based Sharyn.[18]

War and Folklore

Such repeated uses and appropriations have made Psalm 91 and its imagery very familiar indeed to believers of many levels of learning or sophistication. But beyond the uses approved by churches, 91 exercises immense vernacular appeal, often of a kind that theologians and clergy would find questionable.

As in earlier eras, 91 has been a special favorite during times of warfare, and elite critics of its use during the First World War had done little to dim its power. During the Second World War, the psalm featured in Allied propaganda. In 1942, William Wyler directed the film *Mrs. Miniver*, a moving tribute to an embattled Great Britain, which was stunningly successful in winning U.S. support for its ally: German propaganda chief Joseph Goebbels was desperately jealous of the film's manipulative power. *Mrs. Miniver* culminates with a rousing sermon in a bombed-out English church, in which the clergyman urges all to join a triumphant people's war against Nazism, but also a war in God's service. His sermon begins with a reading of Psalm 91 vv. 2–6, although with the verses oddly presented out of sequence, as the scriptwriter felt the need to improve on the biblical original. Reputedly, this scene of itself increased demand for easily portable copies of the New Testament that incorporated the psalms. The U.S. government distributed pamphlet copies of the speech text widely across occupied territories.[19]

Many Allied soldiers during this war made a point of learning by heart two key psalms appropriate for times of crisis and death—namely, 23 and 91. The words of 91 conditioned their memories of their combat experience. One of the finest memoirs of the British and Canadian bomber campaigns of these years, which proved extremely costly in lives, is titled *A Thousand Shall Fall*. And of course, the psalm was still believed to offer its supernatural protection. According to legend, 91 secured British survival during the "miracle of Dunkirk." Through the decades, a great many sermons have cited stories of soldiers whose lives were saved by bullets stopped in Bibles, commonly at the very page of 91, although the actual wars in which those tales are set evolve over time.[20]

Nor did Russians waver in their devotion to their Psalm 90. The Great Patriotic War against Hitler produced a rich crop of psalm-related stories from Soviet soldiers:

> When he went to the front, my mother gave me a leaflet with the prayer "Alive in the help of Vyshnyago" and ordered me to sew it into the tunic. I know that for many soldiers this prayer was sewn up. Someone [*sic*] in tunic, someone in lining overcoat. It was still popularly called "Living Aid" or even "Living Aid," sometimes "Soldier Aid." They knew that she works miracles—usually mothers were given a leaflet with a prayer written by hand.

One man reported how the psalm might have stopped the advance of General Guderian's German tanks on Moscow. In 1941,

> I remember all autumn talking about some Guderian: "Guderian went up to Tula; Guderian creeps up to Moscow . . . For me, a child, this word— "Guderian"—for some reason was associated with some huge snake—an asp, a basilisk, I saw such in the book.

Scarcely less dangerous were the postwar years, when every young boy had his collection of leftover grenades and other weaponry, which resulted in many lethal accidents. But the psalm again came into play:

> This aunt with a prayer sheet, wrapped in a handkerchief, sewed to my sleeveless jacket. When she washed it, she pulled off a handkerchief with a prayer, and then sewed it again. When I grew up, my aunt made me memorize prayer. I grew up in the yard, on the street, and my mother's prayer, I believe, saved me more than once.[21]

The psalm provides convenient language for framing war and its disasters as they affected civilian and resisters as much as actual combatants. Several German memoirs of the Second World War years invoke the psalm in their titles, suggesting the extreme dangers faced by people living through those events, and their need for extraordinary intervention just in order to survive. One such work, *Mama Luise*, tells the story of a family's escape from eastern Germany at the end of the Second World War; it is subtitled *Lest You Dash Your Foot Against a Stone*. The story of a Seventh-day Adventist who resisted service in the wartime German military bears the translated title *A Thousand Shall Fall*. One German Christian recorded his experiences in the Soviet Gulag Archipelago, in a book similarly titled *Ob tausend fallen*. Another example concerned Gereon Goldmann, who was about to be ordained a Catholic priest before he was drafted into the German SS, and who eventually joined the bomb plot to assassinate Hitler. His 1964 memoir of those years, which enjoyed great popularity in Catholic circles worldwide, is called *The Shadow of His Wings*. That phrase occurs in several psalms, but the reference here is usually taken to be to 91.[22]

The tradition continues to the present day. Psalm 91 materials, cards, and memorabilia were popular in Vietnam. In the decade after 2006, the Christian nonprofit Operation Bandanas distributed hundreds of thousands of camouflage-print bandanas inscribed with Psalm 91 to U.S. personnel serving in Iraq and Afghanistan. Each of these campaigns has attracted its tales of individuals and units who experienced miraculous escapes due to the psalm, commonly by daily repetition. In Iraq, we are told, one such unit was the 130th Engineer Brigade, "and all soldiers and all vehicles had a Psalm 91 card. Though often working on the front lines, not one of 6,000 plus soldiers were wounded." The brigade in question is an authentic and respected unit, which in reality suffered a number of combat deaths in Iraq.[23]

Nor are modern-day Americans alone in their myth-making. If Americans had their tales of the 130th Brigade, then Russian Christians told stories of Soviet soldiers fighting jihadis in Afghanistan in the 1980s. The mother of one officer going to the front told him to take a small icon with the psalm, and instructed him that if his situation became difficult, he should read it three times. Fighting the Afghan guerrillas, the dushmans, his force finds itself surrounded and running out of ammunition. But then he reads the prayer, "and then a miracle happened: he suddenly felt that it became very quiet, as if he had been covered by an invisible cover, or a cap." The survivors regroup and break through to safety. "After that, he believed in God and the power of prayer, read it before each sortie to the rear of the enemy, fought until the end of the war, returned home without a scratch."[24]

Wars by Other Means

In an age of popular mobilization and mass conscription, the psalm's use spread easily into civilian life in many nations, where it was very familiar to veterans, and to anyone with military aspirations. Irregular or pseudo-military uses of the psalm have become commonplace.

After the attacks of September 11, 2001, one often saw bumper stickers of U.S. flags with the words "PSALM 91" printed across them to invoke divine protection. As Brennan Breed reports, "Actor and political activist Chuck Norris urged Americans to aggressively confront Islamo-fascism, which was only possible if they would 'remember the God of 911, Psalm 91:1 that is.'" In 2003, Jim Goll of the evangelical television program *The 700 Club* outlined a Homeland Security Prayer Initiative, which would involve praying 91 every day for ninety-one days over the United States and Israel:

> We will call forth a Holy Spirit Border Patrol guard of angelic protection all around the entrances of our nation—our seaports, airports, landmarks, large public gatherings, waterways and sources, military installations. . . . It is the Lord Who guards the city!

Beyond the strictly military realm, 91 has been a mainstay of evangelical movements to promote Christian manhood, and of "prayer warrior" groups. The psalm has a vigorous life among athletes.[25]

Since early times, the psalm has attracted many believers who find themselves incarcerated, whether as overt political prisoners, like Thomas More, or as regular criminals who nevertheless see their confinement as an act of repression. A Qabalistic tradition recommended that reciting the psalm seventy-two times could help deliver a prisoner to freedom. In the Soviet context, Pasternak notes that the psalm enjoyed new popularity during the Stalinist purges of the 1930s, when "arrested people started sewing it into their clothing, and convicts in prison repeated it to themselves when they were summoned to the investigators for night interrogations." As we will see, these carceral uses have become very prominent in Global South contexts, over and above military activities.[26]

A distinct corpus of legends describes the benefits befalling those righteous individuals held captive by evil forces but who secure release by invoking the psalm. One oft-reported story stems from Corrie ten Boom, whose courage in sheltering Jews in the wartime Netherlands gave her a venerated place in evangelical popular culture, alongside martyrs like Jim Elliot. Her deeds resulted in the arrest and imprisonment of her family, and her aged father died in captivity, after placing himself under the protection of 91. Corrie ten Boom herself cited the psalm as one of her favorite scriptures, and its first verse is usually cited as the source of the title of her best-selling book, *The Hiding Place*. Among other stories, she reports how a British prisoner of war escaped a German camp by invoking 91 and asserting loudly that he was under the protection of the Most High. The guards reportedly understood him as stating that he was serving Hitler, whom they knew under that title, so they let him pass. There is a theological lesson here, in that the Germans are deceived into attributing that "highest" status to a mere man, which is idolatrous, while victory belongs to the one who recognizes that the term applies only to God. Although the tale is generally quoted as factual—how could the saintly Corrie ten Boom have invented a falsehood?—it is pure fable. But in its sense of permitting the individual to pass through dangers unscathed, it epitomizes so much of the psalm's lore in the context of prisons and camps. Incidentally, evangelical media attached inordinate significance to the fact that ten Boom died at the precise age of ninety-one.[27]

In the United States, one of the text's odder deployments came in 1984, when a group of neo-Nazis began a terrorist campaign in California, beginning with a successful raid on a Brink's armored truck. The group, who described themselves as The Order, saw themselves as launching a general war against a Jewish-dominated United States. After completing all their material preparations for the Brink's attack, the dozen or so terrorists invoked spiritual protection with a devout collective recitation of our psalm. Beyond its military context, the militants had learned this usage from the psalm's popularity in prison settings, of which some had recent experience. There is a certain grim circularity in this story, as a militant in this same larger Order campaign carried out murders for which he was eventually executed in 1995, on the same day as the Oklahoma City bomb attack. Almost certainly, that atrocity was committed both to commemorate and avenge that execution. And as we have seen, it was the mourning for the victims of the attack that so enhanced the popularity of "On Eagle's Wings."[28]

Spiritual Combat, Once More

However skeptically devils and demons might be viewed by liberal and mainline Christians, belief in such supernatural beings is very much alive in the contemporary West, and so is the accompanying worldview that is reflected in 91. In 1941, theologian Rudolf Bultmann famously wrote, "It is impossible to use the electric light and the wireless and to avail ourselves of modern medical and surgical discoveries, and at the same time to believe in the New Testament world of daemons and spirits." Yet a belief in just such spiritual enemies has been a powerful current in modern Christianity, and in some of the most technologically advanced nations. Such ideas found a renewed warrant in the respectable and mainstream writings of C. S. Lewis, and especially of his *The Screwtape Letters* (1942). But Lewis's fiction foreshadowed a much larger and less critical later literature, and themes of exorcism, possession, and "deliverance" enjoyed a huge vogue in the 1970s. This owed much to popular culture phenomena such as the 1973 film *The Exorcist* and its many imitators.[29]

The new interest in demons sparked a controversial revival of exorcism among Catholics. Their rituals continue to draw on familiar texts derived from 91, directly following the *Rituale Romanorum* of the seventeenth century. As in those earlier times, the priest prays to Christ, "who gave to your holy apostles the power to tramp underfoot serpents and scorpions." He then addresses the demon: "Therefore, I adjure you, profligate dragon, in the name of the spotless Lamb, who has trodden down the asp and the basilisk, and overcome the lion and the dragon, to depart from this man."[30]

It was especially the charismatics and evangelicals who most zealously adopted the old-new ideas, and who turned wholeheartedly to 91 and its promises. Ever since the Pentecostal movement arose in the early twentieth century, its ministers and missionaries had often expressed a deeply literal faith in the protective powers of 91 against plagues and diseases, and they made ambitious claims about its effectiveness. That appeal easily segued into the later era of deliverance. The influential charismatic leader Derek Prince, a pioneer of such ministries, was a special advocate for 91 as "the Atomic Age Psalm." Evangelical publishers enjoyed enormous success with books depicting spiritual warfare in modern-day settings, with literal demons combated by angels, who in turn were assisted by the powers of believers' prayers, of "prayer warriors." Some landmark best-sellers included Don Basham's *Deliver Us from Evil* (1972), *Pigs in the Parlor*, by Frank and Ida Mae Hammond (1973), and Mark Bubeck's *The Adversary* (1975). Although Billy Graham did not endorse the deliverance theme in anything like the same way, he argued for the extensive involvement of angels in the everyday life of Christians in his 1975 book *Angels: God's Secret Agents*. The commercial success of such works was amazing—*Pigs in the Parlor* alone has sold one and a half million copies in a dozen languages—and all made frequent allusion to 91. Through the 1980s and 1990s, such ideas reached vast audiences through the writings of Frank Peretti, whose books have sold fifteen million copies worldwide. Satanic and demonic elements are often prominent in end-times speculations, including the novels of Jerry Jenkins and Tim LaHaye. Jenkins, incidentally, describes the first two verses of 91 as his favorite scripture.[31]

Warriors of Prayer

The early 1990s was a fruitful time for books like this, such as Tom White's *The Believer's Guide to Spiritual Warfare* (1990) and Timothy Warner's *Spiritual Warfare* (1991). The chronology should be noted, following from the decisive and low-casualty victory in the brief Gulf War against Iraq in 1991. That did much to reduce the deep suspicion of military rhetoric arising from the Vietnam War, as combat-related language and metaphor became respectable once more in American culture. These spiritual warfare themes found a home in the flourishing ministries and megachurches that are collectively known as the New Apostolic Reformation, which emerged in the 1990s as a third wave of the charismatic revival. One visible leader and theoretician of that movement, and a staunch advocate of spiritual warfare against demons, was C. Peter Wagner. Through the 1990s, Wagner published his series of Prayer Warrior books, all with military-sounding titles, including *Engaging the Enemy*, *Warfare Prayer*, *Prayer Shield*, and *Confronting the Powers*.[32]

Since that point, spiritual combat has usually been visualized in strongly material and territorial terms: witness the idea of the Holy Spirit Border Patrol. Our psalm features frequently as a scripture recommended for the practice of prayerwalking, in which believers seek to bring God's presence to places considered open to spiritual peril. This might include a school or home, or else a location associated with some form of evil, such as drug abuse or violence. Grave centers of potential evil are identified through detailed research, through "spiritual mapping." Believers seek to erect spiritual defenses against such menaces, and ideally to purge them.[33]

Popular authors in the spiritual warfare genre include Chuck D. Pierce and Rebecca Wagner Sytsema, author of *The Spiritual Warfare Handbook* (Rebecca is the daughter of C. Peter Wagner). In a 1999 text, *Ridding Your Home of Spiritual Darkness*, the authors recommend creating a suitably spiritual atmosphere through playing spiritual music and reading scriptures in affected rooms within the house. At that point, the warrior is told to "plead the blood of Jesus over yourself, your family, your animals, and your property," and then "pray Psalm 91 out loud."[34]

Texas-based Peggy Joyce Ruth has made 91 the basis of extensive ministries and a sizable publishing enterprise. Through her books, such as *Psalm 91: God's Umbrella of Protection*, devotees can learn how to pray the psalm and discover its countless benefits. A blog quotes numerous testimonies citing relief and release from afflictions and complaints ranging from shyness, drug abuse, and depression, to natural disasters. One story grows out of the catastrophic Hurricane Andrew that ravaged southern U.S. states in 1992. Reportedly, one family that prayed 91 experienced a miraculous escape:

> Their property looked like an oasis in the desert and soon became like a tourist attraction. Neighbors were appalled when they saw the damage in the neighborhood compared to their home. One man was suspicious and said, "you've been praying again, haven't you?" Pat explained that she had walked the property and prayed Psalm 91. He asked her to extend her prayer borders!

Ruth also offers a book titled *Psalm 91 for Mothers*, and materials for athletes. Her site reports that half a million copies of the military edition of her Psalm 91 book have been sent to U.S. forces serving in Iraq and Afghanistan.[35]

Naming and Claiming

A potent phenomenon in modern Christianity is the Prosperity Gospel, the idea that God will supply material rewards of health and wealth to his faithful believers. Usually, that faith is to be expressed in financial donations to a ministry, in return for which the believer is promised a tenfold or hundredfold return in their own lives. Its most common scriptural justification is a verse in Malachi promising that if a person properly pays tithe, God will "open you the windows of heaven, and pour you out a blessing, that there shall not be room enough to receive it." But Psalm 91 occupies a special place in this movement, as an unequivocal statement of its core doctrines. According to the teaching, which is also known as the Word of Faith movement, the divine promises already exist without further supplication: the believer just has to "name it and claim it."[36] The objections to such doctrines are clear enough, in potentially allowing cynical pastors to exploit simple followers for their own profit. In the context of 91, Prosperity teachings flatly ignore the arguments and insights arising from centuries of debate about its promises, and what we have termed the "facts of life" argument that the virtuous and pious genuinely do suffer. But whatever the qualms, practical or theological, that gospel has proved wildly popular worldwide.[37]

One prominent exponent of Prosperity teachings is Texas-based evangelist Kenneth Copeland, who is associated with the New Apostolic Reformation. Copeland is the center of a very substantial transnational ministry, KCM (he has a reputed fortune of half a billion dollars). The virtues of praying Psalm 91 are regularly stressed on the Copeland website, particularly the paraphrased and modernized version known as the "personalized declaration." As we are told, "Don't wait until you're faced with trouble to declare protection over your life. Use this personalized declaration of Psalm 91 to unleash the power of God's protection in your life." But the Copeland ministry stresses that the individual is not asking or petitioning God for anything. Rather, this is a declaration: "When you pray, you can declare scriptures in faith. You don't have to ask if it is God's will to protect you—His Word already says so!"[38]

The rewards of praying 91, says the ministry, are evident:

In 2019, 2,320 Partners were contacted by our team in the middle of disasters, and only 12 reported damage. In 2020, 1,256 were contacted and only six reported damage. By praying out God's promises of protection and applying the principles of faith they have learned from KCM, our Partners have been supernaturally covered in the anointing during times of disaster—proving the Word works for anyone who will use it. This means it will work for you, too, in the midst of anything the devil tries to do— including pandemics, civil unrest, fires and hurricanes, to name just a few![39]

Quotes from 91 frame the detailed advice that believers are offered on entering a new home in order to promote a spiritual atmosphere, with all the protections that implies. Among other things, this means surrounding oneself with religious audio (worship music and Bible reading) and watching the appropriate evangelistic television. Anointing the house with oil is also desirable, as is invoking angels with the words cited at the beginning of this chapter.[40]

Although the Copeland ministry is especially visible, similar teachings are readily found online. Richard Roberts, son of the legendary evangelist Oral Roberts, declares that

God has put the gift of His divine protection in His Word, but it's up to us to receive it and walk in it. The promises of God found in Psalm 91 are available for everyone. When your spirit has been attacked with fear, worry, poverty, sin, sickness or lack, go to the Word of God for His spiritual answers.[41]

Kenneth Hagin Ministries stress that "we need to claim the 91st Psalm over our families." We note the language: we are not petitioning for anything, but rather are *claiming* what is already and infallibly promised. Joel Osteen emphasizes the act of claiming through explicitly saying the words. Yes, he says, the psalm offers promises, but there is a vital condition, in the act of saying:

> It doesn't say if you believe He's your refuge, if you think He's your shield. Something supernatural happens when you say it. "God, I want to thank You that You're my protector. Thank You that You're my provider, my healer, my way maker. Thank You that You're bigger than what I'm facing. Thank You that You're bringing my dreams to pass." When you say it, the Creator of the Universe goes to work.[42]

Creflo Dollar recommends beginning each day with a recitation of 91, to be assured of safety and well-being. One prominent Prosperity teacher is Paula White-Cain, whose role as a leading advocate of President Donald Trump attracted controversy. She invites believers to support her efforts: "Maybe you'd like to sow a $91 seed, putting your faith with Psalm 91."[43]

Pandemic and Plague, Revisited

The coronavirus pandemic that began in 2020 offered potent new grounds for seeking protection and drew special attention to 91. Many Christians with little or no exposure to Prosperity teachings sought solace and protection in the scriptures, and very soon found the psalm's reassuring words. One evangelical website aptly notes, with only a little hyperbole, "Most of us remember when Covid-19 initially hit and how almost every church and Christian was reciting, praying, and faithfully standing on the scripture in Psalm 91." When Biden recited "On Eagle's Wings" in November 2020, he was specifically seeking to comfort those who had lost relatives to the pandemic. A great many churches and ministries of all denominational shades featured 91 prominently in their online materials.[44]

Several ingenious writers and manufacturers noted a numerical coincidence, as they juxtaposed Psalm 91 with COVID-19—what some termed a "palindromic confrontation" of 91 versus 19. Meanwhile, the rich array of psalm-related objects, amulets, and memorabilia (of which more shortly) now placed far more emphasis on the specific words about plague. The psalm text, in whole or in part, became a fixture on face masks, sometimes accompanied by images of warrior angels. But that mask usage involved a degree of irony. As in earlier times, the psalm inspired a variety of reactions, from those who believed firmly in the psalm's promises to others who took comfort in the knowledge of God's ultimate plan. Psalm 91 became a regular proof text for those conservative believers who rejected mask wearing and asserted their right to depend directly on spiritual defenses. Similar attitudes reinforced the determination of those who wished to keep their places of worship open and operating through the pandemic, despite risks of spreading infection.[45]

The Prosperity ministries themselves made much of the psalm, and of the language of plague and disease that had hitherto been chiefly metaphorical. Kenneth Copeland earned some notoriety for minimizing the practical impact of the disease. Among other resources, his website naturally recommended faithful recitation of the personalized version of 91. As a critic notes of the pastors affiliated with the New Apostolic Reformation, "They claim that 'prophetic proclamation'—especially the proclamation of Psalm 91—is the key to breaking the grip of coronavirus and launching a worldwide revival." The virus crisis, and the role of 91, became a special theme for Peggy Joyce Ruth. In New Zealand, popular pastor Brian Tamaki assured his listeners that "for Bible-believing, born-again Christians who pay their tithes, God assures them protection from the virus in Psalm 91. . . . You will not fear the terror of night, nor the arrow that flies by day, nor the pestilence that stalks in the darkness, nor the plague that destroys at midday. We needn't fear it." When President Donald Trump was himself diagnosed with COVID, Steve Shultz of the Elijah List urged followers to "lift up a prayer shield right now over President Trump, his family and staff. We decree Psalm 91!"[46]

But a great many believers, including evangelicals and charismatics, rejected any simplistic clutching for absolute protection. During the fraught months of early and mid-2020, congregational websites became the setting for thoughtful debates over such fundamental issues as the nature and purpose of prayer, the special protections accorded to believers (or the lack of them), and quite far-reaching questions of theodicy. Classic statements of

Christian attitudes to plague, such as those of Luther and Osiander, were widely reproduced online, and at every stage references to 91 were unavoidable. Of course, the easily visible materials online are only the tip of a larger iceberg of discussions featuring in sermons and small group discussions, most of which would not become easily available to a wider public.

So numerous were the statements and meditations on this theme, all the essays and Bible studies, that it is invidious to focus on particular ones. In themselves, no single example might have been distinctive or influential—they were the product of one middling-size church in Georgia, or a megachurch in Illinois, or even a single pastor—but the overall effect for any consumer seeking enlightenment online was overwhelming. It was as if the lengthy early modern debates over plague and the psalm were recapitulated in the novel setting of the internet, and decades of such controversy distilled into a few months. Also as in earlier times, writers often harked back to the wilderness scenes in the gospels, noting how the Devil himself had quoted the psalm, and that any religion based on hopes of easy miracles was a counterfeit. While not attacking the psalm, such critiques sought to discredit mechanical or miraculous interpretations.

Text and Object

Even before its recent celebrity appearance in the pandemic crisis, Psalm 91 occupied a remarkable role in religious culture via material objects through which believers seek refuge from evils of various kinds. That devotion has produced a dazzling range of items, on a scale paralleled by few other scriptural texts. Some are moving, but many constitute religious kitsch at its most flamboyant. It would scarcely be possible to give a comprehensive catalogue of such materials, or to assess the volume in which they circulate, but a quick and nonscientific survey of Google Images is instructive. We find the psalm's text in whole or in part on jewelry (rings and pendants), yard signs, bumper stickers, wall decals, car decals, T-shirts, baby clothing, stickers, mousepads, and tattoos. In theory, a believer could live a whole Psalm 91 lifestyle, not to mention pursuing a lively collecting hobby. An equivalent search in other languages is just as rewarding. The term "Salmo 91" reveals a comparable range of Spanish- and Portuguese-language materials.

The choice of text to be displayed on such objects varies widely. As in ancient times, the first verse is popular, but so is v. 11, the promise of angelic guardianship, and most parts of the psalm can be found in some context. Items inscribed simply with the words "Psalm 91" are commonplace, as if the mere name recapitulates the whole. Although tattoos naturally favor short extracts, such as v. 11, some enthusiasts have had the entire psalm tattooed on their bodies. Such uses are very popular in prison contexts and among gang members. Beyond the simple text, material objects might include further prayers or slogans, including "This house protected by Psalm 91," "Come in from the storm. Shelter in place in God," and "The psalm of protection." Recalling the use of 911 as the standard number for emergency calls, another poster or placard invokes "the Christian emergency psalm."

Little can be said about the active religious involvement of those who purchase and display such items. Quite probably, many would fit into the category of "Nones," those who reject any religious affiliation while not necessarily forsaking supernatural beliefs as such. Although the majority of consumers of such merchandise are presumably Christian by background, Jewish-oriented items also circulate on a significant scale. The psalm plays a major role in Orthodox Jewish popular culture, in which it is usually known as the Yosheiv BeSeiser (or Yoshev BeSeter, "He that dwelleth in the secret place"). It is esteemed as a source of protection, as well as of *bitachon* (trust) in the divine. Some films have depicted the psalm in the context of specifically Jewish exorcism and demon-fighting, in striking contrast to the robustly Catholic environment of the original *Exorcist*. Psalm 91 features prominently in such films as *The Unborn* (2009) and *The Possession* (2012), both of which depict struggles against the Jewish folklore figure of the dybbuk.[47]

Among material objects, psalm texts in Hebrew might be targeted toward Jews but would also appeal to Christians who seek the greater authenticity of the original words. Definitely Jewish are the mezuzoth accompanied by a psalm verse, and a related car mezuzah is available. The upsurge of popular "Kabbalah" movements has also revived interest in such amulets, among Jews but also among many interested non-Jews.47

The Psalm as Magic

Again harking back to the psalm's earliest history, the question raised by such objects involves the intersection of the user, and when piety shades into superstition or outright magic. What exactly does it mean for a person to wear the psalm's words on a face mask? Is it a prayer or a talisman? In some

Prosperity teachings, for instance, actual spoken words are needed to spur God into protective action, and we are explicitly told that interior faith is not sufficient for this purpose. In other lessons, power lies in specific words, spoken correctly, and according to ritual formulae. Depending on the source, the psalm is to be repeated ninety-one times, or ninety-nine times, or on ninety-one successive days. It is difficult to avoid applying the magical label to such practices. A "Psalm 91 7 Day Hoodoo Ritual Candle" available online retails for $23.27 and is advertised to "Keep You Safe from Disease, Illness, Unfortunate Accidents, Protect Your Health."[48]

In some instances, the protective theme notionally remains within a main-stream Christian framework. While examples can be produced from any and all denominations, some Orthodox uses stand out. As we have seen, the psalm has a long-standing popularity in Russian Orthodoxy, in which it has often inspired superb liturgical settings. One extensive website makes the psalm the foundation of an intense neo-medieval spirituality, as devotees are urged to repeat the psalm at least forty times, commemorating the number of Jesus's days in the wilderness. Recalling the passage we encountered from *Dr. Zhivago*, the author insists that the psalm is to be read in Church Slavonic rather than in modern Russian translation.[49]

In words that could have come from the Egypt of the fifth century, we are told how vital it is to keep the psalm physically close to one's person:

> Rewrite the text on paper, leather or fabric—any natural material. The obtained amulet should be worn with the body—in the pocket of the underwear, in underwear (for example, in bras there are often pockets for push-ups—you can stuff it there), you can sew it on to the lining. In general, decide for yourself how to make the text of the Psalm always with you, preferably with the body. (That is, not in a bag somewhere nearby. Although even this option is better than not defending yourself).[50]

The text goes on to illustrate the psalm's power through typical tales of healing and rescue.

Psalm 91 enjoys immense popularity in the Global South, in regions where Christianity is a relatively new growth. Viewing that popularity, it might be tempting to assume that this reflects the simple or even backward character of religious belief in societies where old animist religions have left such a strong inheritance, and where belief in demons and exorcism still prevails. As time goes by, Westerners might think, such benighted societies will evolve to our own level of spiritual maturity. But such a condescending approach is utterly contradicted by the wide and superstitious manifestations that are so prevalent in Western societies, and in lands where Christianity can now look back over a millennium and more of evolution and growth. Whether in the Global South or North, our psalm continues to offer irresistible attractions to millions who may or may not accept formal religious dogmas and structures. Such an appeal is likely to survive even if religious institutions themselves falter and fail.

10

Under His Wings Shalt Thou Trust

Global South Readings of Psalm 91

> She would not have survived the genocide had a friend not given her a tiny book of Psalms on the eve of the killing and urged her to read Psalm 91. . . . She held the book open over her heart as killers searched a room where she stood in plain sight and could not see her, and again as a guard at a roadblock raised a machete over her head that somehow never fell. "There is no word for that but miracle."[1]
>
> —Agathe Rumanyika, 2004

In 1994, a long-running conflict between two ethnic groups in the Central African nation of Rwanda reached an appalling climax. The Hutu people began a genocidal campaign against the Tutsi, which ultimately claimed some 800,000 lives. Both communities contained large proportions of self-described Christians, and both used biblical and religious language to frame and comprehend the carnage. Indeed, some of the worst massacres occurred in and around churches and church properties. Agathe Rumanyika, a Tutsi and then a Catholic, believed that she owed her preservation to 91. As in all such reports, we ask the obvious theological question: why did the miraculous preservation of one person not extend to the many equally innocent and faithful who perished at the same time?[2]

Over the past century, one of the most important stories in the development of Christianity has been the very rapid expansion of numbers in the Global South, especially in Africa, but also in Asia. By midcentury, Africa should be in numerical terms by far the largest Christian continent. Meanwhile, new Protestant and Pentecostal churches have boomed in Latin America. Often, those churches draw heavily on U.S. styles of worship and praise music, and megachurches on the familiar U.S. model have proliferated around the world. Throughout these new and emerging congregations, many

He Will Save You from the Deadly Pestilence. Philip Jenkins, Oxford University Press. © Oxford University Press 2023.
DOI: 10.1093/oso/9780197605646.003.0010

millions of believers have made a new encounter with the Bible and begun a love affair with scripture comparable to those of Europeans during the Reformation five centuries ago. Just like those earlier generations, Christians in the Global South today turn with hope and excitement to Psalm 91 and use it in ways that would have been immediately comprehensible to their predecessors through the millennia. Then as now, they find ways of singing and commemorating it in daily life.[3]

That Christian expansion is of course part of a larger globalization, but that term does not just imply a spread of global North or "Western" values. Rather, we see a process of cross-fertilization, as different parts of the world influence others from which they had previously been remote. As in the case of Psalm 91, beliefs and practices have flowed northward as well as southward.

Ancient and Modern

One of the finest scholars of modern global or world Christianity is Andrew Walls, who stresses the resemblance of contemporary African practice to that of the very early church, particularly in Egypt. In that sense, the ancient church of that part of the African continent is enjoying a kind of resurgence, rather than a wholly new birth. Walls shows the many analogies between an ancient Christian monastic founder like St. Antony and modern-day African healers and exorcists, who are no less focused on combatting what they see as a threatening demonic realm. In both eras too, spiritual warriors turn to the same array of scriptures, especially to 91, and to its echo in Luke 10:19. Modern churches find a powerful appeal in the promise of protection from spiritual evil.[4]

The psalm's spiritual or demonic elements have long given 91 a special appeal for African believers. As far back as 1974, the psalm was the subject of a pioneering exercise in understanding distinctively African readings of the Bible, in this case in a study from Malawi. A British cleric, F. H. Welshman, asked a range of local respondents to comment on the psalm and how it resonated with their own society and its worldview. Repeatedly, Welshman was struck by the many analogies between modern-day Africa and the ancient Hebrew society that originally produced the psalm. Demons of various kinds were well known in the Malawian context, with an abundance and diversity that closely recalled the ancient Near East. Several verses generated detailed discussion of modern-day African witchcraft beliefs and practices, including the witch-hunts and purges that might be carried out by ritual specialists or *nganga*, what the missionaries termed "witch-doctors." Welshman hoped that this study might offer lessons for pastoral practice and evangelization:

> In Psalm 91 the Psalmist is assuring the people of his day that the way to be safe from demons and witchcraft is not to trust in magic or charms but to trust in God. Today in Malawi, among "weak" Christians, or non-Christians with a similar background and in similar situations, this is still the Christian message. . . . [T]he Christian faith proclaims that only trust in God can counter-act the assault of evil in the form of witchcraft, and sorcery.

But the author was overly optimistic in hoping that such threats would fade rapidly with the spread of Christianity and would be only of concern to "weak" believers. Both witches and demons persisted mightily, and 91 became a powerful remedy against them. The psalm has indeed become a regular feature of the very amulets and charms that he was condemning.[5]

Beyond the resemblances of worldview, those ancient and modern societies experience many similar dangers and stress in life, crises of disease and violence, and disasters both human-driven and natural. Addressing the dilemma of why God would permit his faithful servants to suffer untimely death, modern African Christians have no need to resort to ancient stories of martyrdom in the primitive church, but can readily point to strictly contemporary examples. They cite individuals killed by evil dictatorships, such as Archbishop Janani Luwum, murdered by Idi Amin in 1977, or Christian clergy subsequently killed by Muslims in Nigeria.[6]

At least among elites, nineteenth-century Europeans and North Americans moved away from the reliance on supernatural protection from disease and turned instead to the growing expertise available from modern scientific medicine. Such options are not available to most modern-day Africans, who suffer from a wide range of deadly diseases yet have little access to advanced medicine. Naturally, they turn to the Bible, and especially (if not exclusively) to 91; the psalm found renewed audiences as the coronavirus spread during 2020. In Ghana, clergy issued urgent statements to combine worldly responses with spiritual weapons including 91. One Ghanaian cleric was "encouraged by the definition someone gave to COVID-19 when he reversed it to read Psalm 91 *Destroys Influenza Virus Outbreak Completely*."[7] As in the ancient Near East, the psalm's reference to deadly serpents has an additional power in tropical regions where snakes and other deadly creatures are a far more familiar quantity than in the North, giving immediate relevance to the comparison with diabolical forces.

Nigeria's Psalm

Just how ubiquitous the psalm is in African life is evident from the nation of Nigeria, where examples and case studies are so readily found. Partly that reflects the solid hold that the psalm has on religious matters in that country, but it is also because opinions can readily be encountered through the country's publishing industry and its very lively internet culture. Although the country is in no sense typical of West Africa, to say nothing of Black Africa as a whole, much of what we find here is more broadly applicable. Numbers alone make Nigeria a critical case study. Since 1900, the number of Nigerian Christians has risen from 100,000 to 100 million, and that number could double by midcentury. By that point, that would place Nigeria among the world's three or four leading Christian nations, as measured simply by population.[8]

Nigerian scholars and writers often stress the significance of 91 and its contemporary relevance. Sunday O. Sangotunde describes how ordinary Christians find the evils described in 91 represent a near-documentary catalog of the ills facing Nigerians in an age of disease, violent crime, and the Islamist terrorism of the Boko Haram movement. Accordingly,

> Psalm 91 is very relevant and familiar to us in Nigeria; and particularly, in Yoruba land. This may be the reason why it is used as inscription on motor vehicle such as "Allahu lakuwata" which means "God is my refuge" or simply "Psalm 91." The undeniable presence of evils, disasters, diseases, attacks from the evil forces and enemies in Yoruba society has made this Psalm to be very familiar to the general situations of safety and well being in Yoruba land, Nigeria in particular and Africa in general.[9]

The psalm is popular among churches oriented to faith healing, such as the Nigerian-founded Aladura movement, but it also has wide currency across the denominational spectrum. The psalm has been much to the fore at times of epidemic disease, including the Ebola that hit West Africa in 2014 and the more recent coronavirus. One contribution to discussions of coronavirus appeared in the *Christian Journal for Global Health*, in which an article published in 2020 stressed the assurance of 91 "that those who receive the lordship of Christ will escape the wrath of God which transcends our present experience." One of the coauthors is an ordained minister in the Redeemed Christian Church of God, a booming church with its roots in the Aladura. Quite apart from times of evident crisis, preachers pray the psalm in daily struggles against spiritual evil, in a society where belief in witchcraft and ancestral curses remains widespread. Many churches recommend it to believers for all manner of special occasions, as well as for travel.[10]

As in the United States, the psalm has given birth to a sizable industry in publishing. Pastor Daniel Okpara, of Lagos's Shining Light Christian Centre, is the author of *Psalm 91: His Secret Place, His Shadow, and the Mystery of His Protection*. As his book promises, "the Psalm contains hidden messages that when understood makes it work, whether confessed or not." Grace K. R. Messenger uses the psalm as the basis of a children's novel, *Keena and the Sword* (2020), an allegorical tale of a brave little girl who uses 91 to defeat a series of dangers and menaces. *Psalm 91* is the title of a popular production from Nigeria's vigorous evangelical film industry, and of course it depicts struggles between holy pastors and the demonically possessed. The psalm features frequently in the gospel music that is so central a part of African Christian culture and has spread worldwide through migration. One elaborate setting is by Henry Nwosu, a Nigerian artist and evangelist based in Russia.[11]

Of Witchcraft and Prosperity

Other uses of the prayer might be controversial for traditional-minded observers, although they indubitably have deep historical roots. The evangelist Joshua Orekhle maintains a substantial presence on the internet and especially YouTube. "Evangelist Joshua" focuses on the surprisingly wide field of Christian dream interpretation. Inevitably, given the perils and strange circumstances of nighttime and darkness, he makes 91 a centerpiece of his ministry. In Evangelist Joshua's words, it is "one of the powerful scriptures against night raiders, spiritual attacks and prayers that guarantee a peaceful sleep . . . Psalm 91 is the answer to so many people night prayers before bedtime." He follows with a detailed encomium of the virtues of 91, which "makes you untouchable by the enemy . . . it goes to the heaven to order the angels to protect you . . . it gives you peace of mind and guarantee your victory." Other more detailed supplications grow out of the 91 framework:

> Any material taken from my body and now placed on a witchcraft altar, be roasted by the fire of God, in Jesus name.
> Any drop of my blood sucked by any witch, be vomited now, in the name of Jesus.
> Any part of me shared out amongst household village witches, I recover you, in the name of Jesus.[12]

Whether or not a believer accepts the full panoply of witchcraft beliefs, many Christians fully accept the psalm's talismanic value. As the distinguished Bible scholar David Adamo notes, 91 "is read repeatedly, memorized and chanted, written in parchment, worn and put under the pillow or hanged at the four corners of the house for divine miracle of protection."[13]

The psalm often serves as a magical or ritual item. At first glance, the Rwandan woman reporting her survival amidst the genocide found amazing power in the material text, which supplies a kind of cloak of invisibility. Recommendations for its regular use often give special conditions for enhancing its power through ritual actions, such as praying the psalm for ninety-one days. Such uses in turn feed into the ever-evolving mythology of the psalm and the wonders it can achieve.

Psalm 91 is integral to the Prosperity Gospel teaching that originated in the United States but which has gained a mass audience in Nigeria. As a pathway to prosperity and success, it has even acquired a corporate dimension. To take one example, a company called Psalm 91 Properties Nigeria handles upscale property acquisitions, with the assurance that "long life and satisfaction is guaranteed when you patronize us." By no means only in Nigeria, "Psalm 91" appears as a well-known name for businesses large and small. In Uganda, we find it applied to fisheries and fish stores, to car rental firms and apartment blocks.[14]

Decolonization

At first sight, the problems with using the psalm in such ways are manifest, but the reshaping of Christianity in modern times casts real doubt on that familiar category of "superstition." I have cited the Nigerian scholar David

T. Adamo, who has written extensively on the psalm in an African context, and on the process of decolonizing the text. That decolonization involves a direct challenge to some basic beliefs of the Euro-American Enlightenment. Adamo takes many of the readings and functions of 91 that the West commonly thinks of as superstitious or distasteful, and unapologetically asserts their authentic religious content.[15]

As he notes, with some justification, biblical scholarship shows how ancient Israelites used the Book of Psalms for "protection, healing, and success in life," in accordance with other Near Eastern cultures of the time.[16] Those three goals form the basis of what he terms an "Africentric" reading, in which 91 speaks to many current and pressing modern concerns. Rather than accusing Africans of falling into superstition, he would rather ask why Western churches moved so far away from those biblical (and Patristic) roots.

As Adamo notes, the fundamental African beliefs in witchcraft, evil spirits, and ancestral curses familiar from Welshman's work demanded many practical forms of spiritual defense. Although Western missionaries had scorned such traditional approaches, with their charms and incantations, they had not recommended efficient Christian replacements. Native believers thus evolved their own, and turned happily to 91. He quotes many religious leaders and modern prophets who have appropriated 91 for protective purposes, and also for the healing work that is viewed so differently from Western norms.[17]

Adamo's conclusion is lavish in its praise of the psalm, which almost becomes an epitome of the Christian worldview:

> To many of the Euro-American scholars, Ps 91 is an eloquent poem on the security of a person who trusts on Yahweh, but to the majority of Africentric biblical scholars and ordinary readers it is more than a poem, it is also an *incantation*, and *talisman* that God has given for divine protection, healing and success. Among the majority of African biblical scholars and ordinary readers, Ps 91 is a covenant, that is, a spiritual contract during difficult days. There is a uniqueness in Ps 91 because there are many promises of protection throughout the Bible, but in Ps 91 all the promises seem to be brought together in one collection and forming a covenant.[18]

Adamo uses the words "amulet" and "talisman" without any of the negative connotations that would commonly be found in mainstream Western discussions.

The Psalm in Asia

Although he offers an "Africentric" reading, Adamo freely admits that his examples are chiefly drawn from Nigeria, and specifically from the Yoruba people, rather than any larger sampling of African societies. Nor can comments derived from Africa necessarily be applied to the amorphous category of the Global South, which comprehends so many different societies and such radically different levels of wealth and poverty. But the "global" terminology is useful in that new and emerging churches across the three southern continents actually do have enough features in common to make some generalization possible. Of itself, the fact of newness involves a fresh encounter with scripture, without the interpretive baggage that has built up in the West, and often these societies have a long familiarity with spirit worlds not unlike those of West Africa. Adamo's categories—protection, healing, and success—are useful for understanding the psalm's role not just in Nigerian life, but across much of the Global South.

Asian Christians turn to the psalm as readily as do Africans, and the phrase "I pray Psalm 91" over a particular city or nation has become a natural reflex to disasters, including both natural calamities and violent political struggles. In such instances, what matters is not that an outside observer believes stories of miraculous interventions, but that the participants themselves do, and as these tales are recounted, they swiftly join the evolving mythology.

Asia's only nation with a heavily Christian majority is the Philippines, where a massive popular revolt against the dictatorship of Ferdinand Marcos in 1986 marked a decisive political turning point in the history of the region. Again, Psalm 91 was (reportedly) at the heart of the struggle, to the point of entering the country's political/religious mythology. Supported by the Catholic church, large portions of the armed forces abandoned the government cause to side with the rebels, but the fear was that enough of the military might remain loyal to precipitate a bloody civil war. The moment of greatest danger came when attack helicopters approached rebel positions held by two key generals. As one of those officers, Honesto Isleta, later reported, he had been praying 91, and most fervently v. 5, against the arrow that flies by day: "Five minutes later, the helicopters put down without attacking, effectively ending the last possibility of civil war." Isleta found subsequently that his fellow commander, Fidel Ramos, "had been praying the same psalm at the very same time." Ramos himself went on to serve as the country's president, head of a state with almost eighty million people, and thus a very significant figure in the politics of the region. It was therefore striking to hear him speaking so openly of his trust in 91 and its role on that crucial morning. In a public address, he confirmed that "some of us sought refuge in Psalm 91 which is known to soldiers of World War I as the Protection Psalm. . . . The victorious outcome is now history, and democracy was regained."[19]

The psalm was much in evidence during the dreadful tsunami that killed some 200,000 in 2004, and was widely used in sermons and the personal testimonies of survivors. A member of a Singaporean church wrote of the miraculous preservation of his family from the tsunami that devastated his native Sri Lanka: "I assured my parents that God's favor surrounds our family and that no harm will come to us because our trust is in the blood of Jesus. My parents saw a thousand fall at their side, ten thousand at their right hand but it did NOT come near them. . . . My family became living proof of Psalm 91 in a situation that saw the deaths of tens of thousands." The psalm is just as commonly employed during the epidemics and outbreaks that have posed a much greater threat in the Global South than in North America: SARS in 2003, Ebola in Africa in 2014, and the coronavirus pandemic, which has had such a ruinous impact on South Asia and Latin America. Pakistan's belea-guered Christian minority turned to 91 with special enthusiasm during the COVID years; in Lahore, believers write the psalm's opening verse on their doorposts as an affirmation of faith, and a plea for safeguarding.[20]

Not just in Africa, Global South readings of 91 are prone to abuse and misinterpretation, with the attendant array of superstitions. Charms and amulets derived from 91 proliferate in languages spoken by many millions of Global South Christians: Tamil and Malayalam, Chinese and Korean. Some problems in interpreting the psalm arise from simple errors in translation—again, a familiar motif in the psalm's history, and a special danger at a time when the Bible is being rendered in so many diverse tongues. One startling instance was narrated by Adoniram Judson, the celebrated American mis-sionary to Burma (Myanmar). In 1835, he married the widow of a fellow missionary, an act that caused consternation to his native Burmese converts. An older native Christian quoted the scriptural promise that God would de-liver his children from the snare of the widow, but to the contrary, "he has not delivered you: you have been snared by the widow!" Consulting the local translation of 91 confirmed that the currently available rendering of v. 3 did indeed use the feminine form for the word "fowler," causing it to be read as "widow." It's a good story (and true), but it does point to a real danger in such translations. As we know from the earlier history of 91, nuances of translation can affect readings for centuries. In a South Asian context, more-over, societies need no additional reasons to discriminate against widows.[21]

The Psalm at the Edge

Also uniting the "Southern" Christian world has been the shared experience of headlong modernization, which has so often been accompanied by rapid and unplanned urbanization, as well as unprecedented mass migration ei-ther within countries or far afield. While vastly raising living standards for many, those processes have also generated social crises, reflected in slum cities, crime, and gang cultures. Often, those troubled communities are home to active churches of various shades, and to a vigorous if sometimes unorthodox Christian culture. Since the 1970s, Pentecostal and *evangélico* churches have grown spectacularly across Latin America, especially in Central American nations such as Guatemala and El Salvador, as well as in much larger southern nations. Today, Protestants of various types make up a quarter of the population of Brazil, and 15 to 20 percent in Chile, Peru, and Colombia. In each society, those newer churches exercise a broad appeal to aspiring and middle-class groups as well as to the urban poor and underclass, but it is in the sprawling cities and slums that they find a special stronghold.[22]

Throughout Latin America, the psalm is extremely popular among the marginalized, including gang members and criminals, in societies in which the spread of Pentecostalism has raised awareness of biblical texts. In part, that is an importation of U.S. customs. The civil wars that ravaged Central American nations during the 1980s caused a substantial migration to the United States, and especially the cities of California. Some younger migrants entered wholeheartedly into the subculture of violent gangs, with all their ritual and jargon, which they subsequently reimported into their original home countries. Psalm 91 was part of this package, and it is a commonplace in the tattoos that have become such a trademark of young gang members, both inside and outside prisons.

That use in tattoos is widespread across the continent. The psalm might appear as a single verse or two, or a whole text, and it is accompanied by cherished or religious-oriented objects—stars, crowns, birds (suggesting the protective wings), and soccer balls. A tattoo might include the simple title "Psalm 91" juxtaposed with an inspiring phrase from another text, such as the Latin acronym VDMA, *Verbum Domini manet in aeternum* (the Word of the Lord endures forever). Images are often found on the person's back, where they are intended to deter surprise knife attacks. It serves the same purpose that tattooed figures of the Virgin do in other contexts, such as the Virgin of Guadalupe among those of Mexican origin. In recent times, the psalm has become a mainstay of people hoping to undertake the dangerous passage of undocumented migration to the United States.[23]

Brazil's Psalm

The psalm is as omnipresent in Brazil as in Nigeria, and in both countries it has an obvious appeal for those facing the many dangers and shortcomings of everyday life. Here too, it serves what David Adamo described as the three crucial functions of protection, healing, and success. It is especially popular with booming churches such as the Universal Church of the Kingdom of God, the IURD, which claims several million members in Brazil alone. The church affects an Old Testament character and is organized in local "temples"; its headquarters is a reproduction of the original Temple in ancient Jerusalem. Fittingly, the church cherishes the psalms that would have been heard in that archaic context. In 2018, all the temples celebrated "91 Days in the Shelter of the Most High," using the psalm to bring long life and well-being to participants and their families. Such invocations were redoubled when Brazil became one of the countries worst affected by the coronavirus of 2020–2022.[24]

Outside the churches, 91 is a staple of Brazil's booming music industry, and not only within the categories of gospel or contemporary Christian music. The sheer scale of these enterprises is hard to exaggerate, although the performers involved are largely unknown to North Americans. Among the most famous are Diante do Trono (Before the Throne), which emerged as the praise band of a charismatic Baptist megachurch, under the leadership of Ana Paula Valadão. In 2003, they attracted an audience of two million to an event in São Paulo that was one of the world's largest events in Christian popular culture, and their albums have sold fifteen million copies worldwide. In 2015, their album *Tetelestai* included "Salmo 91 Recitado," a reading of 91 with their customarily large accompaniment, including harps and multiple guitars. The video is ambitious, with the group performing in what appears to be ancient Jerusalem. When Marine Friesen left Diante do

Trono to launch a very successful solo career, she in turn recorded her own version of 91. The 2017 video of the song shows her as a white-clad angel with beating wings.[25]

Plenty of other artists have recorded versions of 91, aimed at a wide variety of genres and audiences. Another worship band originally linked to a church is Trazendo a Arca, which also sells albums in the multimillions. In 2009, they recorded "Aquele Que Habita" (The One Who Dwells). The annual showcase for Brazil's gospel bands is the Festival Promessas, a rock festival that was initiated in 2011 with "an explosion of fluorescent lights, a deafening drum roll and, finally, an extract from Psalm 91. 'A thousand shall fall at thy side, and ten thousand at thy right hand; but it shall not come nigh thee.'" Meanwhile, the popular pastor and gospel singer Fernandinho recorded "Mil Cairão" (A Thousand May Fall). "Salmo 91" features in the work of rap groups like Brazil's Sound Food Gang, and the Brazilian-US heavy metal band Soulfly offers a Portuguese-language reading of the text. The psalm is almost a musical world in its own right, and there is a 91 for every taste.[26]

As in Africa, psalm features prominently in Brazil's visual landscape. "Salmo 91" is a common element in the names of businesses seeking to project an air of success and prosperity: it is used by bakeries, restaurants, department stores, convenience stores, gas stations, gift shops, embroidery boutiques, and (of course) lottery firms. But often the psalm is most closely associated with marginalized areas and their population. References to 91 commonly appear in graffiti and murals that adorn Brazil's notoriously poor favelas, where gangbangers young and old cleave to the promise that "a thousand may fall." It is not the only scripture used thus, but it is among a handful of absolutely predictable choices.[27]

As an aspect of criminal subcultures (evidenced, for instance, by tattoos), the psalm regularly appears in crime-related fiction and popular culture. In the celebrated Brazilian crime film *City of God* (2002), the psalm is heard as a gangster reforms and turns to the church, and we see him passing unharmed through his enemies—in this instance, police detectives and rival criminals. It also appears in significant dramatic work. In 1992, the Brazilian prison of Carandiru was the scene of a horrific massacre when military police intervened to suppress a prison riot; over a hundred dred inmates perished. The incident focused public attention on inmate subcultures, which in 2007 was reflected in a major theatrical production by Dib Carneiro Neto. His play was titled *Salmo 91*, after the text to which convicts so often resort.[28]

Globalization

The fact of globalization spreads the psalm worldwide and helps build the body of lore surrounding it. Modern forms of communication and media mean that ideas and images spread almost instantly. In terms of a broad movement, the prosperity gospel of American celebrity preachers has become well established around the Pacific Rim. One visible practitioner is Singapore evangelist Joseph Prince, who heads the New Creation megachurch, NCC. The main facility seats some five thousand, and NCC also has a network of related campuses and business affiliates. Pastor Prince had originally preached on disease threats during the threatened epidemic of SARS that afflicted parts of Asia in 2003, but that interest became stronger and more immediate when coronavirus struck. In 2020, Prince preached on the theme "Protection from Deadly Viruses: Answers from Psalm 91." He drew heavily on understanding the exact Hebrew words and letters that constituted the psalm, and stressed their numerological significance. Focusing on multiple biblical references to the number 20 gave a special relevance to the year 2020, when the psalm came into its own. Although he did not tell his congregation that they would escape bodily ills and afflictions, nevertheless the psalm offered a total and comprehensive protection: "Every area of your life is covered in the promises of Psalm 91."[29]

Technically, Prince's sermon occurred in the Global South, but it scarcely represented any kind of religious view that would not have been quite at home in the United States. The same is true of NCC's lively ventures in contemporary Christian music, in which 91 naturally features: little distinguishes such songs from what we might expect in the United States, Britain, or Australia. Similarly, when we find publications extolling 91 in Global South nations and in local languages, quite often they are translations of writing by Texas's Peggy Joyce Ruth, whom we encountered in Chapter 9. Her works are available in Spanish, Portuguese, Korean, Japanese, and Chinese, among other languages. The fact that these books circulate so widely means that they find ready and enthusiastic consumers, but the ideas they present are born and bred in the United States.[30]

In turn, the psalm's popularity in emerging churches has repeatedly caught the attention of U.S. Christians, who are intoxicated by the passionate spirituality they witness in those societies, where Christian numbers are conspicuously growing apace. North Americans encounter those experiences in different ways. Some of the leading evangelicals have personal experience of Global South settings through missionary work; to take one example of many, C Peter Wagner was a veteran of the Bolivian mission field. Others have read about those distant experiences and seek to emulate them, but often they can witness the new devotion at first hand, as migrant churches become such a visible presence in North American cities. I have already mentioned the practice of spiritual mapping, of identifying areas where sin and evil are concentrated, to be confronted by acts of prayer and exorcism, usually with the use of 91. The story began in the late 1980s with Kenyan pastor Thomas Muthee and his wife, Margaret, who initially targeted a notorious Nairobi slum, and reportedly purified it of evil influences. That story inspired the then-emerging prayer warrior movement in the United States, and encouraged its interest in the territorial nature of the evils to be fought.[31]

Western churches frequently report stories of miracles claimed for the psalm in Global South contexts, just as Euro-American preachers through the decades have used spectacular missionary-derived tales to illustrate their sermons. As in earlier decades, it is all but impossible to tell whether we should classify these as in any sense authentically African or Asian, or as Euro-American constructs, situated in the romanticized spiritual powerhouse of Global South Christianity. Citing the experience of Liberia during the 2014 Ebola outbreak, the ministry Young Life Africa reported that health officials initially predicted over a million people would die within the space of three months. However,

> the Lord led us to pray Psalm 91 every day for 91 days and invite others to do the same. We did. The very same week we completed the 91 days an article in the *New York Times* declared the Ebola virus outbreak finished in its epicenter, Liberia—much to the amazement of scientists and health officials. Our Lord is mighty to save.[32]

An outside observer is free to interpret that sequence of actions and to decide whether indeed it constitutes a miracle, but it is assuredly being presented as one, of a kind believed to be commonplace in the Global South. Despite its African setting, the story derives from a U.S. operation, founded in Texas and based in Colorado Springs, and it can be found on the websites of multiple U.S. churches, with exhortations to be faithful in praying the psalm. It is a reasonable assumption that this Ebola example will often reappear in sermons and devotionals, and will likely morph and evolve through repeated use, with the exact location and numbers shifting over time. Probably the disease in question will change into the far better-known coronavirus.

Such tales readily cross cultural boundaries. CBN, for instance, is the Christian Broadcasting Network, a conservative evangelical enterprise founded by evangelist Pat Robertson and associated with his *700 Club*. It is thoroughly American in its content, but it covers relevant or inspiring stories from around the world, with a strong commitment to emerging Global South congregations. One lengthy report told of U.S. missionaries living in northern Ghana, in a mainly Muslim area with powerful undercurrents of black magic and voodoo. When attacked, the missionaries use 91—or rather "claim" its promises—and are saved from death. The takeaway message is that any true Christian facing danger should use the same spiritual resources. Again, the question arises: should this story be counted as part of American or African religious lore, or have the two once disparate components now merged into a globalized whole? That synthesis acquires transitional dimensions through repetition on CBN broadcasts, and subsequently on the network's website.[33]

In every sense, 91 has always been a psalm for the borders, whether the frontiers involved separate the worldly and spiritual realms, or good and evil, or light and darkness, day and night. But those borders can also be material, and 91 comes into its own when a religion spreads into a new territory and encounters whole new realities there. These might be the new social conditions of modernizing cities, or the political divisions of emerging nations. Everywhere, it seems, there are new evils to be confronted, new forces of evil, and, all too often, new kinds of pestilence. In all these settings, believers turn again to the psalm, with its assurances of a safety and protection that seem so elusive otherwise. And in turn, as they use the psalm with such fervor, that usage in turn draws new frontiers with an older Christian world that has grown skeptical of the psalm's power and the worldview it represents.

But regardless of any critiques, Psalm 91 remains a mainstay in a vastly expanded Christian world. Arguably, the psalm's great age in the churches is yet to come.

11

To Keep Thee in All Thy Ways

How Can We Pray Psalm 91?

Fear lurks in everyone. The one who always asserts to not know fear
is mentally damaged or a fool.[1]

—Max Horkheimer

Back in the Wilderness

When Satan quoted 91 to Jesus in the wilderness, he was urging him to exploit the ostentatious miracle it promised. Jesus rejected the specific challenge, although not the psalm itself. At first, he scorned such signs and
wonders as an improper testing or temptation of divine goodwill, although
he subsequently endorsed such miracles, for himself and his followers.
Throughout its long history, those who have read or heard 91 have often
debated the meaning and significance of the material miracles that it seems
to promise, and its possible role in affecting conditions in the everyday
world. In a modern setting, the question obviously arises: is it still possible
to use 91, even to treasure it, if we reject many of the key beliefs that have become so closely associated with it?

So many of the purposes for which the psalm has been used through the
centuries now seem inappropriate or outmoded. In a larger context, the
whole concept of prayer has to be examined very closely in a scientific age
that knows a great deal about the causes of natural disaster and the workings
of viruses and bacteria. If we pray Psalm 91—or any form of words—do we
think it makes a difference in the material world, whether against war, or terrorism, or coronavirus? What about purely natural calamities, such as floods
or fires? If we don't think prayer makes such a material difference, why do
we do it? If those worldly disasters continue, does that mean that prayer has
failed and that divine promises are void?

He Will Save You from the Deadly Pestilence. Philip Jenkins, Oxford University Press. © Oxford University Press 2023.
DOI: 10.1093/oso/9780197605646.003.0011

Sometimes great spiritual truths can be found in surprising settings. While writing the present book, I was using the historic Oxford bookstore of Blackwell's, where customers are greeted with a sign starkly proclaiming that "Religion is in the Basement." As well as offering useful directions, those words offer a reasonable commentary on the state of faith in contemporary Europe, and increasingly in North America. Religious institutions of all kinds are contracting, but more important, so are specifically religious ideas concerning matters such as prayer and providential action. If a government minister or church leader during a modern pandemic said anything like Spurgeon did so confidently about the psalm's prophylactic powers, that that person would be mocked and denounced so sharply that they would be instantly driven from public life. Religious ideas that would once have been very mainstream and orthodox have become deeply unfashionable, and indeed have been confined to the cultural basement.

To some degree, accounts of the rise of modernity have been greatly exaggerated. In terms of raw numbers of believers, tales of miracle pose no difficulty whatever for a large share of the Christian community at least, and that share is actually growing substantially when we consider the global expansion of faith and faiths. Many millions of people are still evidently prepared to pray Psalm 91 over a house, city, or nation, and, moreover, to expect results. But where does such confidence leave others who are not able to find such faith?

The fact of the psalm's appeal is beyond doubt, but we have to understand just why it has been so persistently popular. Every community, and perhaps even every individual, that has turned to 91 has seen it according to its own needs and interests, and has told its story accordingly. If all those very diverse understandings have any one theme in common, it is that of hope—and, commonly, hope for those who otherwise would have none. The psalm has flourished in settings where other forms of worldly hope have been in short supply, and where believers compensate by expecting miracles or direct divine interventions. It would be a grave mistake to see these expectations as naive or deluded: rather, they were, and are, ways of comprehending and confronting an often frightening array of worldly menaces.

Viewed over the long term, there is a certain irony here. It was just as belief in the demonic was vanishing from respectable thought that modern states were constructing technologies and ideologies that would inflict evils on a scale beyond the most extravagant imaginations of the so-called Dark Ages. Arguably, if ever a world needed defenses against the assaults of outright evil, it was that of the twentieth and twenty-first centuries. In such a world, the psalm continues to offer certain hope in an unshakable reality, whether or not that belief is framed in visions of demons and miracles. For figures like Max Horkheimer or Elizabeth Elliot (to take two utterly different individuals), the fact of those continuing problems and even catastrophes is not a cause to abandon prayer or biblical faith, but is rather a renewed reason to turn to it, to seek refuge in the fortress that is described in 91. Such believers found, and find, here an expression of the highest spiritual value, despite all the trappings that the psalm has acquired though long centuries. That appeal, that assurance, extends to those who do not necessarily have any faith in religious institutions, and it appeals especially outside the organized churches.

For more than two millennia, 91 has offered consolation and strength to those assailed by darkness or the fear of death. As long as those realities persist, it is difficult to imagine a world in which the psalm will not continue to be a mainstay of faith.

The Latin Vulgate Text of Psalm 90/91

1. Laus cantici David. Qui habitat in adjutorio Altissimi, in protectione Dei caeli commorabitur.
2. Dicet Domino: Susceptor meus es tu, et refugium meum; Deus meus, sperabo in eum.
3. Quoniam ipse liberavit me de laqueo venantium, et a verbo aspero.
4. Scapulis suis obumbrabit tibi, et sub pennis ejus sperabis.
5. Scuto circumdabit te veritas ejus: non timebis a timore nocturno.
6. a sagitta volante in die, a negotio perambulante in tenebris, ab incursu, et daemonio meridiano.
7. Cadent a latere tuo mille, et decem millia a dextris tuis; ad te autem non appropinquabit.
8. Verumtamen oculis tuis considerabis, et retributionem peccatorum videbis.
9. Quoniam tu es, Domine, spes mea; Altissimum posuisti refugium tuum.
10. Non accedet ad te malum, et flagellum non appropinquabit tabernaculo tuo.
11. Quoniam angelis suis mandavit de te, ut custodiant te in omnibus viis tuis.
12. In manibus portabunt te, ne forte offendas ad lapidem pedem tuum.
13. Super aspidem et basiliscum ambulabis, et conculcabis leonem et draconem.
14. Quoniam in me speravit, liberabo eum; protegam eum, quoniam cognovit nomen meum.
15. Clamabit ad me, et ego exaudiam eum; cum ipso sum in tribulatione: eripiam eum, et glorificabo eum.
16. Longitudine dierum replebo eum, et ostendam illi salutare meum.[1]

Notes

Chapter 1

1. For the Devil's style of argument in this scene, see Michael J. Morris, *Warding Off Evil: Apotropaic Tradition in the Dead Sea Scrolls and Synoptic Gospels* (Tübingen: Mohr Siebeck, 2017), 185.

2. Brennan W. Breed, "Reception of the Psalms: The Example of Psalm 91," in William P. Brown, ed., *The Oxford Handbook of the Psalms* (New York: Oxford University Press, 2014), 297–310. In a concise space, Dr. Breed offers an excellent and wide-ranging survey of the psalm's reception. I have learned much from this exemplary work—although, obviously, I feel that I have a great deal more to say on the topic(!). That applies to expanding the range of topics substantially, as well as including many additional illustrations. See also Susan Gillingham, *Psalms Through the Centuries*, 3 vols. (Chichester: Wiley-Blackwell, 2012–2022), III, 87–94; Matthias Henze, "Psalm 91 in Premodern Interpretation and at Qumran," in Matthias Henze, ed., *Biblical Interpretation at Qumran* (Grand Rapids, MI: William B. Eerdmans, 2005), 168–193. For the reception of psalms through history, see Katherine J. Dell, "Psalms," in Michael Lieb, Emma Mason, and Jonathan Roberts, eds., *The Oxford Handbook of the Reception History of the Bible* (New York: Oxford University Press, 2011), 37–51; Susan Gillingham, "Psalms 90–92: Text, Images and Music," *Revue des Sciences Religieuses* 89, no. 3 (2015): 255–276, at https://journals.openedition.org/rsr/2686.

3. Gerrit C. Vreugdenhil, *Psalm 91 and Demonic Menace* (Leiden, Netherlands: Brill, 2020).

4. For "biographies" of other psalms, see Susan Gillingham, *A Journey of Two Psalms: The Reception of Psalms 1 and 2 in Jewish and Christian Tradition* (New York: Oxford University Press, 2013); David W. Stowe, *Song of Exile: The Enduring Mystery of Psalm 137* (New York: Oxford University Press, 2016).

5. The text is taken from https://www.biblegateway.com/passage/?search=psalm+91&version=KJV.

6. Vreugdenhil, *Psalm 91 and Demonic Menace*, 346–368. For the image of wings, see S. Schroer, "Im Schatten deiner Flügel," in Rainer Kessler et al., eds., *Ihr Völker alle, klatscht in die Hände!* (Münster: Verlag Münster, 1997), 296–316.

7. Augustine of Hippo, *Expositions on the Book of Psalms*, translated by A. Cleveland Coxe, Nicene and Post-Nicene Fathers, series 1, vol. 8 (Grand Rapids, MI: Eerdmans, n.d.), https://www.ccel.org/ccel/schaff/npnf108/npnf108.ii.i.html. Augustine's commentary on Psalm 91 is at https://www.ccel.org/ccel/schaff/npnf108.ii.XCI.html. For Luther, see Chapter 6.

8. William L. Holladay, *The Psalms Through Three Thousand Years: Prayerbook of a Cloud of Witnesses* (Minneapolis: Fortress Press, 1993), 360–362.

9. Philip Jenkins, *Crucible of Faith* (New York: Basic Books, 2017).

10. T. J. Kraus, "Greek Psalm 90 (Hebrew Psalm 91)—the Most Widely Attested Text of the Bible," *Biblische Notizen* 176 (2018): 47–63; Regine Hunziker-Rodewald, "Bild und Wort im Gespräch mit Gott: Gedanken zur Kommunikationspragmatik in Psalm 91," in W. Gräb and J. Cottin, eds., *Imaginationen der inneren Welt. Theologische, psychologische und ästhetische Reflexionen zur spirituellen Dimension der Kunst* (Frankfurt: Peter Lang, 2012), 123–140. For modern uses of the text in material objects, see Drew Brooks, "Operation Bandanas Continues Decade-Long Ministry to Deployed Troops," *Fayetteville Observer*, April 15, 2017, https://www.fayobser ver.com/news/20170415/operation-bandanas-continues-decade-long-ministry-to-deployed-troops.

11. From a large literature on gender, masculinity, and religious practice, see, for instance, Kristin Kobes Du Mez, *Jesus and John Wayne: How White Evangelicals Corrupted a Faith and Fractured a Nation* (New York: Liveright, 2020).

12. See the Appendix for the Vulgate text.

13. For the Douce Ivory, see https://medieval.bodleian.ox.ac.uk/catalog/manuscript_4 546. The image may be seen at https://en.wikipedia.org/wiki/Christ_treading_on_ the_beasts#/media/File:Ivory_book_cover_MS_Douce_176.jpg.

14. Edmée Kingsmill, "The Psalms: A Monastic Perspective," in William P. Brown, ed., *The Oxford Handbook of the Psalms* (New York: Oxford University Press, 2014), 596–607.

15. Andrew Solomon, *The Noonday Demon: An Atlas of Depression* (New York: Simon and Schuster, 2001); Dom Jean-Charles Nault, *The Noonday Devil: Acedia, the Unnamed Evil of Our Times* (San Francisco: Ignatius Press, 2015).

16. Kate Bowler, *Blessed: A History of the American Prosperity Gospel* (New York: Oxford University Press, 2013).

17. Job 5:17–26, and see especially vv. 21–22 (KJV). See Mark Larrimore, *The Book of Job: A Biography* (Princeton, NJ: Princeton University Press, 2013); Kyle C. Dunham, *The Pious Sage in Job: Eliphaz in the Context of Wisdom Theodicy* (Eugene, OR: Wipf and Stock, 2016).

18. Jerome, Letter 68, to Castrutius, at https://www.newadvent.org/fathers/3001068. htm; Jerome, Homily 20, "On Psalm 90 (91)," in *The Homilies of Saint Jerome*, vol. 1, *1–59 on the Psalms* (Washington, DC: Catholic University of America Press, 1964), 156–163.

19. The folk music quote is attributed to various figures including Louis Armstrong, but Ellington is the source most commonly cited.

20. The actual number of days of prayer required for 91 varies according to source. See, for instance, Susan Chamberlain Shipe, *31 Days of Praying Psalm 91* (n.p.: CreateSpace Independent Publishing Platform, 2018).

21. Vreugdenhil, *Psalm 91 and Demonic Menace*, 265–273. Throughout this book I have made use of a number of concordances and word guides for both Greek and Hebrew, most frequently the classic work of James Strong, which in its earliest form dates back to 1890. His *Exhaustive Concordance of the Bible* (for both Hebrew and Greek terms) can now easily be accessed online through https://biblehub.com/strongs.htm. See

also https://biblehub.com/greek/ and https://biblehub.com/hebrew/. For *pachad*, for instance, see https://biblehub.com/hebrew/6343.htm.

22. Thomas More, *Dialogue of Comfort Against Tribulation*, edited by Monica Stevens (London: Sheed and Ward, 1951), ii, 13, at https://ccel.org/ccel/more/comfort/comf ort.iii.xiii.html; Matthew Henry, *Matthew Henry's Commentary on the Whole Bible* (Grand Rapids, MI: Christian Classics Ethereal Library, n.d.), vol. 3. For psalms, see https://www.ccel.org/ccel/henry/mhc3.Ps.i.html. "When we are retired" is taken from https://ccel.org/ccel/henry/mhc3/mhc3.Ps.xcii.html.

23. Princeton University Press produced a distinguished sequence of studies in its series Lives of Great Religious Books, which included Larrimore, *The Book of Job*. See https://press.princeton.edu/series/lives-of-great-religious-books.

Chapter 2

1. Midrash Tehillim 91, Part 1, at https://www.matsati.com/index.php/midrash-tehillim/.

2. "The song of evil spirits" is quoted from Shevuot 15b, at https://www.sefaria.org/Shev uot.15b?lang=bi.

3. Two of the outstanding books specifically on the psalm are Pirmin Hugger, *Jahwe meine Zuflucht: Gestalt und Theologie des 91. Psalms* (Münsterschwarzach: Vier-Türme-Verlag, 1971); and Gerrit C. Vreugdenhil, *Psalm 91 and Demonic Menace* (Leiden: Brill, 2020).

4. Major sources on the Book of Psalms that I have used throughout this book include Hans-Joachim Kraus, *Psalms 60–150: A Continental Commentary* (Minneapolis, MN: Fortress, 1993); J. Clinton McCann Jr., "The Book of Psalms," in *The New Interpreters Bible*, vol. 4 (Nashville, TN: Abingdon, 1996); Patrick D. Miller and Peter W. Flint, eds., *The Book of Psalms: Composition and Reception* (Leiden: Brill, 2004); Walter Brueggemann and William Bellinger, eds., *Psalms* (New York: Cambridge University Press, 2013); Susan Gillingham, ed., *Jewish and Christian Approaches to the Psalms: Conflict and Convergence* (New York: Oxford University Press, 2013); William P. Brown, ed., *The Oxford Handbook of the Psalms* (New York: Oxford University Press, 2014); William P. Brown, "The Psalms and Hebrew Poetry," in Stephen B. Chapman and Marvin A. Sweeney, eds., *The Cambridge Companion to the Hebrew Bible/Old Testament* (Cambridge University Press, 2016); W. Dennis Tucker Jr. and William H. Bellinger Jr., eds., *The Psalter as Witness: Theology, Poetry, and Genre* (Waco, TX: Baylor University Press, 2017); Bruce K. Waltke and James M. Houston, *The Psalms as Christian Praise: A Historical Commentary* (Grand Rapids, MI: William B. Eerdmans, 2019).

5. "It also does not" is from Robert Alter, *The Book of Psalms: A Translation with Commentary* (New York: W. W. Norton, 2007), 321. "It is not a hymn" is from Samuel Terrien, *The Psalms: Strophic Structure and Theological Commentary* (Grand Rapids, MI: Eerdmans, 2003), 652. Mika S. Pajunen and Jeremy Penner, eds., *Functions of*

Psalms and Prayers in the Late Second Temple Period (Berlin: De Gruyter, 2017); Vreugdenhil, *Psalm 91 and Demonic Menace*, 175–207.

6. The "bewildering" characterization is from Alexander MacLaren, "The Psalms," in W. Robertson Nicoll, ed., *The Expositor's Bible* (New York: A. C. Armstrong and Son, 1894), III:20. For 91, see https://ccel.org/ccel/maclaren/expositorpsalms3/ expositorpsalms3.iii.html. For discussions of the nature and purpose of 91, see A. Caquot, "Le Psaume XCI," *Semitica* 8 (1958): 21–37; Pierre Auffret, " 'Je suis avec lui.' Étude structurelle du psaume 91," in Pierre Auffret, ed., *Voyez de vos yeux* (Leiden: Brill, 1993), 279–300; Konrad Schaefer, *Psalms* (Collegeville, MN: Liturgical Press, 2001), 227–230: Erich Zenger, "Psalm 91," in Frank-Lothar Hossfeld and Erich Zenger, *Psalms 2: A Commentary on Psalms 51–100*, ed. Klaus Baltzer, Hermeneia (Minneapolis: Fortress, 2005), 426–433; John Goldingay, *Psalms: Volume 3, Psalms 90–150* (Grand Rapids, MI: Baker, 2008), 37–50; Beth L. Tanner, "Psalm 91," in Nancy L DeClaissé-Walford, Rolf A. Jacobson, and Beth Laneel Tanner, eds., *The Book of Psalms* (Grand Rapids, MI: William B. Eerdmans, 2014), 697–701; Vreugdenhil, *Psalm 91 and Demonic Menace*, 123–130.

7. C. C. Broyles, "Psalms Concerning the Liturgies of Temple Entry," in Patrick D. Miller and Peter W. Flint, eds., *The Book of Psalms: Composition and Reception* (Leiden: Brill, 2004), 248–287; Kevin Cathcart, "Phoenician Inscriptions from Arslan Tash and Some Old Testament Texts," in James K. Aitken, Katharine J. Dell, and Brian A. Mastin, eds., *On Stone and Scroll: Essays in Honour of Graham Ivor Davies* (Berlin: Walter de Gruyter, 2011), 87–100; Vreugdenhil, *Psalm 91 and Demonic Menace*, 368–375.

8. Vreugdenhil, *Psalm 91 and Demonic Menace*, 175–207, 415–437; Rainer Albertz, "Family Religion in Ancient Israel and Its Surroundings," in J. Bodel and S. M. Olyan, eds., *Household and Family Religion in Antiquity* (New York: Oxford University Press, 2008), 89–112; Rainer Albertz and Rüdiger Schmitt, *Family and Household Religion in Ancient Israel and the Levant* (Winona Lake, IN: Eisenbraun's, 2012).

9. Sanhedrin 103a, at https://www.sefaria.org/Sanhedrin.103a.14?lang=bi.

10. Goldingay, *Psalms: Volume 3, Psalms 90–150*, 37–50.

11. Alter, *The Book of Psalms*, 322; Warren C. Robertson, *Drought, Famine, Plague and Pestilence: Ancient Israel's Understandings of and Responses to Natural Catastrophes* (Madison, WI: Gorgias Press, 2010).

12. For *deber*, see https://biblehub.com/hebrew/1698.htm.

13. The other psalms with possible plague or disease references are 38, 41, 73, 78, 89, 103, and 106. The speaker of 41 recounts the diseases that he has suffered. Diseases appear as symbols of divine wrath in Psalm 78, and 103 tells us how God will deliver from sins and diseases. Psalm 106 recalls the historical plague that befell the children of Israel in the wilderness as a consequence of their lack of faith. *Deber's* other appearance in a psalm is at Ps 78:50.

14. 2 Samuel 24:15–17.

15. For Hezekiah, see 2 Kings 19:35–37; Isaiah 37:33–36. "Blessed David" is quoted from Theodoret of Cyrus, *Commentary on the Psalms 73–150* (Washington, DC: Catholic University of America Press, 2001), 103.

16. Zenger, "Psalm 91."

17. A major source for the view of the psalms at Qumran is "The Great Psalms Scroll, 11Q5," in Peter W. Flint, *The Dead Sea Psalms Scrolls and the Book of Psalms* (Leiden: Brill, 1997). Brown, *The Oxford Handbook of the Psalms*; Mika S. Pajunen, "The Influence of Societal Changes in the Late Second Temple Period on the Functions and Composition of Psalms," *Scandinavian Journal of the Old Testament* 33, no. 2 (2019): 164–184.

18. Gerald H. Wilson, "Shaping the Psalter: A Consideration of Editorial Linkage in the Book of Psalms," in J. Clinton McCann, ed., *The Shape and Shaping of the Psalter* (Sheffield: JSOT Press, 1993), 72–82; Nancy L. deClaissé-Walford, ed., *The Shape and Shaping of the Book of Psalms: The Current State of Scholarship* (Atlanta: Society of Biblical Literature Press, 2014).

19. Michael G. McKelvey, *Moses, David and the High Kingship of Yahweh: A Canonical Study of Book IV of the Psalter*, Gorgias Biblical Studies 55 (Madison, WI: Gorgias Press, 2010); Philip Jenkins, *Crucible of Faith* (New York: Basic Books, 2017).

20. Zenger, "Psalm 91."

21. A. F. Kirkpatrick, *The Book of Psalms* (Cambridge: Cambridge University Press, 1951), 553–554.; David M. Howard Jr., "A Contextual Reading of Psalms 90–94," in J. Clinton McCann, ed., *The Shape and Shaping of the Psalter* (Sheffield: JSOT Press, 1993), 108–123; DeClaissé-Walford, Jacobson, and Tanner, eds., *The Book of Psalms*; Nancy deClaissé-Walford, "Feminine Imagery and Theology in the Psalter: Psalms 90, 91, and 92," in W. Dennis Tucker Jr. and William H. Bellinger Jr., eds., *The Psalter as Witness: Theology, Poetry, and Genre* (Waco, TX: Baylor University Press, 2017).

22. Frederick J. Gaiser, "'It Shall Not Reach You': Talisman or Vocation? Reading Psalm 91 in Time of War," *Word and World* 25 (2005): 191–202.

23. For continuing Mosaic theories, see Chapter 4.

24. Susan Gillingham, *Psalms Through the Centuries* (Chichester: Wiley-Blackwell, 2022), III:82–98; Susan Gillingham, "Psalms 90–92: Text, Images and Music," *Revue des Sciences Religieuses* 89, no. 3 (2015): 255–276, at https://journals.openedition.org/rsr/2686.

25. Samuel E. Balentine, "Wisdom," in Stephen B. Chapman and Marvin A. Sweeney, eds., *The Cambridge Companion to the Hebrew Bible/Old Testament* (New York: Cambridge University Press, 2016); Donn F. Morgan, ed., *Oxford Handbook of the Writings of the Hebrew Bible* (New York: Oxford University Press, 2019).

26. Phil J. Botha, "Psalm 91 and Its Wisdom Connections," *Old Testament Essays* 25, no. 2 (2012): 260–276; Diane Jacobson, "Wisdom Language in the Psalms," in William P. Brown, ed., *The Oxford Handbook of the Psalms* (New York: Oxford University Press, 2014); William P. Brown, "Psalms," in Samuel L. Adams and Matthew Goff, eds., *The Wiley Blackwell Companion to Wisdom Literature* (Hoboken, NJ: Wiley Blackwell, 2020), 67–86; W. H. Bellinger Jr., "Wisdom Psalms," in Will Kynes, ed., *The Oxford Handbook of Wisdom and the Bible* (New York: Oxford University Press, 2021).

27. Bruce K. Waltke, *The Book of Proverbs* (Grand Rapids, MI: William B. Eerdmans, 2004–2005). For uses of *pachad*, see https://biblehub.com/hebrew/6343.htm.

28. Job 22:21–30.

29. Jenkins, *Crucible of Faith*.

30. William O. E. Oesterley, *A Fresh Approach to the Psalms* (New York: Charles Scribner's Sons, 1937), 278–288.

31. Miryam T. Brand, *Evil Within and Without: The Source of Sin and Its Nature as Portrayed in Second Temple Literature* (Göttingen: Vandenhoeck & Ruprecht, 2013).

32. Besides 91, psalms with angelic references include 34, 35, 78, 103, 104, and 148.

33. Oesterley, *A Fresh Approach to the Psalms,* 278–288; A. Caquot, "Sur quelques demons de l'Ancien Testament: Reshep, Qeteb, Deber," *Semitica* 6 (1956): 56–58; J. M. Blair, *De-Demonising the Old Testament: An Investigation of Azazel, Lilith, Deber, Qeteb and Reshef in the Hebrew Bible* (Tübingen: Mohr Siebeck, 2009); Kevin Cathcart, "Phoenician Inscriptions from Arslan Tash and Some Old Testament Texts," in James K. Aitken, Katharine J. Dell, and Brian A. Mastin, eds., *On Stone and Scroll: Essays in Honour of Graham Ivor Davies* (Berlin: Walter de Gruyter, 2011), 87–100; Vreugdenhil, *Psalm 91 and Demonic Menace.*

34. Peter Riede, *Im Netz des Jägers: Studien zur Feindmetaphorik der Individualpsalmen* (Neukirchen-Vluy: Neukirchener Verlag, 2000); Ida Fröhlich, "Demons and Illness in Second Temple Judaism: Theory and Practice," in Siam Bhayro and Catherine Rider, eds., *Demons and Illness from Antiquity to the Early-Modern Period* (Leiden: Brill, 2017), 81–96. The role of Psalm 91 is often stressed in the sizable literature on Jewish magical texts: see the work of Gideon Bohak, especially his *Ancient Jewish Magic: A History* (Cambridge: Cambridge University Press, 2008).

35. Esther Eshel, "Apotropaic Prayers in the Second Temple Period," in E. Chazon, ed., *Liturgical Perspectives: Prayer and Poetry in Light of the Dead Sea Scrolls* (Leiden: Brill, 2003), 69–88.

36. T. J. Kraus, "Septuaginta-Psalm 90 in apotropäischer Verwendung: Vorüberlegungen für eine kritische Edition und (bisheriges) Datenmaterial," *Biblische Notizen* 125 (2005): 39–73; Siegfried Kreuzer, ed., *Introduction to the Septuagint* (Waco, TX: Baylor University Press, 2019); Staffan Olofsson, "The Psalter," in Alison G. Salvesen and Timothy Michael Law, eds., *The Oxford Handbook of the Septuagint* (New York: Oxford University Press, 2021).

37. Joachim L. W. Schaper, "The Septuagint Psalter," in William P. Brown, ed., *The Oxford Handbook of the Psalms* (New York: Oxford University Press, 2014), 173–184.

38. Brennan W. Breed, "Reception of the Psalms: The Example of Psalms 91," in William P. Brown, ed., *The Oxford Handbook of the Psalms* (New York: Oxford University Press, 2014), 297–310; Panagiotis Stamatopoulos, "A Mistranslation or a Liberal Rendering in Ps. 91/90:6 (LXX)?," accessible at https://www.academia.edu/4167142/_English_ A_mistranslation_or_a_liberal_rendering_in_Psalm_91_90_6_L%20XX; Jenkins, *Crucible of Faith.* The word I cite that also "appears in another psalm" refers to Ps 106:37: compare https://biblehub.com/hebrew/7700.htm and https://biblehub.com/ hebrew/7736.htm.

39. Vreugdenhil, *Psalm 91 and Demonic Menace,* 130–132.

40. For *pragmatos,* see https://biblehub.com/greek/pragmatos_4229.htm.

41. Robertson, *Drought, Famine, Plague and Pestilence.*

42. "Jackal," in *International Standard Bible Encyclopedia Online* at https://www.interna tionalstandardbible.com/J/jackal.html; Philip Jenkins, "Dragons, Jackals, and Bible

Translators," *Anxious Bench* (blog), October 25, 2021, at https://www.patheos.com/blogs/anxiousbench/2021/10/dragons-jackals-and-bible-translators/.

43. For the animals enumerated and their mythological dimensions, see Vreugdenhil, *Psalm 91 and Demonic Menace*, 311–331; Manfred Gorg, "Schreiten über Löwe und Otter: Beobachtungen zur Bildsprache in Ps 91,13a," in Johannes Frühwald-König, Ferdinand Prostmeier, and Reinhold Zwick, eds., *Steht nicht geschrieben? Studien zur Bibel und ihrer Wirkungsgeschichte* (Regensburg: Pustet, 2001), 37–48.

44. See Appendix 1.

45. Scott Goins, "Jerome's Psalters," in William P. Brown, ed., *The Oxford Handbook of the Psalms* (New York: Oxford University Press, 2014), 185–199; "Labor Tam Utilis: The Creation of the Vulgate," *Vigiliae Christianae* 50, no. 1 (1996): 42–72. For Jerome's Hebrew-derived text of 91 (his 90), see http://www.latinvulgate.com/verse.aspx?t=0&b=21&c=90. The two versions can be compared at https://vulgate.org/ot/psalms_90.htm.

46. Vreugdenhil, *Psalm 91 and Demonic Menace*, 293–297; Harry F. Van Rooy, "The Psalms in Early Syriac Tradition," in Patrick D. Miller and Peter W. Flint, eds., *The Book of Psalms: Composition and Reception* (Leiden: Brill, 2004), 537–550; Ignacio Carbajosa, *The Character of the Syriac Version of Psalms: A Study of Psalms 90–150 in the Peshitta* (Leiden: Brill, 2008); Richard A Taylor, George Kiraz, and Joseph Bali, eds., *The Psalms According to the Syriac Peshitta Version with English Translation* (Madison, WI: Gorgias Press, 2020). For a later scholarly understanding of the *simoom*, see Augustus Tholuck, *A Translation and Commentary of the Book of Psalms* (Philadelphia: William S. and Alfred Martien, 1858), 375–376.

47. The extract from 91 cited here is taken from http://www.targum.info/pss/ps4.htm#_ftnref6; see also David M. Stec, ed., *The Targum of Psalms* (Collegeville, Minn: Liturgical Press, 2004).

48. Y. Shabb., in Jacob Neusner, ed., *The Talmud of the Land of Israel: Shabbat* (Chicago: University of Chicago Press, 1991), 11:198–199. Compare the close parallel in Y. Erubin 10.11, in Jacob Neusner, ed., *The Talmud of the Land of Israel: Erubin* (Chicago: University of Chicago Press, 1991) 12:290–291.

49. P. S. Alexander, "The Demonology of the Dead Sea Scrolls," in P. W. Flint and J. C. VanderKam, eds., *The Dead Sea Scrolls: A Comprehensive Assessment* (Leiden: Brill, 1999), 2:331–353; David Flusser, *Qumran and Apocalytpticism* (Grand Rapids, MI: Eerdmans, 2007); B. H. Reynolds, "A Dwelling Place of Demons: Demonology and Apocalypticism in the Dead Sea Scrolls," in Sidnie White Crawford and Cecilia Wassen, eds., *Apocalyptic Thinking in Early Judaism: Engaging with John Collins' The Apocalyptic Imagination* (Leiden: Brill, 2018), 23–54. For the extensive use of Psalms at Qumran, see Bodil Ejrnæs, "David and His Two Women: An Analysis of Two Poems in the Psalms Scroll from Qumran (11Q5)," in Anssi Voitila and Jutta Jokiranta, eds., *Scripture in Transition: Essays on Septuagint, Hebrew Bible, and Dead Sea Scrolls in Honour of Raija Sollamo* (Leiden: Brill, 2008), 581.

50. Hermann Lichtenberger, "Ps 91 und die Exorzismen in 11QPsApa," in Armin Lange, Hermann Lichtenberger, and K. F. Diethard Römheld, eds., *Die Dämonen: Die Dämonologie der israelitisch-jüdischen und frühchristlichen Literatur im Kontext*

ihrer Umwelt (Tübingen: J. C. B. Mohr, 2003), 416–421; Matthias Henze, "Psalm 91 in Premodern Interpretation and at Qumran," in Matthias Henze, ed., *Biblical Interpretation at Qumran* (Grand Rapids, MI: William B. Eerdmans, 2005), 168–193; Mika S. Pajunen, "Qumranic Psalm 91: A Structural Analysis," in Anssi Voitila and Jutta Jokiranta, eds., *Scripture in Transition: Essays on Septuagint, Hebrew Bible, and Dead Sea Scrolls in Honour of Raija Sollamo* (Leiden: Brill, 2008), 591–605; Hermann Lichtenberger, "Demonology in the Dead Sea Scrolls and the New Testament," in Ruth Clements and Daniel R. Schwartz, eds., *Text, Thought, and Practice in Qumran and Early Christianity* (Leiden: Brill, 2009), 267–280; Corinna Körting, "Text and Context—Ps 91 and 11QPsaPa," in Erich Zenger, ed., *The Composition of the Book of Psalms* (Leuven: Peeters, 2010), 567–577; Craig A. Evans, "Jesus and Psalm 91 in Light of Exorcism Scrolls," in Peter W. Flint, Jean Duhaime, and Kyung S. Baek, eds., *Celebrating the Dead Sea Scrolls: A Canadian Collection* (Atlanta: Society of Biblical Literature, 2011), 541–555; Ida Fröhlich, "Magical Healing at Qumran (11Q11) and the Question of the Calendar," in H. R. Jacobus, A. K. de Hemmer Gudme, and P. Guillaume, eds., *Studies on Magic and Divination in the Biblical World* (Piscataway, NJ: Gorgias Press, 2013), 39–49; Mika S. Pajunen, "How to Expel a Demon: Form- and Traditional-Critical Assessment of the Ritual of Exorcism in 11QApocryphal Psalms," in Mika S. Pajunen and H. Tervanotko, eds., *Crossing Imaginary Boundaries: The Dead Sea Scrolls in the Context of Second Temple Judaism* (Helsinki: Finnish Exegetical Society, 2015), 128–161.

51. Gideon Bohak, "Jewish Exorcism Before and After the Destruction of the Second Temple," in D. R. Schwartz and Z. Weiss, eds., *Was 70 CE a Watershed in Jewish History? On Jews and Judaism Before and After the Destruction of the Second Temple* (Leiden: Brill, 2012), 277–300; Gideon Bohak, "Exorcistic Psalms of David and Solomon," in Richard Bauckham, James R. Davila, and Alex Panayotov, eds., *Old Testament Pseudepigrapha: More Noncanonical Scriptures* (Grand Rapids, MI: William B. Eerdmans, 2013), I:287–297; Gideon Bohak, "Expelling Demons and Attracting Demons in Jewish Magical Texts," in G. Melville and C. Ruta, eds., *Experiencing the Beyond: Intercultural Approaches* (Berlin: De Gruyter, 2019), 170–185.

Chapter 3

1. Tertullian, "The Five Books Against Marcion," IV:24, at http://www.earlychristianw ritings.com/text/tertullian124.html.

2. Craig A. Evans, "Jesus and Psalm 91 in Light of Exorcism Scrolls," in Peter W. Flint, Jean Duhaime, and Kyung S. Baek, eds., *Celebrating the Dead Sea Scrolls: A Canadian Collection* (Atlanta: Society of Biblical Literature, 2011), 541–555; Andrew J. Schmutzer, "Psalm 91: Refuge, Protection and Its Use in the New Testament," in Andrew J. Schmutzer and David M. Howard Jr., eds., *The Psalms: Language for All Seasons of the Soul* (Chicago: Moody, 2013), 85–108; David B. Sloan, "Interpreting Scripture with Satan? The Devil's Use of Scripture in Luke's Temptation Narrative,"

Tyndale Bulletin 66 (2015): 231–250; Michael J. Morris, *Warding Off Evil: Apotropaic Tradition in the Dead Sea Scrolls and Synoptic Gospels* (Tübingen: Mohr Siebeck, 2017).

3. Susan Gillingham, *Psalms Through the Centuries*, 3 vols. (Chichester: Wiley-Blackwell, 2012–2022). "Thou art my Son" is from Psalm 2:7.

4. Carl Pace, "Dashing a Foot, Trashing a Tradition: On the Use of Psalm 91 in Matthew 4," paper delivered to the Society of Biblical Literature, 2011; Michael J. Morris, "Apotropaic Tactics in the Matthean Temptation," *Journal of Postgraduate Research*, 2014, 134–146; Michael J. Morris, "Apotropaic Inversion in the Temptation and at Qumran," in Jan Dochhorn, Susanne Rudnig-Zelt, and Benjamin Wold, eds., *Das Böse, der Teufel und Dämonen—Evil, the Devil, and Demons* (Tübingen: Mohr Siebeck, 2016), 93–100; Michael J. Morris, *Warding Off Evil: Apotropaic Tradition in the Dead Sea Scrolls and Synoptic Gospels* (Tübingen: Mohr Siebeck, 2017); Donald C. McIntyre, "Demons, DSS, and Jesus: Psalm 91 and the Need for Text Critical Pastors," 2020, at https://academic.logos.com/demons-dss-and-jesus-psalm-91-and-the-need-for-text-critical-pastors/.

5. Jesus's responses are drawn as follows: "Man shall not live by bread alone," Deuteronomy 8:3; "Thou shalt worship the Lord thy God," Deuteronomy 6:13; and "Do not put the Lord your God to the test," Deuteronomy 6:16.

6. Sloan, "Interpreting Scripture with Satan?"

7. *Origen: Homilies on Luke*, trans. Joseph T. Lienhard (Washington, DC: Catholic University of America Press, 1996), 128.

8. The sequence of stories is found in Luke 9:1–10:23.

9. For Peter's acknowledgment, see Luke 9:18–20. The transfiguration follows at Luke 9:28–36.

10. Luke 10:17–19.

11. Darrell L. Bock, *Luke*, Baker Exegetical Commentary on the New Testament, 2 vols. (Grand Rapids, MI: Baker, 1994–1996); the two volumes cover Luke 1:1–9:50 and Luke 9:51–24:53, respectively. For the use of the word "enemy" in a Satanic context, see Matthew 13:25.

12. Deuteronomy 8:15.

13. Matthew 22:15. See also Benjamin Wold, "Apotropaic Prayer and the Matthean Lord's Prayer," in Jan Dochhorn, Susanne Rudnig-Zelt, and Benjamin Wold, eds., *Das Böse, der Teufel und Dämonen—Evil, the Devil, and Demons* (Tübingen: Mohr Siebeck, 2016), 101–112.

14. R. T. France, *The Gospel of Matthew* (Grand Rapids, MI: Eerdmans, 2007).

15. Matthew 12:22–29 and 12:33–37.

16. The "generation of vipers" occurs at Matthew 12:33.

17. Mark 5:6–8.

18. "He took many captives" is from Ephesians 4:7. Gustaf Aulén, *Christus Victor: An Historical Study of the Three Main Types of the Idea of Atonement* (New York: Macmillan, 1961); Barry D. Smith, *The Meaning of Jesus' Death: Reviewing the New Testament's Interpretations* (London: Bloomsbury T. & T. Clark, 2017).

19. For the use of psalms as messianic texts, see Wenceslaus Mkeni Urassa, *Psalm 8 and Its Christological Re-Interpretations in the New Testament Context: An Inter-Contextual*

Study in Biblical Hermeneutics (New York: P. Lang, 1998); Andrew Streett, *The Vine and the Son of Man: Eschatological Interpretation of Psalm 80 in Early Judaism* (Minneapolis, MN: Fortress Press, 2014); Paul M. Blowers and Peter W. Martens, eds., *The Oxford Handbook of Early Christian Biblical Interpretation* (New York: Oxford University Press, 2019).

20. Philip Jenkins, *Crucible of Faith* (New York: Basic Books, 2017); Susan Gillingham, *Psalms Through the Centuries* (Chichester: Wiley-Blackwell, 2012), 28–29; *Origen: Homilies on Luke*, trans. Lienhard, 126–128. For later corrections of the "exegetical error," see Derek A. Olsen, *Reading Matthew with Monks* (Collegeville, MN: Liturgical Press, 2015), 132.

21. Isaiah 11:6–8.

22. The trampling verse is Malachi 4:3. For the larger theme of trampling or treading, see Gerrit C. Vreugdenhil, *Psalm 91 and Demonic Menace* (Leiden: Brill, 2020), 331–336.

23. J. H. Charlesworth, *The Good and Evil Serpent: How a Universal Symbol Became Christianized* (New Haven, CT: Yale University Press, 2010).

24. For the Hebrew *ramas*, see https://biblehub.com/hebrew/strongs_7429.htm. For the "treading" word in Luke 10:19, see https://biblehub.com/greek/3961.htm.

25. Jenkins, *Crucible of Faith*.

26. *The Explanation of the Apocalypse by Venerable Bede*, ed. and trans. Rev. Edw. Marshall (Oxford: James Parker, 1878), 84.

27. Romans 16:20.

28. Psalm 8:5–6. For New Testament allusions, see 1 Corinthians 15:25–27; Hebrews 2:5–8. Urassa, *Psalm 8 and Its Christological Re-Interpretations*.

29. Irenaeus, *Against Heresies*, book II, 20:3, at http://www.earlychristianwritings.com/text/irenaeus-book2.html; Stephen O. Presley, *The Intertextual Reception of Genesis 1–3 in Irenaeus of Lyons* (Leiden: Brill, 2015), 116, 123–131.

30. Irenaeus, *Against Heresies*, book III, 23:7, at http://www.earlychristianwritings.com/text/irenaeus-book3.html.

31. The Latin text is taken from https://www.biblegateway.com/passage/?search=psalm+91&version=VULGATE.

32. For the "old serpent," see Tertullian, *Against Praxeas,* 1, at https://www.newadvent.org/fathers/0317.htm.

Chapter 4

1. Midrash Tanchuma Mishpatim Sinan 19:4–5, at https://www.sefaria.org/Midrash_Tanchuma%2C_Mishpatim.19.4-5?lang=bi.

2. The Egyptian book referred to here is today known as AMS 9. Marvin W. Meyer and Richard Smith, *Ancient Christian Magic: Coptic Texts of Ritual Power* (Princeton, NJ: Princeton University Press, 1999), 311–322; Joseph Emanuel Sanzo, *Scriptural Incipits on Amulets from Late Antique Egypt: Text, Typology, and Theory* (Tübingen: Mohr Siebeck, 2014), 82–83; T. J. Kraus, "Greek Psalm 90 (Hebrew Psalm

91)—the Most Widely Attested Text of the Bible," *Biblische Notizen* 176 (2018): 47–63; Joseph E. Sanzo, "Early Christianity," in David Frankfurter, ed., *Guide to the Study of Ancient Magic* (Leiden: Brill, 2019); "Religion in the Coptic Magical Papyri VIII: The Bible and Magic," February 15, 2019, at https://www.coptic-magic.phil.uni-wuerzb urg.de/index.php/2019/02/15/religion-in-the-coptic-magical-papyri-vii-the-bible-and-magic/.

3. For the *Glossa Ordinaria*, see Brennan W. Breed, "Reception of the Psalms: The Example of Psalms 91," in William P. Brown, ed., *The Oxford Handbook of the Psalms* (New York: Oxford University Press, 2014), 297–310.

4. Midrash Tanchuma Mishpatim Sinan 19:4–5, at https://www.sefaria.org/Midrash_Tanchuma%2C_Mishpatim.19.4-5?lang=bi.

5. Andrew J. Schmutzer, "Psalm 91: Refuge, Protection and Its Use in the New Testament," in Andrew J. Schmutzer and David M. Howard Jr., eds., *The Psalms: Language for All Seasons of the Soul* (Chicago: Moody, 2013), 85–108. Gerrit C. Vreugdenhil, *Psalm 91 and Demonic Menace* (Leiden: Brill, 2020), 5–10. Compare Lawrence H. Schiffmann and M. Swartz, eds., *Hebrew and Aramaic Incantation Texts from the Cairo Genizah* (Sheffield: JSOT Press, 1992). For a much later example, see Margaretha Folmer, "A Jewish Childbirth Amulet from the Bibliotheca Rosenthaliana," in W. Th. van Peursen and J. W. Dyk, eds., *Tradition and Innovation in Biblical Interpretation* (Leiden: Brill, 2011), 223–241.

6. Vreugdenhil, *Psalm 91 and Demonic Menace*, 5–10; J. Naveh and S. Shaked, *Amulets and Magic Bowls: Aramaic Incantations of Late Antiquity* (Jerusalem: Magnes, 1985); Dan Levene, *A Corpus of Magic Bowls: Incantation Texts in Jewish Aramaic from Late Antiquity* (London: Kegan Paul, 2003); Dan Levene, *Jewish Aramaic Curse Texts from Late-Antique Mesopotamia* (Leiden: Brill, 2014).

7. For Rashi, see A. Cohen, *Everyman's Talmud* (New York: Dent and Dutton, 1949 [1932]), 269. Nancy Benovitz, "Psalm 91:1 and the Rabbinic Shema in Greek on a Byzantine Amuletic Armband," *Textus* 26 (2016): 143–171.

8. The phrase "the Most Holy and glorious Names" occurs frequently in magical texts and grimoires, but see, for instance, Richard Cavendish, *The Black Arts* (New York: Penguin, 1967), 239.

9. For Jewish magic, see Joshua Trachtenberg, *Jewish Magic and Superstition: A Study in Folk Religion* (Philadelphia: University of Pennsylvania Press, 2004); Yuval Harari, "The Sages and the Occult," in Shmuel Safrai et al., eds., *The Literature of the Sages, Second Part: Midrash and Targum, Liturgy, Poetry, Mysticism, Contracts, Inscriptions, Ancient Science and the Languages of Rabbinic Literature* (Assen: Royan Van Gorcum, 2006), 521–566; Gideon Bohak, *Ancient Jewish Magic: A History* (Cambridge: Cambridge University Press, 2008); Yuval Harari, *Jewish Magic Before the Rise of Kabbalah* (Detroit: Wayne State University Press, 2017). For the Shoshan Yesod ha-'Olam, see J. H. Chajes, *Between Worlds: Dybbuks, Exorcists, and Early Modern Judaism* (Philadelphia: University of Pennsylvania Press, 2003), 65.

10. W. G. Braude, *The Midrash on Psalms*, 2 vols. (New Haven, CT: Yale University Press, 1959); Midrash Tehillim, at https://www.matsati.com/index.php/midrash-tehillim/. Psalm 91 is also attributed to Moses in Numbers Rabbah.

11. *The Zohar*, edited by Daniel Chanan Matt, 12 vols. (Stanford, CA: Stanford University Press, 2004–2017).

12. Pesachim 111b, at https://www.sefaria.org/Pesachim.111b.7?lang=bi; Vreugdenhil, *Psalm 91 and Demonic Menace*, 293–297.

13. *Midrash Rabbah VII Lamentations*, edited by H. Freedman and Maurice Simon (London: Soncino, 1939), 98–99.

14. "Covered with scale upon scale" is from Braude, *The Midrash on Psalms*, 2:102–103. Rashi is quoted from his commentary on Psalms 91:6, at https://www.sefaria.org/Rashi_on_Psalms.91.5?lang=bi.

15. Berakhot 55b, at https://www.sefaria.org/Berakhot.55b?lang=bi. See also Sanhedrin 103a:13, at https://www.sefaria.org/Sanhedrin.103a.13?lang=bi.

16. Sanhedrin 103a:14, at https://www.sefaria.org/Sanhedrin.103a.14?lang=bi.

17. "When a man performs" is from Midrash Tanchuma Mishpatim 19:1, at https://www.sefaria.org/Midrash_Tanchuma%2C_Mishpatim.19?lang=bi; see also https://www.sefaria.org/Midrash_Tanchuma%2C_Vayetzei.3.1?lang=bi. For the ministering angels, see also Taanit 11a:9, at https://www.sefaria.org/Taanit.11a.9?lang=bi and Chagigah 16a:17, at https://www.sefaria.org/Chagigah.16a.17?lang=bi. *Midrash Tanhuma-Yelammedenu: An English Translation of Genesis and Exodus from the Printed Version of Tanhuma-Yelammedenu*, edited by Samuel A. Berman (Hoboken, NJ: KTAV, 1996), 514.

18. Brigitte (Rivka) Kern-Ulmer, "The Depiction of Magic in Rabbinic Texts," *Journal for the Study of Judaism in the Persian, Hellenistic, and Roman Period* 27 (1996): 289–303.

19. Shevuot 15b:11–12, at https://www.sefaria.org/Shevuot.15b.11-12?lang=bi. For Rabbi Yehoshua ben Levi, see "Joshua b. Levi," at https://www.jewishencyclopedia.com/articles/8919-joshua-b-levi.

20. William L Holladay, *The Psalms Through Three Thousand Years: Prayerbook of a Cloud of Witnesses* (Minneapolis, MN: Fortress Press, 1993), 141–143. For funeral practices, see Blu Greenberg, *How to Run a Traditional Jewish Household*, reprint ed. (New York: Touchstone, 2011).

21. Origen cites the "serpents and scorpions," for instance, at *De Principiis*, IV:5, at http://www.earlychristianwritings.com/text/origen125.html or Origen, *Contra Celsum*, II:48, at http://www.earlychristianwritings.com/text/origen162.html. For the high praise of the psalm in the early Christian era, see Quentin F. Wesselschmidt, ed., *Psalms 51–150*, Ancient Christian Commentary on Scripture, Old Testament Volume 8 (Downers Grove, IL: IVP Academic, 2007), 170–175.

22. Jeffrey Spier, "Medieval Byzantine Magical Amulets and Their Tradition," *Journal of the Warburg and Courtauld Institutes* 56 (1993): 25–62; Thomas J. Kraus, "'He That Dwelleth in the Help of the Highest': Septuagint Psalm 90 and the Iconographic Program on Byzantine Armbands," in C. A. Evans and H. D. Zacharias, eds., *Jewish and Christian Scripture as Artifact and Canon* (London: T. & T. Clark, 2009), 137–147; Theodore de Bruyn, *Making Amulets Christian: Artefacts, Scribes, and Contexts* (New York: Oxford University Press, 2017).

23. David Frankfurter, "The Binding of Antelopes: A Coptic Frieze and Its Egyptian Religious Context," *Journal of Near Eastern Studies* 63, no. 2 (2004): 97–109; David

Frankfurter, *Christianizing Egypt: Syncretism and Local Worlds in Late Antiquity* (Princeton, NJ: Princeton University Press, 2017). For older Egyptian precedents, see Carol Andrews, *Amulets from Ancient Egypt* (Austin: University of Texas Press, 1994).

24. For the sarcophagus, see Fritz Saxl, "The Ruthwell Cross," *Journal of the Warburg and Courtauld Institutes* 6 (1943): 12.

25. "Lamp with Christ Trampling the Beasts 5th Century," at https://www.metmus eum.org/art/collection/search/447998; Bert Jan Lietaert Peerbolte, "Protection Against Evil: Jesus Christ as Shield and Buckler (Psalm 91)," in R. Zimmermann and S. Joubert, eds., *Biblical Ethics and Application: Purview, Validity, and Relevance of Biblical Texts in Ethical Discourse* (Tübingen: Mohr Siebeck, 2017), 27–43.

26. The item is P. Duk. inv. 778: Csaba Láda and Amphilochios Papathomas, "A Greek Papyrus Amulet from the Duke Collection with Biblical Excerpts," *Bulletin of the American Society of Papyrologists* 41 (2004): 93–114.

27. Sanzo, *Scriptural Incipits on Amulets from Late Antique Egypt*.

28. Joseph E. Sanzo, "Magic and Communal Boundaries: The Problems with Amulets in Chrysostom, Adv. Iud. 8, and Augustine, In Io. tra. 7," *Henoch* 38, no. 2 (2017): 227–346.

29. For Laodicea, see Joseph E. Sanzo, "Ancient Amulets with Incipits: The Blurred Line Between Magic and Religion," 2015, at https://www.biblicalarchaeology.org/daily/ biblical-artifacts/artifacts-and-the-bible/ancient-amulets-with-incipits/.   Claudia Rapp, "Holy Texts, Holy Men, and Holy Scribes: Aspects of Scriptural Holiness in Late Antiquity," in William E. Klingshirn and Linda Safran, eds., *The Early Christian Book* (Washington, DC: Catholic University of America Press, 2007), 201; Ciaran Arthur, *"Charms," Liturgies, and Secret Rites in Early Medieval England* (Woodbridge, Suffolk: Boydell and Brewer, 2018).

30. Origen is quoted from *Origen: Homilies on Luke*, translated by Joseph T. Lienhard (Washington, DC: Catholic University of America Press, 1996), 128. Augustine, "Exposition on Psalm 91," at https://www.newadvent.org/fathers/1801091.htm. For Theodoret, see Theodoret of Cyrus, *Commentary on the Psalms 73–150* (Washington, DC: Catholic University of America Press, 2001), 106.

31. Vassiliki Foskolou, "The Virgin, the Christ-Child and the Evil Eye," in Maria Vassilaki, ed., *Images of the Mother of God* (London: Routledge, 2004), 251–262.

32. Frankfurter, *Christianizing Egypt*.

33. Athanasius, "Life of Antony," at http://medieval.ucdavis.edu/120A/Antony.html.

34. "That the demons" is quoted from Athanasius, "Life of Antony." Frankfurter, *Christianizing Egypt*. Denis F. Sullivan, "Life of St Ioannikios," in Alice-Mary Talbot, ed., *Byzantine Defenders Of Images: Eight Saints' Lives In English Translation* (Washington, D.C.: Dumbarton Oaks Research Library and Collection, 1998), 285–286.

35. Columba Stewart, *Cassian the Monk* (New York: Oxford University Press, 1998).

36. Jerome, "Letter XXII to Eustochium," at https://www.newadvent.org/fathers/3001 022.htm.

37. "So then you bring forward" is from John Cassian, *Seven Books on the Incarnation of the Lord, Against Nestorius*, ch. 16, at https://www.ewtn.com/catholicism/libr

ary/seven-books-on-the-incarnation-of-the-lord-against-nestorius-11532. John Cassian, *The Conferences of John Cassian,* at https://www.newadvent.org/fathers/ 3508.htm; John Cassian, *The Twelve Books on the Institutes of the Coenobia, and the Remedies for the Eight Principal Faults,* at https://www.newadvent.org/fathers/ 3507.htm.

38. Susan Gillingham, *Psalms Through the Centuries* (Chichester: Wiley-Blackwell, 2012), 51–55.

39. Jacqueline Borsje, "Druids, Deer, and 'Words of Power': Coming to Terms with Evil in Medieval Ireland," in K. Ritari and A. Bergholm, eds., *Approaches to Religion and Mythology in Celtic Studies* (Cambridge: Cambridge Scholars, 2008), 122–149.

40. "This psalm has marvelous power" is from *Cassiodorus: Explanation of the Psalms,* vol. 2, edited by P. G. Walsh (New York: Paulist Press, 1990), 387. For his career, see *The Selected Letters of Cassiodorus: A Sixth-Century Sourcebook,* edited by M. Shane Bjornlie (Oakland: University of California Press, 2020).

41. "Everyone who is guided" is from Theodoret of Cyrus, *Commentary on the Psalms 73–150,* 103.

42. "Complin," *Catholic Encylopedia,* at https://www.newadvent.org/cathen/04187a.htm.

43. Thomas Merton, *Bread in the Wilderness* (New York: J. Laughlin, 1953), 124.

44. Thomas Aquinas, *Summa Theologica,* 5 vols. (Westminster, MD: Christian Classics, 1981), 1 284.

45. "This is akin to dejection" is from John Cassian, Institutes X 1, at https://www.newadv ent.org/fathers/350710.htm. Roger Caillois, *Les démons de midi* (Montpellier: Fata Morgana, 1991 [1937]).

46. Robert E. Sinkewicz, ed., *Evagrius of Pontus: The Greek Ascetic Corpus* (New York: Oxford University Press, 2003), 99; Rüdiger Augst, *Lebensverwirklichung und christlicher Glaube. Acedia—Religiöse Gleichgültigkeit als Problem der Spiritualität bei Evagrius Ponticus* (Frankfurt: Peter Lang, 1990).

47. Basil is quoted from "Works: Ascetic," at https://www.ccel.org/ccel/schaff/npnf208. vi.ii.iv.html; "it is not unlikely that those schemers" is from Theodoret of Cyrus, *Commentary on the Psalms 73–150,* 104. W. H. Worrel, "The Demon of Noonday and Some Related Ideas," *Journal of the American Oriental Society* 38 (1918): 160–166; Joseph F. Gillet, "El mediodía y el demonio meridiano en España," *Nueva Revista de Filología Hispánica* 7 (1953): 307–315; R. Arbesmann, "The Daemonium Meridianum and Greek and Latin Patristic Exegesis," *Traditio* 14 (1958): 17–31; Dietrich Grau, *Das Mittagsgespenst (Daemonium Meridianum): Untersuchungen über seine Herkunft, Verbreitung und seine Erforschung in der europäischen Volkskunde* (Bonn: F. Schmitt, 1966); David Scott-Macnab, "The Many Faces of the Noonday Demon," *Journal of Early Christian History* 8, no. 1 (2018): 22–42.

48. Bernard of Clairvaux, Sermon 33, in "Commentary on the Song of Songs," http://www.clerus.org/bibliaclerusonline/en/c0z.htm.

49. Bernard of Clairvaux, Sermon 33. For Cistercian monastics falling prey to such temptations, see Barbara Newman, "Possessed by the Spirit: Devout Women, Demoniacs, and the Apostolic Life in the Thirteenth Century," *Speculum* 73, no. 3 (1998): 740–742.

50. Quoted from Walter Hilton, *The Scale of Perfection*, at https://ccel.org/ccel/hilton/ladder/ladder.ii_1.ii.ii.vii.html. See also Walter Hilton, *The Scale of Perfection*, translated by John P. H. Clark and Rosemary Dorward (New York: Paulist Press, 1991).

51. Hilton is quoted from J. P. H. Clark, "Walter Hilton and the Psalm Commentary *Qui Habitat*," *The Downside Review* 100 (1982): 244. The modernization of the Middle English text is my own work. Walter Hilton, *Qui habitat*, in *An Exposition of "Qui habitat" and "Bonum est" in English*, edited by Björn Wallner (Lund: Gleerup, 1954).

52. Reinhard Kuhn, *The Demon of Noontide: Ennui in Western Literature* (Princeton, NJ: Princeton University Press, 1976); Andrew Solomon, *The Noonday Demon: An Atlas of Depression* (New York: Simon and Schuster, 2001); Dom Jean-Charles Nault, *The Noonday Devil: Acedia, the Unnamed Evil of Our Times* (San Francisco: Ignatius Press, 2015); Donald Grayston, *Thomas Merton and the Noonday Demon: The Camaldoli Correspondence* (Eugene, OR: Cascade Books, 2015).

53. Oliver Farrar Emerson, "Some of Chaucer's Lines on the Monk," *Modern Philology* 1 (1903): 105–115.

54. Augustine of Hippo, *Expositions on the Book of Psalms*. The commentary on Psalm 91 is at https://www.ccel.org/ccel/schaff/npnf108.ii.XCI.html.

55. Jerome is quoted from Wesselschmidt, ed., *Psalms 51–150*, 171. Geoffrey Chaucer, "The Second Nun's Tale," at https://chaucer.fas.harvard.edu/pages/second-nuns-prologue-and-tale; Emerson, "Some of Chaucer's Lines on the Monk."

56. Emerson, "Some of Chaucer's Lines on the Monk."

Chapter 5

1. Augustine, "Exposition on Psalm 91," 17, at https://www.newadvent.org/fathers/1801091.htm.

2. Judith Herrin, *Ravenna: Capital of Empire, Crucible of Europe* (London: Allen Lane, 2020).

3. Robert W. Baldwin, "'I Slaughter Barbarians': Triumph as a Mode in Medieval Christian Art," *Konsthistorisk Tidskrift* 59, no. 4 (1990): 225–242.

4. Bart D. Ehrman, ed., *The Apostolic Fathers*, 2 vols., Loeb Classical Library (Cambridge, MA: Harvard University Press, 2003).

5. *Passio Sanctarum Perpetuae et Felicitatis*, at https://www.thelatinlibrary.com/perp.html.

6. "Marcion reads the scriptures" is from *Origen: Homilies on Luke*, translated by Joseph T. Lienhard (Washington, DC: Catholic University of America Press, 1996), 126–128.

7. Romans 16:17–20.

8. Jerome, Homily 20, in *The Homilies of Saint Jerome, Volume 1 (1–59 on the Psalms)*, edited by Marie Liguori Ewald (Washington, DC: Catholic University of America Press, 2010), 158.

9. "When some heretics promise" is from David Scott-Macnab, "The Many Faces of the Noonday Demon," *Journal of Early Christian History* 8, no. 1 (2018): 22–42.

10. "Deserters from the heavenly army" is from Augustine, *Confessions*, book 7:21, at https://www.newadvent.org/fathers/110107.htm.

11. Augustine, "Exposition on Psalm 91," 1.

12. "The persecution is very hot" is from Augustine, "Exposition on Psalm 91," 8. "But what is said to Christ" is from Augustine, "Tractate 10 (John 2:12–21)," at https://www.newadvent.org/fathers/1701010.htm.

13. Jerome is quoted from Scott-Macnab, "The Many Faces of the Noonday Demon," 33.

14. M. Shane Bjornlie, *Politics and Tradition Between Rome, Ravenna and Constantinople* (New York: Cambridge University Press, 2013).

15. "Thrice three tens" is from *Cassiodorus: Explanation of the Psalms*, edited by P. G. Walsh (New York: Paulist Press, 1990), 2:387.

16. "The terror of the night, then," is from *Cassiodorus: Explanation of the Psalms*, 2: 382.

17. Rudolf Leeb, *Konstantin und Christus: Die Verchristlichung der imperialen Repräsentation unter Konstantin dem Grossen als Spiegel seiner Kirchenpolitik und seines Selbstverständnisses als christlichen Kaiser* (Berlin: Walter de Gruyter, 1992), 51–52; Eusebius, "Life of Constantine," III:3, at https://sourcebooks.fordham.edu/basis/vita-constantine.asp.

18. Baldwin, "'I Slaughter Barbarians'"; Juliana Dresvina, *A Maid with a Dragon: The Cult of St Margaret of Antioch in Medieval England* (Oxford: Oxford University Press, 2016); Ildar Garipzanov, *Graphic Signs of Authority in Late Antiquity and the Early Middle Ages, 300–900* (New York: Oxford University Press, 2018).

19. Cyril Mango and Roger Scott, eds., *The Chronicle of Theophanes Confessor* (Oxford: Clarendon Press, 1997), 523.

20. J. Romilly Allen, "The Crosses at Ilkley," *Journal of the British Archaeological Association* 40 (1884): 158–172; F. Saxl, "The Ruthwell Cross," *Journal of the Warburg and Courtauld Institutes* 6 (1943): 1–19; Éamonn Ó Carragáin, "Christ over the Beasts and the Agnus Dei: Two Multivalent Panels on the Ruthwell and Bewcastle Crosses," in Paul E. Szarmach and Virginia Darrow Oggins, eds., *Sources of Anglo-Saxon Culture* (Kalamazoo, MI: Medieval Institute Publications, Western Michigan University, 1986), 377–403; Maidie Hilmo, *Medieval Images, Icons, and Illustrated English Literary Texts: From Ruthwell Cross to the Ellesmere Chaucer* (Aldershot, UK: Ashgate, 2004), 38; Éamonn Ó Carragáin, *Ritual and the Rood: Liturgical Images and the Old English Poems of the Dream of the Rood Tradition* (Toronto: University of Toronto Press, 2005). For a differing interpretation of the stone crosses, see Richard N. Bailey, "In Medio Duorum Animalium: Habakkuk, the Ruthwell Cross and Bede's Life of St Cuthbert," in Elizabeth Mullins and Diarmuid Scully, eds., *Listen, O Isles, unto Me: Studies in Medieval Word and Image in Honour of Jennifer O'Reilly* (Cork: Cork University Press, 2011), 243–252. For the overwhelming role of psalms in the Christian culture of the time, see Tamara Atkin and Francis Leneghan, eds., *The Psalms and Medieval English Literature: From the Conversion to the Reformation* (Woodbridge: D. S. Brewer, 2017).

21. Janet L. Nelson, *King and Emperor: A New Life of Charlemagne* (Oakland: University of California Press, 2019).

22. "Drawing of the Reliquary of Einhard," at https://izi.travel/en/1c9a-drawing-of-the-reliquary-of-einhard/en.

23. Celia Martin Chazelle, *The Crucified God in the Carolingian Era: Theology and Art of Christ's Passion* (Cambridge: Cambridge University Press, 2001); Robert Favreau, "Le Thème iconographique du lion dans les inscriptions médiévales," *Comptes Rendus des Séances de l'Académie des Inscriptions et Belles-Lettres* 135, no. 3 (1991): 613–636; Juliet Mullins, Jenifer Ní Ghrádaigh, and Richard Hawtree, eds., *Envisioning Christ on the Cross: Ireland and the Early Medieval West* (Dublin: Four Courts Press, 2013). The Genoels-Elderen ivory is depicted at https://www.flickriver.com/photos/28433765@N07/7985873435/ and at https://inpress.lib.uiowa.edu/feminae/DetailsPage.aspx?Feminae_ID=31200. For the Lorsch Gospels, see https://en.wikipedia.org/wiki/Christ_treading_on_the_beasts#/media/File:Ivory_back_cover_of_the_Lorsch_Gospels,_c._810,_Carolingian.jpg. For a tenth-century image of Christ trampling, from the abbey of Corbie, see https://gallica.bnf.fr/ark:/12148/btv1b10546770w/f201.image. The image is from a manuscript of the Venerable Bede, *De Templo Salomonis*. A "trampling" image from a French sacramentary around 1060 can be found at http://ica.themorgan.org/manuscript/page/15/126589. For the Utrecht Psalter, see Jill Bradley, *"You Shall Surely Not Die": The Concepts of Sin and Death as Expressed in the Manuscript Art of Northwestern Europe, c. 800–1200*, 2 vols. (Leiden: Brill, 2008), 100–106.

24. "Because our sleep has some likeness" is quoted from "Psalm 90—Introduction to Psalm 90," March 6, 2019, at https://psallamdomino.blogspot.com/2019/03/psalm-90-introduction-to-psalm-90.html. William L Holladay, *The Psalms Through Three Thousand Years: Prayerbook of a Cloud of Witnesses* (Minneapolis, MN: Fortress Press, 1993), 176–184; Bruce K. Waltke and James M. Houston, with Erika Moore, *The Psalms as Christian Worship: A Historical Commentary* (Grand Rapids, MI: William B. Eerdmans, 2010); Bruce K. Waltke and James M. Houston, *The Psalms as Christian Praise: A Historical Commentary* (Grand Rapids, MI: William B. Eerdmans, 2019).

25. "And listen to David giving thee" is from Philip Schaff and Henry Wace, eds., *A Select Library of the Nicene and Post Nicene Fathers of the Christian Church* (New York: Christian Literature Company, 1894), 364. "Thou whom none can deceive" is quoted from Alexander Roberts, ed., *The Ante-Nicene Fathers*, at http://www.tertullian.org/fathers2/ANF-07/anf07-49.htm.

26. Vassiliki Foskolou, "The Virgin, the Christ-Child and the Evil Eye," in Maria Vassilaki, ed., *Images of the Mother of God* (London: Routledge, 2004), 251–262.

27. *"Qui habitat in adiutorio altissimi,"* March 7, 2017, at http://chantblog.blogspot.com/2017/03/qui-habitat-in-adiutorio-altissimi-lent.html.

28. Celia Martin Chazelle, *The Crucified God in the Carolingian Era* (Cambridge: Cambridge University Press, 2001), 260–261.

29. K. M. Openshaw, "The Battle Between Christ and Satan in the Tiberius Psalter," *Journal of the Warburg and Courtauld Institutes* 52 (1989): 14–33; Hilmo, *Medieval Images, Icons, and Illustrated English Literary Texts.*

30. Honorius of Autun, "Super Aspidem et Basiliscum Ambulabit: A Sermon for Palm Sunday from the Speculum Ecclesię," at https://sicutincensum.wordpress.com/2021/

03/23/super-aspidem-et-basiliscum-ambulabit-a-sermon-for-palm-sunday-from-the-speculum-ecclesiae/.

31. Marleen Cré, "London, Westminster Cathedral Treasury, MS 4: An Edition of the Westminster Compilation," *Journal of Medieval Religious Cultures* 37, no. 1 (2011): 1–59. J. P. H. Clark, "Walter Hilton and the Psalm Commentary *Qui Habitat*," *The Downside Review* 100 (1982): 235–262.

32. Openshaw, "The Battle Between Christ and Satan in the Tiberius Psalter"; Kathleen M. Openshaw, "Weapons in the Daily Battle: Images of the Conquest of Evil in the Early Medieval Psalter," *Art Bulletin* 75, no. 1 (1993): 17–38; Stella Panayatova, "The Illustrated Psalter: Luxury and Practical Use," in Susan Boynton and Diane J. Reilly, eds., *The Practice of the Bible in the Middle Ages: Production, Reception, and Performance in Western Christianity* (New York: Columbia University Press, 2011), 247–271; Bradley, "You Shall Surely Not Die."

33. Janet Backhouse, *The Luttrell Psalter* (London: British Library, 1989), 42; Michelle P. Brown, ed., *The Luttrell Psalter: A Facsimile* (London: British Library, 2006).

34. Chris Wickham, *Medieval Europe* (New Haven, CT: Yale University Press, 2016).

35. M. Stroll, *Symbols as Power: The Papacy Following the Investiture Contest* (Leiden: Brill, 1991).

36. Baldwin, "'I Slaughter Barbarians.'" For Nicholaus the sculptor, see Christine Verzár Bornstein, "Matilda of Canosssa, Papal Rome, and the Earliest Italian Porch Portals," in Arturo Carlo Quintavalle, ed., *Romanico padano, romanico europeo* (Parma: Artegrafica Silva, 1982), 143–159; Christine Verzár Bornstein, "Victory over Evil: Variations on the Image of Psalm 90:13 in the Art of Nicholaus," in Roberto Salvini, ed., *Scritti di Storia dell'arte in onore di Roberto Salvini* (Florence: Sansoni, 1984), 45–51; Christine Verzár Bornstein, *Portals and Politics in the Early Italian City-State: The Sculpture of Nicholaus in Context* (Parma: Università degli Studi di Parma, Istituto di Storia dell'Arte, Centro di Studi Medievali, 1988).

37. Baldwin, "'I Slaughter Barbarians.'" Pisa's Pantokrator mosaic is depicted at https://commons.wikimedia.org/wiki/File:Pisa_Cathedral_Pantokrator_UP.jpg. For Jewish appropriations of the theme, see Ephraim Shoham-Steiner, "The Clash over Synagogue Decorations in Medieval Cologne," *Jewish History* 30 (2016): 129–164; Illia Rodov, "Dragons: A Symbol of Evil in Synagogue Decoration?," *Ars Judaica* 1 (2005): 63–84.

38. Baldwin, "'I Slaughter Barbarians.'"

39. Kevin Cathcart, "Phoenician Inscriptions from Arslan Tash and Some Old Testament Texts," in James K. Aitken, Katharine J. Dell, and Brian A. Mastin, eds., *On Stone and Scroll: Essays in Honour of Graham Ivor Davies* (Berlin: Walter de Gruyter, 2011), 97; Christoph T. Maier, ed., *Crusade Propaganda and Model Sermons for the Preaching of the Cross* (New York: Cambridge University Press, 2006).

40. "These words were inscribed on the marble pillar in Kosovo," at http://manasija.rs/history/despot-stefan/inscription-on-the-marble-pillar-at-kosovo/?lang=en.

41. Irving Lavin, "Pisanello and the Invention of the Renaissance Medal," in J. Poeschke, ed., *Italienische Frührenaissance und nordeuropäisches Spätmittelalter: Kunst der frühen Neuzeit im europäischen Zusammenhang* (Munich: Hirmer, 1993), 67–84.

Chapter 6

1. Martin Luther, "Lectures on Genesis 49," in *Luther's Works*, vol. VIII, edited by Jaroslav Pelikan (St. Louis: Concordia, 1966), 251.

2. "The Law Is Not for You," January 28, 2014, at https://allegralaboratory.net/the-law-is-not-for-you/; Susan Tipton, "Super aspidem et basiliscum ambulabis. Zur Entstehung der Mariensäulen im 17. Jahrhundert," in Dieter Breuer, ed., *Religion und Religiosität im Zeitalter des Barok* (Wiesbaden: Harrassowitz, 1995), 375–398; Hubert Glaser and Elke Anna Werner, "The Victorious Virgin: The Religious Patronage of Maximilian I of Bavaria," in Klaus Bussmann and Heinz Schilling, eds., *1648, War and Peace in Europe: Art and Culture* (Münster: Landschaftverband Westfalen-Lippe, 1998). For the wider artistic context, see Steven F. Ostrow, "Paul V, the Column of the Virgin, and the New Pax Romana," *Journal of the Society of Architectural Historians* 69 (2010): 352–377.

3. "A most distinguished jewel" is from Martin Luther, *A Manual of the Book of Psalms* (London: R. B. Seeley and W. Burnside, 1837), 241. Martin Luther, "Lectures on Psalm 91," in *Luther's Works*, vol. XI, edited by Hilton C. Oswald (St. Louis: Concordia, 1976), 208–258.

4. "If I believe the promise of God" is from Martin Luther, "Lectures on Genesis 48," in *Luther's Works*, vol. VIII, edited by Jaroslav Pelikan (St. Louis: Concordia, 1966), 167.

5. "This faith alone lasts" is from Matrtin Luther, "The Gospel for St. Stephen's Day," in *Luther's Works*, vol. LII, edited by Hans J. Hillerbrand (Philadelphia: Fortress Press, 1974), 97. Scott H. Hendrix, *Martin Luther: Visionary Reformer* (New Haven, CT: Yale University Press, 2015).

6. Hannibal Hamlin, *Psalm Culture and Early Modern English Literature* (Cambridge: Cambridge University Press, 2004), 127.

7. Edward Henry Lauer, "Luther's Translation of the Psalms in 1523–24," *Journal of English and Germanic Philology* 14, no. 1 (1915): 1–34.

8. The text of Luther's 1545 translation of 91 can be found at https://newchristianbib lestudy.org/bible/german-luther-1545/psalms/91/. Martin Luther, "Defense of the Translation of the Psalms, 1531," in *Luther's Works*, vol. XXXV, edited by E. Theodore Bachmann (Philadelphia: Muhlenberg Press, 1960), 216–218.

9. "There is a ministry of the angels" is from Martin Luther, "Lectures on Isaiah 63," in *Luther's Works*, vol. XVII, edited by Hilton C. Oswald (St. Louis: Concordia, 1972), 357.

10. For the noonday demon, see, for instance, Martin Luther, "Lectures on Psalm 59," in *Luther's Works*, vol. X, edited by Hilton C. Oswald (St. Louis: Concordia, 1974), 274. For the basilisk, see J. H. M. D'Aubigné, *History of the Reformation of the Sixteenth Century* (London: Blackie and Son, 1846), II:92.

11. For Vehus, see Martin Luther, "Luther at the Diet of Worms (1521)," in *Luther's Works*, vol. XXXII, edited by George W. Forell (Philadelphia: Muhlenberg Press, 1958), 116–117. The Murnarus illustration is reproduced at https://commons.wikimedia.org/wiki/File:Luther_et_Murner_en_dragon_par_Matthias_Gnidius-1521_(BNUS)_(2).jpg. George Clutton, "Two Early Representations of Lutheranism in France,"

Journal of the Warburg Institute 1 (1938): 287–291. The trampling image was a familiar one in controversial texts in these years; see Desiderius Erasmus, *Collected Works of Erasmus: Controversies*, edited by Denis L. Drysdall (Toronto: University of Toronto Press, 1993), 73:136.

12. "For what are these [enemies] but the voices" is from Martin Luther to Nicholas von Amsdorf, May 30, 1525, in *Luther's Works*, vol. XLIX, edited by Gottfried G. Krodel (Philadelphia: Fortress Press, 1972), 112–114.

13. "He is commanded to avoid" is from Martin Luther, "Against the Roman Papacy, an Institution of the Devil, 1545," in *Luther's Works*, vol. XLI, edited by Eric W. Gritsch (Philadelphia: Fortress Press, 1966), 359.

14. "This entire psalm is an exhortation" is from Luther, "Lectures on Psalm 91," 208; see also 216 for the terror of the night, and 212 for "ungodly teachings."

15. For Jan Hus, see Martin Luther, "Lectures on Psalm 112," in *Luther's Works*, vol. XIII, edited by Jaroslav Pelikan (St. Louis: Concordia, 1956), 416–417.

16. Rowland Prothero, *The Psalms in Human Life* (New York: E. P. Dutton, 1904), 185–186; Herman J. Selderhuis, ed., *Psalms 73–150*, in Timothy George, ed., *Reformation Commentary on Scripture: Old Testament VIII* (Downers Grove, IL: IVP, 2018): 118–122.

17. John Calvin, "Commentary on Psalm 91," at https://www.ccel.org/ccel/calvin/calcom10/calcom10.xxvi.html.

18. "The obstacles which Satan throws" is quoted from John Calvin, "Commentary on Psalm 91," at https://ccel.org/ccel/calvin/calcom10/calcom10.xxvi.iv.html." Mention is made" is at https://www.ccel.org/ccel/calvin/calcom10.xxvi.ii.html.

19. "Troubles, it is true" is from Calvin, "Commentary on Psalm 91," at https://ccel.org/ccel/calvin/calcom10/calcom10.xxvi.iii.html.

20. Martin Luther to Hans Luther, February 15, 1530, in *Luther's Works*, vol. XLIX, edited by Gottfried G. Krodel (Philadelphia: Fortress Press, 1972), 270. Lewis Bayly, *The Practice of Piety*, at https://www.ccel.org/ccel/bayly/piety.iv.v.i.html.

21. Susan Gillingham, *Psalms Through the Centuries* (Chichester: Wiley-Blackwell, 2012). For de Rohan, see Prothero, *The Psalms in Human Life*, 212.

22. Jason McCloskey, "Spain Succored by Religion: Titian and Lope de Vega's *La Dragontea*," in Jason McCloskey and Ignacio López Alemany, eds., *Signs of Power in Habsburg Spain and the New World* (Lewisburg, PA: Bucknell University Press, 2013). For the title page of *La Dragontea*, see https://www.alamy.com/drake-dragon-la-dragontea-etc-a-poem-against-sir-francis-dra-p-p-mey-valecia-1598-title-page-of-an-epic-poem-written-to-celebrate-drakes- sudden-death-the-illustration-depicts-the-spanish-eagle-above-the-dying-drake-dragon-image-taken-from-la-dragontea-etc-a-poem-against-sir-francis-drake-originally-publishedproduced-in-p-p-mey-valecia-1598-source-g10925-title-page-image227161102.html.

23. Jean Le Frère de Laval, *La Vraye et entière histoire des troubles et guerres civiles, avenuë de nostre temps, pour le faict de la religion, tant en France, Allemaigne que pays bas. Recueillie de plusieurs discours françois & latins, & réduite en vingtz livres* (Paris: Chez Jean Hulpeau, 1575), 345–346.

24. Thomas More, *Dialogue of Comfort Against Tribulation*, edited by Monica Stevens (London: Sheed and Ward, 1951), book II, sec. 9–16, at https://ccel.org/ccel/more/comfort/comfort.i.html.

25. Christopher Fowler, *Dæmonium Meridianum. Satan at Noon. Or, Antichristian Blasphemies, Anti-Scripturall Divelismes, Anti-Morall Uncleanness, Evidenced in the Light of Truth, and Published by the Hand of Justice* (London: Francis Eglesfield, 1655).

26. For the Anabaptists, see Thieleman J. Van Braght, ed., *The Bloody Theater or Martyrs' Mirror of the Defenseless Christians* (Scottsdale, PA: Herald Press, n.d.). "Yea, we must fight" is from the correspondence of Jerome Segers, at https://www.ccel.org/ccel/vanbraght/mirror.iv.v.html?scrBook=Eph&scrCh=3&scrV=20#highlight.

27. "The proud pope" is quoted from *The Acts and Monuments of John Foxe* in *The Church Historians of England*, vol. II, part 1 (London: Seeley's, 1854), 195–196: spelling modernized. Gillian B. Elliott, "Victorious Trampling at Sts. Peter and Paul at Andlau and the Politics of Frederick Barbarossa," *Zeitschrift für Kunstgeschichte* 72 (2009): 145–164.

28. Kurt Stadtwald, *Roman Popes and German Patriots: Antipapalism in the Politics of the German Humanist Movement from Gregor Heimburg to Martin Luther* (Geneva: Librairie Droz, 1996). The Cornelius story is from Acts 10:26.

29. Robert Greene, *The Spanish Masquerado* (London, 1589).

30. Abbie Findlay Potts, *The Ecclesiastical Sonnets of William Wordsworth* (New Haven, CT: Yale University Press, 1922), 245. See also https://www.public-domain-poetry.com/william-wordsworth/ecclesiastical-sonnets-part-i-xxxviii-scene-in-venice-4374.

31. Wycliffe's translation of the psalm is from "John Wycliffe Bible 1382," at http://textusreceptusbibles.com/Wycliffe/19/90. Elizabeth Solopova, ed., *The Wycliffite Bible: Origin, History and Interpretation* (Leiden: Brill, 2016).

32. The Coverdale version can be found, for instance, at https://www.bibliatodo.com/en/parallel-bible/?l=psalm&cap=91&i=en&v=Coverdale&ii=en&vv=Coverdale.   See also William Aldis Wright, *The Hexaplar Psalter* (Cambridge: Cambridge University Press, 2015), 227–228.

33. Wright, *The Hexaplar Psalter*, 227–228; Kevin Killeen, Helen Smith, and Rachel Willie, eds., *The Oxford Handbook of the Bible in Early Modern England, c. 1530–1700* (Oxford: Oxford University Press, 2015); Hannibal Hamlin, "The Renaissance Bible," in Hannibal Hamlin, ed., *The Cambridge Companion to Shakespeare and Religion* (New York: Cambridge University Press, 2019).

34. The Geneva text can be found at https://www.biblegateway.com/passage/?search=psalm+91&version=GNV; Hamlin, *Psalm Culture and Early Modern English Literature*; Hannibal Hamlin, "Reading the Bible in Tudor England," Oxford Handbooks Online, 2015, at https://www.oxfordhandbooks.com/view/10.1093/oxfordhb/9780199935338.001.0001/oxfordhb-9780199935338-e-77.

35. "Decree Concerning the Canonical Scriptures," at https://www.ewtn.com/catholicism/library/decree-concerning-the-canonical-scriptures-1494.

36. For the Douay-Reims version of "Psalm 90," see https://www.biblegateway.com/passage/?search=psalm+90&version=DRA.

37. *Sermons of Saint Robert Cardinal Bellarmine, S.J., Part III: Sermons 56 to 87: Twelve Sermons on the Catholic Faith; Eight Sermons on Tribulation; Twelve Sermons on Psalm 90 (91)*, edited by Kenneth Baker (Saddle River, NJ: Keep the Faith, 2018).

38. Maximilian von Eynatten, *Manuale Exorcismorum; Continens Instructiones et Exorcismos* ... (Antwerp, 1648), 2, 55, 155, 232; compare Fr. Bernardo Sannig, *Rituale Franciscanum* (Prague, 1693), 318, For a semifictional use of that ritual with those words, set in the 1630s, see Aldous Huxley, *The Devils of Loudun* (London: Chatto and Windus, 1952). Moshe Sluhovsky, *Believe Not Every Spirit: Possession, Mysticism, and Discernment in Early Modern Catholicism* (Chicago: University of Chicago Press, 2007); Francis Young, *A History of Exorcism in Catholic Christianity* (Cham: Springer, 2016). The witch-hunter's manual is Francesco Maria Guazzo, *Compendium Maleficarum: The Montague Summers Edition* (North Chelmsford, MA: Courier, 2012), 168.

39. Rubens's "The Virgin as the Woman of the Apocalypse" is reproduced at http://www.getty.edu/art/collection/objects/762/peter-paul-rubens-the-virgin-as-the-woman-of-the-apocalypse-flemish-about-1623-1624/.

40. Joseph de San Miguel y Barco, *Biblia Mariana ex pluribus authoribus collecta* (Burgis, 1674). For an early sculptural depiction, see, for instance, "Santa Maria in Celsano," at https://romanchurches.fandom.com/wiki/Santa_Maria_in_Celsano. For the Callot etching, see https://www.metmuseum.org/art/collection/search/420704. The same theme appears in other depictions of saints from these years. Stefano della Bella (1610–1664) shows a saint heroically trampling a two-headed monster, with the *super aspidem* verse as inscription. The saint is identified as the medieval monastic founder St. John Gualbert, but another source credits it as St. Anthony: François Etienne Joubert, *Manuel de l'amateur d'estampes* (Paris: Chez l'auteur, 1821), 176–177.

41. Diantha Steinhilper, "An Emperor's Heraldry, a Pope's Portrait, and the Cortés Map of Tenochtitlan: The *Praeclara Ferdinadi Cortesii* as an Evangelical Announcement," *Sixteenth Century Journal* 47 (2016): 371–399; Fernando Cervantes, *The Devil in the New World: The Impact of Diabolism in New Spain* (New Haven, CT: Yale University Press, 1997).

42. For the Jesuits of New France, see Reuben Gold Thwaites, ed., *The Jesuit Relations and Allied Documents* (Cleveland, OH: Burrows Brothers, 1897), vol. 6, at https://www.gutenberg.org/files/51262/51262-h/51262-h.htm.

43. Antonio Ruiz de Montoya, *Conquista espiritual hecha por los religiosos de la Compañía de Jesús en las provincias del Paraguay, Paraná, Uruguay y Tape* (Madrid, 1639); D. Francisco Jarque, *Ruiz Montoya en Indias 1608–1652* (Madrid: Victoriano Suarez, 1900), IV:105; Barbara Ganson, "Antonio Ruiz de Montoya, Apostle of the Guarani," *Journal of Jesuit Studies* 3 (2016): 197–210.

44. Alonso Ramos, *Los prodigios de la omnipotencia y milagros de la gracia en la vida de la venerable sierva de Dios, Catarina de San Juan*, books II, III, and IV, edited by Robin Ann Rice (New York: IDEA/IGAS, 2016), 197.

45. Gerry Ronan, "Zorro of Wexford?," *The Past: The Organ of the Uí Cinsealaigh Historical Society* 22 (2000): 3–50.

46. Johann Albrecht Widmanstetter, ed., *Liber sacrosancti evangelii de Iesu Christo Domino et Deo nostro* (Vienna: M. Zimmermann, 1555); Grażyna Jurkowlaniec, "Masterpieces, Altarpieces, and Devotional Prints," *Religions* 10 (2019): 11–14.

47. Moshe Lazar, "Scorched Parchments and Tortured Memories: The 'Jewishness' of the Anussim (Crypto-Jews)," in Mary Elizabeth Perry and Anne J. Cruz, eds., *Cultural Encounters: The Impact of the Inquisition in Spain and the New World* (Berkeley: University of California Press, 1991), 176–206.

48. Silvia Hamui Sutton, "Discursos de los judaizantes novohispanos en torno al Mesías: desde la devoción de Luis de Carvajal hasta la influencia de la Ilustración en Rafael Gil Rodríguez," in Silvia Hamui Sutton, ed., *Criptojudíos siglos XVI–XVIII* (Mexico City: Centro de Documentación e Investigación Judía de México, 2019), 73; Silvia Hamui Sutton, ed., *El judaizante Rafael Gil Rodríguez y el declive de la Inquisición: Nueva España, siglo XVIII* (Mexico City: Universidad Iberoamericana, 2020); Teresa Farfán Cabrera, Jazmín Hernández Moreno, and Javier Meza González, *La risa del profeta o Rafael Gil Rodríguez* (Mexico City: Universidad Autónoma Metropolitana, 2020).

49. Leeman L. Perkins, "Josquin's *Qui habitat* and the Psalm Motets," *Journal of Musicology* 26, no. 4 (2020): 512–565. For musical settings of the psalms in early modern Europe, see Susan Gillingham, *Psalms Through the Centuries* (Chichester: Wiley-Blackwell, 2012), 180–190.

50. The Scottish psalter is quoted from https://thewestminsterstandard.org/psalm-91/

51. "Wer heimlich seine Wohnestatt" was the work of Kaspar Ulenberg: https://www.newadvent.org/cathen/15120b.htm.

52. For the full text of "Wer sich des Höchsten Schirm vertraut," see https://www.cpdl.org/wiki/index.php/Wer_sich_des_H%C3%B6chsten_Schirm_vertraut,_SWV_1 89_(Heinrich_Sch%C3%BCtz).

53. Frederick J. Gaiser, "'I Sing to You and Praise You' (Psalm 30): Paul Gerhardt and the Psalms," *Word and World* 27 (2007): 195–205; Frederick J. Gaiser, "'It Shall Not Reach You': Talisman or Vocation? Reading Psalm 91 in Time of War," *Word and World* 25 (2005): 200–202.

54. For Watts's rendering of Psalm 91, see http://www.cgmusic.org/workshop/watts/psalm_91.htm.

55. *The Poems of Alexander Pope*, edited by John Butt (New Haven, CT: Yale University Press, 1963), 113–114.

56. Todd M. Johnson and Gina A. Zurlo, *World Christian Encyclopedia*, 3rd ed. (Edinburgh: Edinburgh University Press, 2019).

Chapter 7

1. C. H. Spurgeon, "The Privileges of the Godly: An Exposition of Psalm 91," in *The General Baptist Magazine* 76 (January 1874): 4.

2. Spurgeon's essay was later expanded into a much larger discussion in his vast series on the psalms, published as *The Treasury of David* (New York: Funk & Wagnalls, 1883). His discussion of Psalm 91 is found at IV:230–262. The expanded Spurgeon commentary on 91 is reproduced at multiple online locations, including https://www.christian ity.com/bible/commentary.php?com=spur&b=19&c=91.

3. See, for instance, the 1498 painting "Saint Sebastian Interceding for the Plague Stricken," at https://art.thewalters.org/detail/6193/saint-sebastian-interceding-for-the-plague-stricken/; Duncan G. Stroik, "Non Timebis a Sagitta Volante in Die," *Institute for Sacred Architecture* 37 (2020), at https://www.sacredarchitecture. org/articles/non_timebis_a_sagitta_volante_in_die. Lori Jones, "Apostumes, Carbuncles, and Botches: Visualizing the Plague in Late Medieval and Early Modern Medical Treatises," in Rinaldo Fernando Canalis and Massimo Ciavolella, eds. *Disease and Disability in Medieval and Early Modern Art and Literature* (Turnhout, Belgium: Brepols, 2021), 173–200.

4. Julia Bolton Holloway, "The 'Sweet New Style': Essays on Brunetto Latino, Dante Alighieri, Geoffrey Chaucer, and Giovanni Boccaccio," (2015) at academia.edu.

5. William R. Newman, "Bad Chemistry: Basilisks and Women in Paracelsus and Pseudo-Paracelsus," *Ambix* 67 (2020): 30–46. For syphilis, see Andrew Stott, "Tiresias and the Basilisk: Vision and Madness in Middleton and Rowley's *The Changeling*," *Revista Alicantiona de Estudios Ingleses* 12 (1999): 165–179.

6. The *Enarratio Psalmorum Davidis* was an enduring best-seller, which appeared in multiple editions. For Jewish uses of 91 as a charm against plagues, see Chen Malul, "Prayers, Amulets and Spells to Ward Off Plagues," *Jerusalem Post*, April 14, 2020, at https://www.jpost.com/judaism/jewish-holidays/prayers-amulets-and-spells-to-ward-off-plague-624517.

7. Rebecca Totaro, ed., *The Plague Epic in Early Modern England Heroic Measures, 1603–1721* (London: Routledge, 2012); Rebecca Totaro and Ernest B. Gilman, eds., *Representing the Plague in Early Modern England* (London: Routledge, 2011); Dean Phillip Bell, ed., *Plague in the Early Modern World: A Documentary History* (London: Routledge, 2019).

8. Martin Luther, "Whether One May Flee From a Deadly Plague," in *Luther's Works*, vol. XLIII, edited by Carl J. Schindler (Philadelphia: Fortress Press, 1968), 115–138.

9. Andreas Osiander, *How and Whither a Christen Man Ought to Flye the Horrible Plage of the Pestilence: A Sermon Out of the Psalme. Qui Habitat in Adsutorio Altissimi* (London: James Nicolson, 1537). Full text at https://quod.lib.umich.edu/e/eebo2/ A06532.0001.001/1:5?rgn=div1;view=fulltext.

10. Osiander, *How and Whither*.

11. Osiander, *How and Whither*.

12. Osiander, *How and Whither*.

13. Lactantius is quoted from Spurgeon, *The Treasury of David*, IV:243. See also John Downame, *Annotations upon All the Books of the Old and New Testament: Wherein the Text Is Explained, Doubts Resolved, Scriptures Parallelled, and Various Readings Observed* (London, 1645), 5.

14. "Almighty God doth govern natural causes" is quoted from Theodore Beza, *A Learned Treatise of the Plague Wherein the Two Questions, Whether the Plague Be Infectious or No, and, Whether and How Farr It May Be Shunned of Christians by Going Aside, Are Resolved* (London, 1665); full text at https://quod.lib.umich.edu/e/eebo/A27 641.0001.001?rgn=main;view=fulltext. See also Amy Nelson Burnett and Emidio Campi, eds., *A Companion to the Swiss Reformation* (Leiden: Brill, 2016); Ronald K. Rittger, "Protestants and Plague: The Case of the 1562/63 Pest in Nürnberg," in Franco Mormando and Thomas Worcester, eds., *Piety and Plague: From Byzantium to the Baroque* (Kirksville, MO: Truman State University Press, 2007), 132–155.

15. Beza, *A Learned Treatise of the Plague*; Theodore Beza, *A Learned Treatise of the Plague*, edited by Ben Castle (Moscow, ID: Canon Press, 2020).

16. *Orders, Thought Meete by His Maiestie, and His Priuie Counsell, to Be Executed Throughout the Counties of This Realme, in Such Townes, Villages, and Other Places, as Are, or May Be Hereafter Infected with the Plague, for the Stay of Further Increase of the Same* (London, 1603). "To lighten his hand" is quoted from J. R. Tanner, *Constitutional Documents of the Reign of James I* (Cambridge: Cambridge University Press, 1961), 24; James Balmford, *A Short Dialogue Concerning the Plagues Infection Published to Preserue Bloud, Through the Blessing of God* (London: Richard Boyle, 1603).

17. T.C., *A Godly and Learned Sermon, vpon the 91. Psalme Declaring How, and to What Place, a Christian Man Ought to Flie in the Daungerous Time of the Pestilence, for His Best Safetie and Deliuerance* (London: E. Allde for Edward White, 1603); Henry Holland, *Spirituall Preseruatiues Against the Pestilence: Or a Treatise Containing Sundrie Questions Both Concerning the Causes of the Pestilence, (Where is Shewed, that the Plague is a Mixt Euill of Knowne and Secret Causes, and Therefore So Hardly Healed by Naturall Curatiues Only) and the Most Pretious Preseruatiues Against the Same and Many Other Euils. Chiefely Collected out of the 91 Psalme* (London: R. Field and T. Scarlet, 1593); Henry Holland, *Spiritual Preservatives Against the Pestilence. Or Seven Lectures on the 91st Psalm* (London, 1603 [1593]).

18. Henoch Clapham, *An Epistle Discoursing upon the Present Pestilence Teaching What It Is, and How the People of God Should Carry Themselves Towards God and Their Neighbor Therein*, reprinted with some additions (London, 1603), at https://quod.lib. umich.edu/e/eebo/A18917.0001.001?view=toc; Henoch Clapham, *Henoch Clapham His Demaundes and Answeres Touching the Pestilence Methodically Handled, as His Time and Meanes Could Permit* (Middelburg, Netherlands, 1604), at https://quod.lib. umich.edu/e/eebo/A18922.0001.001/1:4?rgn=div1;view=toc.

19. "Appeareth to be deadly" is quoted from Clapham, *Henoch Clapham His Demaundes and Answeres*, 11; "That stroke which the angel inflicteth" is from the same source, n.p.

20. Clapham, *Henoch Clapham His Demaundes and Answeres*.

21. Robert Horne, *The Shield of the Righteous: or, the Ninety-first Psalm, Expounded, with the Addition of Doctrines and Verses. Verie Necessarie and Comfortable in These Dayes of Heauinesse, Wherein the Pestilence Rageth So Sore in London, and Other Parts of This Kingdome* (London, 1628), 3.

22. Martin Luther, "Defense of the Translation of the Psalms, 1531," in *Luther's Works*, vol. XXXV, edited by E. Theodore Bachmann (Philadelphia: Muhlenberg Press, 1960), 209–223.

23. Matthew Henry, "Commentary on Psalm 91," at https://ccel.org/ccel/henry/mhc3/mhc3.Ps.xcii.html.

24. John Newton, "Hymn 47," in *Olney Hymns*, at https://ccel.org/ccel/newton/olneyhymns.h1_47.html.

25. Martin Luther, "Lectures on Genesis 46," in *Luther's Works*, vol. VIII, edited by Jaroslav Pelikan (St. Louis: Concordia, 1966), 94.

26. Weller is quoted from Herman J. Selderhuis, ed., *Psalms 73–150*, in Timothy George, ed., *Reformation Commentary on Scripture: Old Testament VIII* (Downers Grove, IL: IVP, 2018), 121.

27. Downame, *Annotations*, 5.

28. Abraham Wright, *A Practical Commentary upon the Psalms* (London 1661), 102–103. The parable of the wheat and tares is found at Matthew 13:24–43.

29. William Bridge, *The Righteous Man's Habitation in the Time of Plague and Pestilence, Being a Brief Exposition of the XCI Psalm* (London, 1665). Quotes are taken from the 1853 edition published as *The Saint's Hiding Place* (London: John Henry Jackson, 1853). Thomas Doolittle, *Man Ashiv le-Yahoweh, or, A Serious Inquiry for a Suitable Return for Continued Life, in and After a Time of Great Mortality by a Wasting Plague* (London, 1665).

30. "Though the danger, evil, and misery of the pestilence" is from Bridge, *The Righteous Man's Habitation*, 7; "Without all doubt he may" is from 20–21.

31. Bridge, *The Righteous Man's Habitation*, 27.

32. Henry, "Commentary on Psalm 91."

33. Henry, "Commentary on Psalm 91."

34. Daniel Defoe, *History of the Plague in London*, in *The Novels and Miscellaneous Works of Daniel Defoe* (London: Bell & Daldy, 1869), 5:12.

35. Manuel Barcia Paz, *The Yellow Demon of Fever* (New Haven, CT: Yale University Press, 2020). Starr is quoted from Donna R. Causey, "John Wesley Starr, Jr. Biography and Genealogy (1830–1853)" at https://www.alabamapioneers.com/biography-john-wesley-starr-jr-1830/. For "Brother Wilkinson," see "John Wilkinson 1834–1875: Obituary," Louisiana Conference, United Methodist Church, at https://www.la-umc.org/obituary/1548261. George Dodd Armstrong, *The Summer of the Pestilence: A History of the Ravages of the Yellow Fever in Norfolk, Virginia, A.D. 1855* (Philadelphia: J. B. Lippincott, 1856), 101. For cholera, see Lucinda Boyd, "Cholera—The Pestilence That Walketh in Darkness and Wasteth at Noonday," in her *Chronicles of Cynthiana and Other Chronicles* (Cincinnati, OH: Robert Clarke, 1892), 119–121.

36. Charles Haddon Spurgeon, *The Treasury of David* (New York: Funk & Wagnalls, 1883), IV:234.

37. Sandra Hempel, *The Strange Case of the Broad Street Pump: John Snow and the Mystery of Cholera* (Berkeley: University of California Press, 2007); Spurgeon, *The Treasury of David*, IV:235–236.

Chapter 8

1. Reinhold Niebuhr, *Beyond Tragedy* (New York: Charles Scribner's Sons, 1937), 97.

2. Peter Mercer-Taylor, ed., *The Cambridge Companion to Mendelssohn* (Cambridge: Cambridge University Press, 2004); Christopher Clark, *Iron Kingdom: The Rise and Downfall of Prussia, 1600–1947* (Cambridge, MA: Belknap Press, 2009).

3. Marijke Jonker, "On Asp and Cobra You Will Tread . . . : Animals as Allegories of Transformation in Delacroix's Liberty Leading the People," at https://archiv.ub.uni-heidelberg.de/artdok/6532/1/Jonker_On_asp_and_cobra_2019.pdf, 194–195; Liz Smith, "A Mighty Force," January 5, 2010, at https://news.americanbible.org/article/a-mighty-force.

4. Jonker, "On Asp and Cobra You Will Tread."

5. Jonker, "On Asp and Cobra You Will Tread."

6. Declaration of the American Anti-Slavery Society Convention, 1833, at https://loc.harpweek.com/LCPoliticalCartoons/IndexDisplayCartoonLarge.asp?SourceIndex=Topics&IndexText=&UniqueID=15&Year=1833. "De fowler caught in his own snare!" is depicted at https://digital.librarycompany.org/islandora/object/digitool%3A37061. Douglass is quoted from David W. Blight, *Frederick Douglass, Prophet of Freedom* (New York: Simon and Schuster, 2018), 420.

   The "Battle Hymn of the Republic" (1861) does not specifically cite 91, although it does draw on other texts we have discussed, including Genesis 3:15 and Malachi 4: "Let the Hero, born of woman, crush the serpent with his heel, / Since God is marching on." For "demonic" ideas in these years, see Edward J. Blum and John H. Matsui, *War Is All Hell: The Nature of Evil and the Civil War* (Philadelphia: University of Pennsylvania Press, 2021); James P. Byrd, *A Holy Baptism of Fire and Blood: The Bible and the American Civil War* (New York: Oxford University Press, 2021).

7. Ernst Wilhelm Hengstenberg, *Commentary on the Psalms*, in *Clark's Foreign Theological Library*, vol. XII (Edinburgh: T. & T. Clark, 1848).

8. Augustus Tholuck, *A Translation and Commentary of the Book of Psalms* (Philadelphia: William S. and Alfred Martien, 1858), 373–375.

9. "The character of the Psalm" is from Hengstenberg, *Commentary on the Psalms*, 137; "It is not the Psalmist" is from 140.

10. Albert Barnes, *Notes, Critical, Explanatory and Practical on the Book of Psalms* (New York: Harper, 1869), III:13.

11. Alexander MacLaren, *The Psalms*, in W. Robertson Nicoll, ed., *The Expositor's Bible* (New York: A. C. Armstrong and Son, 1894), III:20. For 91, see https://ccel.org/ccel/maclaren/expositorpsalms3/expositorpsalms3.iii.html.

12. Joseph S. Exell and Henry Donald Maurice Spence-Jones, eds., *Preacher's Complete Homiletical Commentary*, at https://www.studylight.org/commentaries/eng/phc/psalms-91.html.

13. C. H. Spurgeon, "The Snare of the Fowler," March 29, 1857, at https://www.spurgeon.org/resource-library/sermons/the-snare-of-the-fowler/#flipbook/.

14. John Perowne, *The Book of Psalms* (London: G. Bell, 1882), ii 173. "The diseases of all hot climates" is quoted from Charles Haddon Spurgeon, *The Treasury of David* (New York: Funk & Wagnalls, 1883), IV:244.

15. Tholuck, *A Translation and Commentary of the Book of Psalms,* 375.

16. Tholuck, *A Translation and Commentary of the Book of Psalms,* 376.

17. Barnes, *Notes, Critical, Explanatory and Practical on the Book of Psalms,* III:12.

18. Barnes, *Notes, Critical, Explanatory and Practical on the Book of Psalms,* III:14.

19. Alexander MacLaren, Psalm 91, at https://ccel.org/ccel/maclaren/expositorpsal ms3/expositorpsalms3.iii.html. The quote about "makes his sun to rise" is from Matthew 5.45.

20. John Ruskin, *The Bible of Amiens* (1882), at https://www.gutenberg.org/files/24428/ 24428-h/24428-h.htm chapter IV, point #34; Elisabeth Everitt and Roy Tricker, *Swaffham-Two-Churches: A Guided Stroll Through the History of the Churches of St Mary, the Virgin and of St Cyriac and St Julitta in Swaffham Prior in the County of Cambridgeshire* (1996), at http://www.swaffham-prior.co.uk/2churches/. The stained glass can be seen at https://commons.wikimedia.org/wiki/File:Church_of_ St_Mary_Swaffham_Prior_Cambridgeshire_%28219897318%29.jpg.

21. C. H. Spurgeon, "The Snare of the Fowler." For shifting views of the nature of evil, see Sarah Bartels, *The Devil and the Victorians: Supernatural Evil In Nineteenth-Century English Culture* (London: Routledge, 2021).

22. Spurgeon, *The Treasury of David.*

23. George Horne, *Commentary on the Psalms* (London: Griffin and Rudd, 1813), 386.

24. "The good Bishop of Marseilles" is from James Anderson, footnote appended to Calvin's commentary on Psalm 91 at https://www.ccel.org/ccel/calvin/calcom10. xxvi.iii.html. The bishop was Henri François Xavier de Belsunce de Castelmoron. Ritchie Robertson, *The Enlightenment: The Pursuit of Happiness, 1680–1790* (New York: Harper, 2021).

25. Stier is cited by Perowne, *The Book of Psalms,* II:172.

26. Dwight L Moody, *Pleasure and Profit in Bible Study* (Chicago: Fleming Revell, 1895), chap. VII, at https://www.gutenberg.org/files/36655/36655-h/36655-h.htm.

27. Oliver Otis Howard, *Autobiography of Oliver Otis Howard, Major General, United States Army,* vol. II, chap. 70, at http://www.perseus.tufts.edu/hopper/text?doc=Pers eus%3Atext%3A2001.05.0174%3Achapter%3D3.36.

28. For Spurgeon's story, see Chapter 7.

29. J. H. Chajes, *Between Worlds: Dybbuks, Exorcists, and Early Modern Judaism* (Philadelphia: University of Pennsylvania Press, 2003); Nimrod Zinger, "Who Knows What the Cause Is? 'Natural' and 'Unnatural' Causes for Illness in the Writings of Ba'alei Shem, Doctors and Patients Among German Jews in the Eighteenth Century," in Maria Diemling and Giuseppe Veltri, eds., *The Jewish Body Corporeality, Society, and Identity in the Renaissance and Early Modern Period* (Leiden: Brill, 2008), 127–156; Bill Rebiger, ed., *Sefer Shimmush Tehillim—Buch vom magischen Gebrauch der Psalmen* (Tübingen: Mohr Siebeck, 2010). For 91, see, for instance, 5–10, 36–39, 268–270.

30. "It is without doubt" is from Rebiger, ed., *Sefer Shimmush Tehillim*, 268, my translation. "If anyone should be in danger" is from Joseph H. Peterson, ed., *The Sixth and Seventh Books of Moses* (Lake Worth, FL: Ibis Press, 2008). For a digital edition, see "The Sixth and Seventh Books of Moses (Part 2)" at http://esotericarchives.com/moses/67moses2.htm.

31. Francis Barrett, *The Magus* (New Hyde Park, NY: University Books, 1967), part II, 67–68.

32. Emanuel Swedenborg, *Apocalypsis Explicata Secundum Sensum Spiritualem* (New York: American Swedenborg Printing and Publishing Society 1894), 7:1628–1629.

33. *The Key of Solomon*, originally edited by S. Liddell MacGregor Mathers, and revised by Joseph H. Peterson, last updated 2021, at http://www.esotericarchives.com/solomon/ksol.htm.

34. R. S. Hawker, "The Botathen Ghost" (1867), at http://victorian-studies.net/ghost-stories-hawker.html; M. R. James, "Canon Alberic's Scrap Book," at https://gutenberg.ca/ebooks/james-alberic2/james-alberic2-00-h.html.

35. E. F. Benson, "Negotium Perambulans," at http://www.lesvampires.org/negotium.html.

36. Montague Summers, *The Vampire—His Kith and Kin* (New York: Dutton, 1929).

37. Charles Williams, *War in Heaven* (London: Gollancz, 1930).

38. Charles Williams, *The Place of the Lion* (London: Gollancz, 1931).

39. F. Scott Fitzgerald, "Sleeping and Waking," *Esquire*, December 1, 1934, https://classic.esquire.com/article/1934/12/1/sleeping-and-waking.

40. Paul Bourget, *Le Démon de midi* (Paris: Plon, 1914).

41. Sir Harry George Wakelyn Smith, *The Autobiography of Lieutenant-General Sir Harry Smith, Baronet of Aliwal on the Sutlej, G.C.B.* (n.p.: Good Press, 2019). The psalm supplies titles for several recent works of military history: see, for instance, Brian Matthew Jordan, *A Thousand May Fall: Life, Death, and Survival in the Union Army* (New York: Liveright, 2021).

42. The author, Huntly Gordon, is quoted from Michael Snape, "The Bible and the British and American Armed Forces in Two World Wars," *Journal of the Bible and Its Reception* 4, no. 2 (2017): 247–286.

43. "And first allow me to record" is from "Report of Lieut. Col. John H. Miller, First Mississippi Cavalry Battalion," at http://www.civilwardata.com/active/hdsquery.dll?RegimentHistory?1530&C. John Beatty, *The Citizen-Soldier; or, Memoirs of a Volunteer* (1879), at http://www.perseus.tufts.edu/hopper/text?doc=Perseus%3Atext%3A2001.05.0005%3Achapter%3D20.

44. For the soldier at Andersonville, see O. B. Chester, "Prison Life," *Annual Reunions of the Tenth Wisconsin Infantry* (1907), at https://content.wisconsinhistory.org/digital/collection/quiner/id/42107/.

45. The ethnographic study is Hanns Bächtold-Stäubli, *Deutscher Soldatenbrauch und Soldatenglaube* (Strasbourg: K. J. Trübner, 1917).

46. "Buy yourself" is from *Der 1. Weltkrieg und seine Auswirkungen auf Schweinfurt* (Schweinfurt: FAG Schaeffler Technologies GmbH & Co. KG, 2014): my translation.

For 91 as the Trench Psalm, see Ronald W. Goetsch, "The Lord Is My Refuge: Psalm 91," *Concordia Journal* 9 (1983): 143. Philip Jenkins, *The Great and Holy War* (San Francisco: HarperOne, 2014).

47. The Somme story is from "Soldiers," https://www.biblesociety.org.uk/what-we-do/england-and-wales/world-war-1/stories/soldiers/soldiers-life-saved-at-the-somme-by-his-bible/; Owen Davies, *A Supernatural War* (New York: Oxford University Press, 2019). Thomas Waters, *Cursed Britain: A History of Witchcraft and Black Magic in Modern Times* (New Haven, CT: Yale University Press, 2019).

48. Leonhard Frank, "Die Mutter," in *Der Mensch ist Gut*, at https://www.gutenberg.org/files/35176/35176-h/35176-h.htm.

49. The quotes are from Boris Pasternak, *Doctor Zhivago* (New York: Pantheon, 2010), 300–301.

50. Pasternak, *Dr. Zhivago*, 301–302.

51. Fyodor Dostoevsky, *The Brothers Karamazov* (Minneapolis, MN: First Avenue Editions, 2015).

52. Reinhold Niebuhr, *Beyond Tragedy* (New York: Charles Scribner's Sons, 1937) 96–97. See also the enlightening discussion of Niebuhr's attitudes and influence in Peter J. Thuesen, *Tornado God* (New York: Oxford University Press, 2020).

53. Frederick J. Gaiser, "'It Shall Not Reach You': Talisman or Vocation? Reading Psalm 91 in Time of War," *Word and World* 25 (2005): 192–193. The original source is Emanuel Hirsch, *Das Alte Testament und die Predigt des Evangeliums* (Tübingen: Mohr Siebeck, 1936).

54. Gaiser, "'It Shall Not Reach You': Talisman or Vocation?"

Chapter 9

1. "7 Strategies for Building a Psalm 91 House," Kenneth Copeland Ministries, 2019, at https://blog.kcm.org/7-strategies-building-psalm-91-house/.

2. The story is found in many locations. See, for instance, "Psalm 91: The Soldier's Psalm," 2016, at http://mcf-a.org.au/articles/the-soldiers-psalm/; Mary Jane Holt, "The Truth About the 91st Psalm," March 9, 2003, at http://archive.thecitizen.com/archive/main/archive-030309/fp-08.html.

3. Pirmin Hugger, *Jahwe meine Zuflucht: Gestalt und Theologie des 91. Psalms* (Münsterschwarzach: Vier-Türme-Verlag, 1971); Gerrit C. Vreugdenhil, *Psalm 91 and Demonic Menace* (Leiden: Brill, 2020); Gideon Bohak, "From Qumran to Cairo: The Lives and Times of a Jewish Exorcistic Formula," in Ildikó Csepregi and Charles Burnett, eds., *Ritual Healing: Magic, Ritual and Medical Therapy from Antiquity until the Early Modern Period* (Florence: Edizioni del Galluzzo, 2012), 31–52.

4. Thomas Merton, *Bread in the Wilderness* (New York: J. Laughlin, 1953), 124.

5. Karl Barth, *Church Dogmatics: The Doctrine of God*, vol. 2, part 2, *The Election of God* (London: Bloomsbury, 2003), 559.

6. Max Horkheimer, "Psalm 91," in Warren S. Goldstein, ed., *Marx, Critical Theory, and Religion: A Critique of Rational Choice* (Boston: Brill, 2006), 115–120; Roland Boer, "Nurturing the Indwelling Protest: Max Horkheimer and the Dialect of Religious Resistance and Betrayal," *Religion and Theology* 18, no. 3 (2011): 380–397. For Horkheimer's mother, see Rudolf J. Siebert, "The Evolution of the Critical Theory of Religion and Society," in Dustin J. Byrd, ed., *The Critique of Religion and Religion's Critique: On Dialectical Religiology* (Leiden: Brill, 2020), 96–97.

7. "A divine homeland" is from Horkheimer, "Psalm 91," 116.

8. Abigail Gilman, *A History of German Jewish Bible Translation* (Chicago: University of Chicago Press, 2018).

9. Elizabeth Elliot, *Shadow of the Almighty: The Life and Testament of Jim Elliot* (San Francisco: HarperCollins, 1989).

10. John Piper, "Your Executioner May Laugh You to Scorn for Quoting Psalm 91," 2012, at https://www.desiringgod.org/articles/your-executioner-may-laugh-you-to-scorn-for-quoting-psalm-91.

11. Billy Graham, *Angels: God's Secret Agents* (Nashville, TN: Thomas Nelson, 1975).

12. "The Company of Heaven," at http://www.emmanuelmusic.org/notes_translations/translations_other/t_britten_the_company_of_heaven.htm.

13. C. S. Lewis, *The Great Divorce* (London: Geoffrey Bles, 1945), 134; Pierre H. Berube, "An Unsourced Poem in Lewis's *Great Divorce*," *Mythlore* 37, no. 2 (2019): 141–146.

14. C. S. Lewis, *Reflections on the Psalms* (New York: HarperCollins, 2017). For the influence of Williams on Lewis, see Brenton Dickieson, "Meeting the Oddest Inkling," 2013, at https://apilgriminnarnia.com/2013/06/27/meeting-the-oddest-inkling-the-early-letters-of-c-s-lewis-and-charles-williams/; Brenton Dickieson, "The Place of the Lion in C.S. Lewis' Fiction," 2015, at https://apilgriminnarnia.com/2015/05/20/cwlion/.

15. "On Eagle's Wings," lyrics, at http://catholichymn.blogspot.com/2015/07/on-eagles-wings.html.

16. Perry D. Jamieson, *Khobar Towers: Tragedy and Response* (Washington, DC: Air Force History and Museum Programs, 2008), 170.

17. Christy DeSmith, "What 'On Eagle's Wings' Means for Joe Biden and the Priest Who Wrote It," *Boston Globe*, November 10, 2020, at https://www.bostonglobe.com/2020/11/10/arts/what-eagles-wings-means-joe-biden-priest-who-wrote-it/.

18. "My Sisters and Brothers," lyrics, at https://whitegum.com/introjs.htm?/songfile/MYSISTER.HTM; "Sharyn—Psalm 91 (ft. Calibleubird)," at https://www.youtube.com/watch?v=yK156zFPDm8. Susan Gillingham, *Psalms through the Centuries* three volumes (Chichester: Wiley-Blackwell, 2012–2022), III, 92–93.

19. The speech in *Mrs. Miniver* can be found at https://www.americanrhetoric.com/MovieSpeeches/moviespeechmrsminiver.html. Michael Snape, "The Bible and the British and American Armed Forces in Two World Wars," *Journal of the Bible and Its Reception* 4, no. 2 (2017): 247–286.

20. "Psalm 91 and the Miracle of Dunkirk," https://kinshipradio.org/home/2020/03/25/psalm-91-and-the-miracle-of-dunkirk/. For tales of miraculous survival, see Ken Onstot, "Faith and False Security," 2016, at http://spcdesmoines.org/spcsermons/

8cfe604c-9cac-4c8a-ae1e-1b1fea9fb628. For an example from Christian radio (concerning the Korean war), see "A Soldier's Story of Angelic Protection" at https://faith hub.net/soldiers-story-of-protection/. For the memoir of the bomber campaign, see Murray Peden, *A Thousand Shall Fall: A Pilot for 214* (Stittsville, ON: Canada's Wings, 1979).

21. The Soviet wartime stories are from "Prayer Alive in Help for What It Is. Orthodox Prayer 'Living in Help,'" at https://vetdryg.ru/en/molitva-zhivyi-v-pomoshchi-dlya-chego-ona-pravoslavnaya-molitva-zhivyi-v-pomoshchi/.

22. Peter Epp, *Ob tausend fallen: Mein Leben in Archipel Gulag* (Weichs: Memra-Verlag, 1988); Gereon Goldmann, *The Shadow of His Wings: The True Story of Fr. Gereon Goldmann, OFM* (Fort Collins, CO: Ignatius, 2000 [1964]); Susi Hasel Mundy, *A Thousand Shall Fall* (Hagerstown, MD: Review and Herald, 2001); Katja Lenssen, *Mama Luise . . . dass du deinen Fuß nicht an einen Stein stoßest* (Leipzig: Einbuch, 2014). "Erfahrungen mit Psalm 91 (Unter dem Schutz des Höchsten) durch Pater Gereon Goldmann," at https://www.youtube.com/watch?v=FOl8oWPaQWk.

23. "And all soldiers and all vehicles" is from Lorraine Joy, "Watchman on the Wall No Fear Psalm 91," *Williams Pioneer*, March 11 2020, at https://williamspioneer.com/2020/opin ion/96671/. For another example from the Iraq War, see "Divine Protection: Psalm 91," at https://www.ananda.org/prayers/articles-on-healing/divine-protection-psalm-91/. For Operation Bandanas, see http://www.operationbandanas.org/.

24. "Prayer Alive in Help for What It Is." Following the Russian invasion of Ukraine in 2022, Psalm 91 provided the basis of a patriotic Ukrainian song of resistance: Anatoliy Lykholai and Kate Osian "There Is Only One Reason: Psalm 91," 2022, at https://www. youtube.com/watch?v=8VMZoQlBafM

25. Norris is quoted from Brennan W. Breed, "Reception of the Psalms: The Example of Psalms 91," in William P. Brown, ed., *The Oxford Handbook of the Psalms* (New York: Oxford University Press, 2014), 297–310. "We will call forth" is from Jim Goll, "Prayer for the Nations," at https://www.cbn.com/spirituallife/prayeran dcounseling/intercession/jim_goll2.aspx?mobile=false&u=1. The practice of "91 for ninety-one days" is common. See, for instance, Steve Allen, "Praying Psalm 91 for 91 Days," 2020, at https://cbcbellevue.com/2minutestogether/2020/3/22/praying-psalm-91-for-91-days; "Praying Psalm 91 Together," 2020, at https://outlookmag.org/pray-91/.

26. "Arrested people started sewing it" is from Boris Pasternak, *Doctor Zhivago* (New York: Pantheon, 2010), 301. For Qabalistic traditions, see F. Levine, "The Use of Scripture in Practical Kabbalah," 2000, at http://kabbalah.fayelevine.com/letters/pk010.php.

27. The story of the airman is from Corrie ten Boom, *Clippings from My Notebook* (Nashville, TN: Thomas Nelson, 1982), 41–42. See also Corrie ten Boom, *The Hiding Place* (Grand Rapids, MI: Chosen Books, 1971). Other sources credit the book's title to Psalm 119.

28. Mark S. Hamm, *Crimes Committed by Terrorist Groups: Theory, Research and Prevention* (Washington, DC: Office of Justice Programs, 2005), 159, at https://www.ojp.gov/pdffiles1/nij/grants/211203.pdf.

29. "It is impossible" is from Rudolf Bultmann, *New Testament and Mythology, and Other Basic Writings*, edited by Schubert M. Ogden (Philadelphia: Fortress, 1984), 4; Michael Cuneo, *American Exorcism* (New York: Random House, 2010).

30. The "Rite of Exorcism" is from https://www.catholic.org/prayers/prayer.php?p= 683. The original Latin text read "Adjuro ergo te, draco nequissime, in nomine Agni immaculati, qui ambulavit super aspidem et basiliscum, qui conculavit leonem et draconem, ut discedas ab hoc homine, discedas ab Ecclesia Dei."

31. Lee Roy Martin, "The Use and Interpretation of the Psalms in Early Pentecostalism as Reflected in the Apostolic Faith from 1906 Through 1915," *Old Testament Essays* 30, no. 3 (2017), at http://www.scielo.org.za/scielo.php?script=sci_arttext&pid=S1010-99192017000300010. For the 1970s, see Don Basham, *Deliver Us from Evil* (Grand Rapids, MI: Chosen Books, 1972); Frank and Ida Mae Hammond, *Pigs in the Parlor: A Practical Guide to Deliverance* (Kirkwood, MO: Impact Christian Books, 1973); Mark I. Bubeck, *The Adversary: The Christian Versus Demon Activity* (Chicago: Moody, 2013 [1975]); Graham, *Angels; Cuneo, American Exorcism;* Sean McCloud, *American Possessions: Fighting Demons in the Contemporary United States* (New York: Oxford University Press, 2015); Daniel Silliman, *Reading Evangelicals: How Christian Fiction Shaped a Culture and a Faith* (Grand Rapids, MI: Eerdmans, 2021). "Jerry B. Jenkins: Interview by C. J. Darlington," at https://www.titletrakk.com/author-int erviews/jerry-jenkins-interview-2.htm.

32. For the larger movement, see Brad Christerson and Richard Flory, *The Rise of Network Christianity: How Independent Leaders Are Changing the Religious Landscape* (New York: Oxford University Press, 2017); J. Gordon Melton, "Women in the New Apostolic Reformation," paper presented at the 45th Annual Meeting of the Society for Pentecostal Studies, Dallas, TX, March 2021; C. Peter Wagner, *Spiritual Power and Church Growth* (Altamonte Springs, FL: Strang Communications, 1986); C. Peter Wagner, *Warfare Prayer* (Ventura, CA: Regal Books, 1992); C. Peter Wagner, *Prayer Shield Prayer* (Ventura, CA: Regal Books, 1992); C. Peter Wagner, *Engaging the Enemy* (n.p.: Gospel Light, 1995); C. Peter Wagner, *Confronting the Powers* (Ventura, CA: Regal Books, 1996).

33. Graham Kendrick and John Houghton, *Prayerwalking* (n.p.: Kingsway, 1990).

34. Chuck D. Pierce and Rebecca Wagner Sytsema, *Ridding Your Home Of Spiritual Darkness* (Colorado Springs, CO: Wagner Institute for Practical Ministry, 1999), at https://www.operationezra.com/uploads/1/0/4/4/10446233/ridding_your_home_of _spiritual_darkness.pdf.

35. "Their property looked like an oasis" is from "Protection from Hurricane Andrew," 2019, at https://www.peggyjoyceruth.org/protection-from-hurricane-andrew--- psalm-91-story/protection-from-hurricane-andrew-psalm-91-story. For Peggy Joyce Ruth ministries, see https://www.peggyjoyceruth.org/. Other testimonies are found at https://www.peggyjoyceruth.org/testimonies-more.html. Ruth's books include *Psalm 91: God's Shield of Protection (Military Edition)* (Kirkwood, MO: Impact Christian Books, 2005) and *Psalm 91: God's Umbrella of Protection* (Kirkwood, MO: Impact Christian Books, 2018). See also Peggy Joyce Ruth and Jose Carlos, *My Own Psalm 91 Book* (Kirkwood, MO: Impact Christian Books, 2007); Peggy Joyce

Ruth and Angelia Ruth Schum, *Psalm 91: Real-Life Stories: of God's Shield of Protection and What This Psalm Means for You and Those You Love* (Lake Mary, FL: Charisma House, 2011); Peggy Joyce Ruth and Angelia Ruth Schum, *Psalm 91 for Mothers: God's Shield of Protection for Your Children* (Lake Mary, FL: Charisma House, 2013). "Over 500,000 of her military Psalm 91 books" is from Peggy Joyce Ruth's Amazon author's site at https://www.amazon.com/gp/product/features/entity-teaser/books-entity-tea ser-ajax.html?ASIN=161638073X&PRODUCT_GROUP=book_display_on_webs ite. Other recent books by other authors include John Galinetti, *Protected: Psalm 91* (n.p.: Bush, 2020).

36. The biblical text is Malachi 3:10. Kate Bowler, *Blessed: A History of the American Prosperity Gospel* (New York: Oxford University Press, 2013).

37. See, for instance, the critique in John Piper, "Your Executioner May Laugh You to Scorn."

38. Kenneth Copeland Ministries, "6 Prayer Points in Response to COVID-19," 2020, at https://blog.kcm.org/6-prayer-points-in-response-to-covid-19/. For the personalized declaration, see https://www.kcm.org/real-help/faith/speak/a-personalized-decl aration-psalm-91-0. Gloria Copeland, *Your Promise of Protection: The Power of the 91st Psalm* (Tulsa: Harrison House, 2001).

39. Kenneth Copeland Ministries, "The Promise of Protection for All Believers in Psalm 91," 2020, at https://blog.kcm.org/the-promise-of-protection-for-all-believ ers-in-psalm-91/. A KCM "Partner" is the source for the story quoted earlier about the U.S. brigade serving in Iraq that used the psalm to escape injuries: "Not One Wounded! Chaplain Hardie Higgins Testimony," at https://www.youtube.com/ watch?v=yDcBJqWzrT4.

40. "7 Strategies for Building a Psalm 91 House."

41. "Psalm 91," at https://oralroberts.com/psalm91/.

42. Craig W. Hagin, "No Fear Here! No Fear Here," at https://www.rhema.org/index. php?option=com_content&view=article&id=2133:no-fear-here&catid=228. For Joel Osteen, see https://www.facebook.com/JoelOsteen/posts/psalm-91-says-i- will-say-of-the-lord-he-is-my-refuge-my-fortress-my-god-in-whom-/101616 97938890227/.

43. For Dollar, see "Start Your Day With Psalm 91," at https://www.facebook.com/watch/ ?v=544593279525037. For Paula White-Cain, see Kerry Cullinan, Lydia Namubiru, and Inge Snip, "Beware the False 'Saviours' and Their Snake-Oil," March 19, 2020, at https://www.dailymaverick.co.za/article/2020-03-19-beware-the-false-saviours- and-their-snake-oil/. The conclusion of the popular 2021 film *The Eyes of Tammy Faye* depicts evangelist Tammy Faye Bakker quoting the psalm as she stages a musical comeback.

44. "Most of us remember when" is from "Should Christians Wear Face Masks?" at https://arechristianssinners.com/2020/07/16/should-christians-wear-face-masks/. Susie Renzema and Becky Sytsema, with contributions by Jack Sytsema, *Meditations on Psalm 91* (Grand Rapids, MI: Lake Effect Church, 2020), available at http://lakeeff ect.church/91-for-91/.

45. Tim Cantrell, "Does Psalm 91 Promise Disease Immunity?," March 2020, at https://sola5.org/does-psalm-91-promise-disease-immunity-beware-of-the-devils-herm eneutic/.

46. "They claim that prophetic proclamation" is from Holly Pivec, "The NAR Antidote to Coronavirus," March 2020, at https://www.hollypivec.com/blog/2020/03/the-nar-antidote-to-coronavirus/9000. Tamaki is quoted from Leonardo Blair, "Tithe-Paying Christians Are Protected from Coronavirus by Psalm 91, Pastor Brian Tamaki Claims," *Christian Post*, March 3, 2020, at https://www.christianpost.com/news/tithe-paying-christians-are-protected-from-coronavirus-by-psalm-91-pastor-brian-tam aki-claims.html. "Lift up a prayer shield right now" is from "From the Desk of Steve Shultz," 2020, at https://elijahlist.com/words/display_word.html?ID=24388. "CBN President Gordon Robertson Prays Psalm 91 over You as Coronavirus Fears Mount," March 2020, at https://www.youtube.com/watch?v=ObpY9DcNhic.

47. Rabbi Yechiel Spero, *The Prayer of Protection: The Soul and Stories of Yosheiv BeSeiser* (Brooklyn, NY: ArtScroll Shaar Press, 2021).

48. "Rita's Psalm 91 7 Day Hoodoo Ritual Candle—Keep You Safe from Disease, Illness, Unfortunate Accidents, Protect Your Health," at https://www.ritasjuju.com/products/ritas-psalm-91-7-day-hoodoo-ritual-candle-keep-you-safe-from-disease-illness-unfortunate-accidents-protect-your-health.

49. "Prayer Alive in Help for What It Is."

50. "Psalm 90 Live in Help. Orthodox Prayer 'Living Aid' in Russian," https://stolicaplus.ru/en/zhilischnye-spory/psaltyr-90-zhivyi-v-pomoshchi-pravoslavnaya-molitva-zhi vye/. This material is found at many sites, with minor variations in content and translation. See, for instance, https://rkcsrp.ru/en/the-health-of-pregnant/psalom-90-zhi vyi-v-pomoshchi-raspechatat-psalom-zhivyi-v-pomoshchi.html; and https://zoopar k63.ru/en/kogda-chitat-psalom-90-zhivyi-v-pomoshchi-pravoslavnaya-molitva-zhi vye-pomoshchi-na/.

Chapter 10

1. Mary Wiltenburg, "Rwanda's Resurrection of Faith," *Christian Science Monitor*, April 12, 2004, https://www.csmonitor.com/2004/0412/p06s02-woaf.html.

2. Wiltenburg, "Rwanda's Resurrection of Faith." For another use of the psalm in this crisis, see Immaculée Ilibagiza, *Left to Tell: Discovering God Amidst the Rwandan Holocaust* (Carlsbad, CA: Hay House, 2014).

3. Madipoane Masenya (Ngwan'a Mphahlele), "Being 'Ādām: A Contextual Reading of the Psalms Today," in Kenneth Mtata, Karl-Wilhelm Niebuhr, and Miriam Rose, eds., *Singing the Songs of the Lord in Foreign Lands: Psalms in Contemporary Lutheran Interpretation* (Geneva: Lutheran World Federation, 2014), 233–243.

4. Andrew F. Walls, *The Missionary Movement in Christian History* (Maryknoll, NY: Orbis, 1996); Andrew F. Walls, *The Cross-Cultural Process in Christian History* (Maryknoll, NY: Orbis, 2001).

5. F. H. Welshman, "Psalm 91 in Relation to a Malawian Cultural Background," *Journal of Theology for Southern Africa* 8 (1974): 24–30.

6. Nupanga Weanzana, Samuel Ngewa, Tewoldemedhin Habtu, and Zamani Kafang, "Psalms," in Tokunboh Adeyemo et al., eds., *Africa Bible Commentary* (Grand Rapids, MI: Zondervan Academic, 2010).

7. "Let Faith Overcome Your Fears—Clergy Admonish Christians," March 22, 2020, at http://www.faapa.info/blog/let-faith-overcome-your-fears-clergy-admonish-chr istians/.

8. Todd M. Johnson and Gina A. Zurlo, *World Christian Encyclopedia*, 3rd ed. (Edinburgh: Edinburgh University Press, 2019).

9. Sunday O. Sangotunde, "A Textual Study of Psalm 91 and its Relevance to an African Milieu," *Global Journal of Human-Social Science* 14, no. 5 (2014), at https://socialscie nceresearch.org/index.php/GJHSS/article/view/1016.

10. A. Fagunwa and O. E. Fagunwa, "Pandemic, Pandemonium, and Psalm 91: In Search of Ultimate Protection and Deliverance," *Christian Journal of Global Health* 7, no. 4 (2020), at https://journal.cjgh.org/index.php/cjgh/article/download/461/859/.

11. Daniel C. Okpara, *Psalm 91: His Secret Place, His Shadow, and the Mystery of His Protection* (n.p.: Author, 2020). For an elaborate music video treatment, see "Henry Nwosu—Psalms 91," at https://www.praiseworldradio.com/henry-nwosu-psalm-91/.

12. "Psalm 91 the Prayer of Protection," at https://www.evangelistjoshua.com/psalm-91-the-prayer-of-protection/.

13. David Tuesday Adamo, "Decolonizing Psalm 91 in an African Perspective with Special Reference to the Culture of the Yoruba People of Nigeria," *Old Testament Essays* 25, no. 1 (2012): 9–26.

14. "Psalm-91 Properties Nigeria Limited—Rc1579339," at https://www.facebook.com/ Psalm91PropertiesNigeriaLtd/; Nelson Kalombo Ngoy, *Neo-Pentecostalism: A Post-Colonial Critique of the Prosperity Gospel in the Democratic Republic of the Congo* (Eugene, OR: Wipf & Stock, 2019).

15. Adamo, "Decolonizing Psalm 91."

16. Quoted from David Tuesday Adamo, "Wisdom Psalms in African Context with Special Reference to Nigeria," *Black Theology* 13, no. 2 (2015): 147–165.

17. Adamo, "Decolonizing Psalm 91."

18. Adamo, "Decolonizing Psalm 91." See also David T. Adamo, "The Use of Psalms in African Indigenous Churches in Nigeria," in Gerald O. West and Musa W Dube, eds., *The Bible in Africa* (Leiden: Brill, 2001), 336–349; David T. Adamo, "Psalms," in Daniel Patte, ed., *Global Bible Commentary* (Nashville, TN: Abingdon, 2004), 151–162.

19. "Five minutes later" is from "Philippines 1988" (2007), at https://www.forerunner. com/forerunner/X0836_Philippines_1988.html. "Speech of President Ramos During the 63rd Anniversary of the Cosmopolitan Church," March 24, 1996, at https://www. officialgazette.gov.ph/1996/03/24/speech-of-president-ramos-during-the-63rd-anni versary-of-the-cosmopolitan-church/.

20. "I assured my parents" is quoted in Philip Jenkins, *New Faces of Christianity* (New York: Oxford University Press, 2006), 108–109. For Pakistan, see Yousaf Sadiq, "Special Psalms Help Pakistani Christians with Persecution, Pandemic, and

Disunity," *Christianity Today*, November 10, 2021, at https://www.christianitytoday.com/ct/2021/november-web-only/pakistan-christians-punjabi-zabur-psalms-persecution-covid.html.

21. William L. Holladay, *The Psalms Through Three Thousand Years: Prayerbook of a Cloud of Witnesses* (Minneapolis, MN: Fortress Press, 1993), 241.

22. Jenkins, *New Faces of Christianity*; Juliano Spyer, *Povo de Deus: Quem são os evangélicos e por que eles importam* (São Paulo: Geração Editorial, 2020).

23. For the mystical speculations surrounding the psalm in Brazil, see Daidson Santos's *A guerra dos onze mil demônios: A maior revelação sobre o Salmo 91* (n.p.: Author, 2020).

24. Philip Jenkins, *The Next Christendom*, 3rd ed. (New York: Oxford University Press, 2011). For the IURD, see https://www.universal.org/noticias/post/91-dias-no-abrigo-do-altissimo-terceira-semana/.

25. Diante do Trono, "Salmo 91 (Recitado)," at https://www.youtube.com/watch?v=Hmbj5bLqoa4; Marine Friesen, "Psalm 91," at https://www.youtube.com/watch?v=9hOqiCgNHt4.

26. The description of Festival Promessas is from Tom Phillips, "Gospel Starts to Strike A Chord in Brazil, the Home of Bossa Nova," *Guardian*, December 27, 2011, at https://www.theguardian.com/world/2011/dec/27/gospel-strikes-chord-brazil.   Trazendo a Arca, "Aquele que habita," https://www.youtube.com/watch?v=XVQqn6gV7Xg; Sound Food Gang, "Salmo 91," https://www.youtube.com/watch?v=okxsHgMnie8; Soulfly, "Salmo 91," at https://www.youtube.com/watch?v=eBh_-7NV3xc.

27. Alex Cuadros, "My Gang Is Jesus," *Harper's Magazine*, January 16, 2020, at https://pulitzercenter.org/stories/my-gang-jesus. Christina Vital da Cunha, *Oração de traficante: uma etnografia* (Rio de Janeiro: Editora Garamond, 2015).

28. Dib Carneiro Neto, *Salmo 91* (São Paulo: Terceiro Nome, 2008); Alberto Tibaji, "Voices from the Inside: An Introduction to Dib Carneiro Neto's *Psalm 91*," *Theater* 45, no. 2 (2015): 82–85; Spyer, *Povo de Deus*.

29. "Protection from Deadly Viruses—Answers from Psalm 91," 2020, https://www.josephprince.com/sermon-notes/protection-from-deadly-viruses-answers-from-psalm-91; Joseph Prince, *The Prayer of Protection: Living Fearlessly in Dangerous Times* (n.p.: FaithWords, 2016).

30. For very Western-looking gospel music in an Asian context, see "Psalm 91—New Creation Church," at https://www.youtube.com/watch?v=kgvx9drZXpk.

31. Jane Lampman, "Targeting Cities with 'Spiritual Mapping,' Prayer," *Christian Science Monitor*, September 23, 1999, at https://www.csmonitor.com/1999/0923/p15s1.html.

32. "The Lord led us" is from Steve Allen, "Praying Psalm 91 for 91 Days," 2020, at https://cbcbellevue.com/2minutestogether/2020/3/22/praying-psalm-91-for-91-days; "Young Life's Ministry to Kids in the Ebola Crisis," at https://buck4good.com/project/young-lifes-ministry-to-kids-in-the-ebola-crisis/. For the actual development of the Liberia outbreak, see Ibrahima Socé Fall, "Ebola Virus Disease Outbreak in Liberia: Application of Lessons Learnt to Disease Surveillance and Control," *Pan African Medical Journal* 33 (2019), at https://www.ncbi.nlm.nih.gov/pmc/articles/PMC6691603/.

33. "Missionaries Claim Psalm 91 and Escape Death," https://www1.cbn.com/700club/missionaries-claim-psalm-91-and-escape-death.

Chapter 11

1. Max Horkheimer, "Psalm 91," in Warren S. Goldstein, ed., *Marx, Critical Theory, and Religion: A Critique of Rational Choice* (Boston: Brill, 2006), 116.

Appendix

1. https://www.biblegateway.com/passage/?search=psalm+91&version=VULGATE

Index

For the benefit of digital users, indexed terms that span two pages (e.g., 52–53) may, on occasion, appear on only one of those pages.

Spurgeon, disease
and Faith   p. 128
    United States, 1778;
" Don't Tread on Me", p. 131
Problem? 149
    Dr. Zhivago story   150